11-2021

Pastor Matt Sti

I would l
thoughts dear pastor as you
read through Revelationary.
May God richly and abundantly
bless you + your family.

Revelationary: Shoshana of David

Three Pillars Restored: Our Jewish Roots, the Prophetic Word, and the Daughters of God with His Sons

O God, you are awesome out
of your holy places. The God of
Israel is He that gives strength
and power unto His people.
Blessed be God. Psalm 68:35

By Christine Elsa Koppel

Joyfully,
Christine E.
Koppel

Revelationary: Shoshana of David

Three Pillars Restored: Our Jewish Roots, The Prophetic Word, and the Daughters of God with His Sons

Trilogy Christian Publishers A Wholly Owned Subsidiary of Trinity Broadcasting Network

2442 Michelle Drive Tustin, CA 92780

Manufactured in the United States of America

10 9 8 7 6 5 4 3 2 1

Library of Congress Cataloging-in-Publication Data is available.

ISBN: 978-1-63769-770-2

E-ISBN: 978-1-63769-771-9

Photo credit to ToddBolen/Bibleplaces.com for the front cover picture of the Jabbok River, eastern tributary to the Jordan River of Israel (Genesis 32).

...Write the Vision

The glory of YHVH is heavy, not lightweight. כבד כבוד Kaved Kavod. Come deep into the waters–let the Glory of God lift you. For it will lift those who know His Word by the power of the Holy Spirit (1 John 2:27-29), who know the God of Israel, who carry the burden of Israel (Zechariah 12, 13 and 14), but will crush those who ignore Him and the prophetic books of the Bible–a Wave of His Glory, a Tsunami.

Come deep (Psalm 42). Reside in the Ark of His Covenant with Israel (never annulled, only renewed, Jeremiah 31:33-34) and all those grafted in–who know Yeshua (ישוע), the King of the Jews and the King of all the earth.

He is coming again! We must be looking for Him.

Habakkuk 2:14: "For the earth shall be filled with the knowledge of the glory of YHVH as the waters cover the sea."

As in the days of Noah...

The earth was cleansed the first time by water. It will be cleansed this time of all apostasy by fire.

They missed Him the first time–the Pharisees, and the Sadducees, the ones who were supposed to know. The Jewish disciples of Yeshua that knew the Word of God brought the good news (*besorah*) to the whole world.

The testimony of Yeshua is the Spirit of Prophecy (Revelation 19:10). Look up your Redeemer (גאולתכם geulat'kem) draws near (כי קרובה).

Write the vision...

I will hasten My Word to perform it...

Thus says YHVH God of Israel (to Jeremiah), saying, "Write all the words that I have spoken to you in a book" (Jeremiah 30:2).

THE PRIESTLY BLESSING OF AARON

And the Lord spoke unto Moses, saying, "Speak unto Aaron and unto his sons, saying, On this wise you shall bless the children of Israel, saying unto them:"

"The Lord bless you and keep (guard, protect) you. The Lord make His face to shine upon you and be gracious to you. The Lord lift up His countenance upon you and give you peace" (Numbers 6:24-26).

Y'verekHa Adonai (YHVH) ve'yishmereKha
Ya'er Adonai (YHVH) panav elekHa vi'cHunekHa
Yisa Adonai (YHVH) panav elekHa, Ve'yasem lekHa Shalom

יברכך יהוה וישמרך
יאר יהוה פניו אליך ויחנך
ישא יהוה פניו אליך וישם לך שלום

Table of Contents

IN ESSENCE–A Preface

This is where the lines are drawn. It has been a fight, and I feel in a spiritual sense, I have gone to my cave to rest, to try to make sense of it all, as many have done before me. Yet, I hear the trumpet call. I hear the still, small voice. "What side will you choose?" "Where will you stand?" "Elijah, come on out. I have work for you to do."

How many times when things looked really bad did everyday heroes of the Bible stand despite how it looked.

MOSES

JOB

JOSEPH

HANNAH

ESTHER

And many more…

This is exactly where we need to be—all eyes on ABBA Father, YHVH, Yeshua (Jesus), to see what He will do when our back is against the Red Sea; when everything looks like it is being or has been taken away; when left in prison waiting for an open door, a birth that is yet to come, a freedom from oppression and release from the enemies' schemes. All eyes on Yeshua (Jesus). All eyes on Him as we pray and seek His face.

We are caught in a net. The promise—the net broke, and we are escaped (Psalm 124:7). No details given of how this will happen, only that it will. Hold on to Hope!

There is a plan, but we have to repent first, and we need to know what it is we need to repent of—the Bride needs to have her feet washed; otherwise, we can have no part with Jesus (John 13:1-17). The testimony of Jesus is the spirit of prophecy (Revelation 19:10). To know Jesus (Yeshua is His Hebrew name) is to have His Law written on your heart. He will fulfill the Law and the Prophets by His Holy Spirit. Our job is to read His Word, the Torah (the first five books)—where did we come from? The writings and the prophets—where are we in time? And the New Covenant (where are we going?). All are equally important. The whole Bible is needed to have understanding, and none of His Word has been done away with.

REVELATION ONE: THE NEW COVENANT IS REALLY THE OLD COVENANT FULFILLED NOT BY OUR STRENGTH BUT PERFECTED IN YESHUA
(more on this in Chapter One).

Jesus says,

> "Think not that I am come to destroy the Law, or the Prophets. I am not come to destroy, but to fulfill. For truly I say unto you, "Until heaven and earth pass away, not one jot or one tittle of the Law shall pass until all be fulfilled. Whosoever therefore shall break one of these least commandments, and shall teach men, so he shall be called the least in the kingdom of heaven; but whosoever shall do and teach them, the same shall be called great in the kingdom of heaven." For I say unto you, "That except your righteousness shall exceed the righteousness of the scribes and Pharisees, you shall in no case enter into the Kingdom of heaven."
>
> Matthew 5:17-20

We have to go deeper, but first, our feet must be washed, and then we will be freed to do the work given us by our Father—not what we think, but what is on His heart for this time, for this hour, for such a time as this.

> O my threshing, and the grain of my floor; that which I have heard of YHVH of hosts (tsava'ot), the God of Israel, have I declared unto you. The burden of Dumah. He calls to me out of Seir, Watchman, what of the night? Watchman, what of the night? The Watchman said, "The morning comes, and also the night; if you will inquire, inquire. Return, come."
>
> Isaiah 21:10-12

The Light grows brighter, even as the dark grows darker. And the Lord YHVH says,

> "Arise, shine; for your Light has come, and the glory of YHVH is risen upon you. For, behold (hinneh), the darkness shall cover the earth, and gross darkness the people; but the Lord YHVH shall arise upon you, and His glory shall be seen upon you. And the Gentiles shall come to your light, and kings to the brightness of Your rising."
>
> Isaiah 60:1-3

The whole of Isaiah 60 is filled with great hope and shows YHVH's plans for the nations, for those who will come to Him and know Him from His Word.

We, His Bride, are grafted into the House of Israel. We are grafted in, or we will be cut off. We have forgotten. We must repent. There is no place for replacement theology, dualism, or grace without understanding. These breaches must be healed.

Here is a place for pause. A Scripture that we must think on. A Selah moment.

> For if the casting away of them be the reconciling of the world, what shall the receiving of them be, but life from the dead? For if the first fruit be holy, the rest of the whole (the lump) is also holy, and if the root be holy, so are the branches. And some of the branches were broken off, and you (Gentiles from all nations) being a wild olive tree, were grafted in among them (the Israelite people), and with them partake of the root and abundance of the olive tree. Do not boast against the branches. But if you boast, (remember) you do not bare the root, but the root bares, supports you. You will say then, the branches were broken off, so I could be grafted in. Yes, well because of unbelief, they were broken off, and you stand by faith. Do not be high-minded, but fear. For if God did not spare the natural branches, take heed (be careful) that He also not spare you. Behold the goodness and severity (holiness) of God. On them which fell, severity; but toward you, goodness, IF you continue in His goodness. Otherwise, you (also) will be cut off. And they also, if they abide not still in unbelief (if the Jewish people come to know Yeshua as their Savior and Messiah), they shall be grafted in (again); for God is able to graft them in again. For if you were cut out of the olive tree which is wild by nature, and were grafted in, contrary to your nature, into a good olive tree, how much more shall these, which be the natural branches, be grafted into their own olive tree? For I would not, children, that you should be ignorant of this MYSTERY, unless you should be wise in your own conceits, that blindness happened IN PART to Israel until the full-

> ness of the Gentiles (the rest of us) come in. And so ALL Israel shall be saved (not replaced!). As it is written, There shall come out of Zion the Deliverer, and shall turn away ungodliness from Jacob (renamed Israel in Genesis 32). For this is MY COVENANT (spoken to the Israelites, the Jewish people in the New Testament, a promise) unto them, when I shall take away their sins.
>
> Romans 11:15-27

We have covered a lot, and this is only the tip of the iceberg, so to speak. A deep teaching of the Holy Spirit—our feet must be washed clean. The Bride must be made spotless by the washing of the water of the Word (Ephesians 5:26), and we must know the *true* prophetic Word (as compared to the warning given many places of false prophesy arising in these days, (Jeremiah 23, Matthew 24:24, 2 Thessalonians 2:9-12). All prophecy must be based on the Word of God. This is our safeguard to know God's Word, all of it; then, we will not be deceived by false teachers, false prophets, false religion.

God's Bride is being called out of the world. We are being grafted in again. We are being deeply rooted to withstand the days ahead. Revelation 18:4 says, "And I heard another voice from heaven saying, 'Come out of her, My people, that you be not partakers of her sins, and that you do not receive of her plagues.'"

We must know what that means. A beginning must start with the controversy between the Old Covenant vs. the New Covenant, Law vs. Grace, Faith vs. Works. What is all the commotion about, and should it even be there at all? What does the Word of God say? What is revealed by the Holy Spirit to heal this breach?

Dear Yeshua, ABBA Father, wash our feet from all false or shallow teaching, misunderstanding of Your Word, blindness to the Truth we need to understand. We submit ourselves to Your Word and the teaching of Your Holy Spirit. In Your Holy and Glorious Name, Jesus, we pray. Amen.

Chapter One

A New Covenant, It's Not What You Think

The Old Covenant vs. the New Covenant. What do we do with all the controversy that surrounds this topic? Has the New Covenant really replaced the Old Covenant? Is the New Covenant really all about grace and the Old Covenant all about the Law? Did Grace replace the Law? What about the issues of "cheap grace" or, on the other side, "we are not under the Law?" Is there a revelation that reconciles these two to the straight and narrow Way of Yeshua? These questions get to the core of what does it mean to be a follower of Yeshua and truly know Him. What does this look like in a Holy Spirit-filled believer in Jesus, our Messiah? What does the Bible say? What does Jesus say Himself?

One morning, as I was praying and spending time in the Word of God and hearing that ABBA Father's heart is yearning for His Bride to be cleansed by the washing of the Water of the Word, I hear or understood as I wrote, the Law is no longer outside us, as something we are trying to do, for we can not in our own human strength. The Law is now within us, something we are as new creations in Yeshua HaMashiach (Jesus the Messiah). This is a revelationary statement given by the Holy Spirit. It may not look like it, but let's look at the Word of God and break it down, rightly dividing the Word of Truth.

First, as many of us know, those who truly know Yeshua, Jesus, our Messiah are new creations.

"Therefore if any person be in Messiah, he is a new creature: old things are passed away; behold all things are become new" (2 Corinthians 5:17).

Second, Yeshua Himself said that He did not come to do away with the Law.

> Think not that I am come to destroy the LAW or the PROPHETS; I am not come to destroy, but to fulfil. For verily I say unto you, Until heaven and earth pass, one jot or one tittle shall in no wise pass from the Law until ALL be fulfilled. Whosoever therefore shall break one of these least commandments and shall teach men so, he shall be called the least in the kingdom of heaven; but whosoever shall do and teach them, the same shall be called great in the kingdom of heaven. For I say unto you, That except your righteousness shall exceed the righteousness of the scribes and Pharisees, you shall not enter into the Kingdom of Heaven.
>
> Matthew 5:17-20

What is Jesus saying here? The Law is still very important. We, as human beings, can not fulfill the Law of our own strength. The people of Israel tried but failed, as we all do when we try to keep the Law in our own strength. So, what is Yeshua saying?

Jesus (Yeshua) is saying, we can not keep the Law, but He can! He will write the Law in our hearts after we ask Him into our hearts, and He will perfect it in us and through us by His Holy Spirit! Let's look at Jeremiah 31:31-34 (which speaks to our Jewish brothers and sisters and also to those who will be grafted in, that's Gentiles from all other nations who know YHVH by His

Word).

> Behold the days come, says YHVH, that I will make a NEW COVENANT with the House of Israel, and with the House of Judah, not according to the covenant that I made with their fathers in that day that I took them by the hand to bring them out of the land of Egypt; which My covenant they broke, although I was a husband unto them, says YHVH. But this shall be the COVENANT that I will make with the House of Israel; After those days says YHVH, I will put MY LAW in their inward parts, and write it in their hearts, and I will be their God, and they shall be MY people. And they shall teach no more every man his neighbor, and every man his brother, saying Know the Lord (YHVH), for they shall all know ME, from the least of them unto the greatest of them, says the Lord YHVH. For I will forgive their iniquity, and I will remember their sin no more.
>
> Jeremiah 31:31-34

Hebrews Chapter 8 repeats this message.

> But now has He obtained a more excellent ministry, by how much also He is the mediator of a better covenant, which was established upon better promises. For if that first covenant had been faultless, then should no place have been sought for the second. For finding fault with them (the people not able to keep the Law themselves), He says, Behold the days come, says YHVH when I will make a new covenant with the House of Israel and with the House of Judah; not according to the covenant I made with their fathers in the day when I took them by the hand to lead them out of the land of Egypt; because they continued not in My covenant and I regarded them not, says YHVH. For this is the covenant that I will make

> with the HOUSE OF ISRAEL, after those days says YHVH, I will put My laws into their minds and write them in their hearts and I will be to them a God, and they shall be unto Me a people. And they shall not teach every man his neighbor and every man his brother saying Know YHVH for all shall know Me from the least to the greatest. For I will be merciful to their unrighteousness and their sins and their iniquities I will remember no more.
>
> Hebrews 8:6-12

In Jeremiah 31, God goes on to say that the promises and covenants made with Israel shall never be annulled. This Old Covenant shall be renewed, not destroyed, just as it says again in Hebrews 8. The New Testament confirms the Old Testament.

So how does this work together?

When we receive Jesus into our hearts, He writes the Law upon our hearts and in our inward parts, and then HE fulfills the Law for us through the power of the Holy Spirit. We are made new, and as a good fruit tree bears good fruit without striving, we now produce good fruit and keep the Law, not from our own efforts, but because the Holy Spirit works this out in us.

Psalm 138:8 says, "The Lord YHVH will perfect and complete that which concerns me; Your mercy, O Lord, endures forever…"

So, grace and mercy are not freedom from the Law, but the only way the Law can be kept perfectly by people. We can only fulfill the Law as Jesus writes it in our hearts and then fulfills it for us through the Holy Spirit. It is a process, though, and as we mature as believers, just as a fruit tree matures, we begin to bear good fruit by His Power, not our own.

So, what does Jesus mean when He said, "Unless your righteousness shall exceed the righteousness of the Scribes and Pharisees, you shall in no case enter into the Kingdom of heaven?"

By the Holy Spirit, let's look at Matthew 23:25-28,

> "Woe unto you, scribes and Pharisees, hypocrites! For you make clean the outside of the cup and of the platter, but within they are full of extortion and excess. You blind Pharisee, cleanse first that which is within the cup and platter, that the outside of them may be clean also. Woe unto you, scribes and Pharisees, hypocrites! For you are like unto whitened sepulchers (tombstones), which indeed appear beautiful outward, but are within full of dead men's bones, and of all uncleanness. Even so you also outwardly appear righteous unto men, but within you are full of hypocrisy and LAWLESSNESS."

So how do we reconcile or heal the breach between the Law and Grace? What does that mean?

The Scribes and Pharisees had the Law on the outside of them. They tried to fulfill it in their own strength. The Scribes and Pharisees are symbolic of all those who are religious and try to work their way into heaven in their own strength. Sadly, because this cannot be done, it produces a false projection of who they really are: either pride and arrogance of putting themselves over others who do not do the Law the way they do, or depression and sadness in realizing that they cannot keep the Law, so they are under constant condemnation. This is where many abandon their belief altogether.

Others who hold on to false grace also have the Law outside of them but keep it far from them, not wanting to know what it says, feeling the Law has nothing to do with them anymore. They are free to do whatever they want as long as they repent again and again. God's mercy is what saves them, so they feel they have little responsibility for what they do in this life. They are covered by the blood of Jesus. This is true if they truly know Him, but Yeshua says in Matthew 7:21-27,

> Not everyone that says unto Me, Lord, Lord, shall enter in the kingdom of heaven; but he that does THE WILL OF MY FATHER which is in heaven. Many will say to Me in that day, Lord, Lord, have we not prophesied in Thy Name (false prophets)? And in Thy Name have cast out devils and in Thy Name done many wonderful works? And then will I profess unto them, I never knew you; depart from Me, you that work iniquity. Therefore, whosoever hears these sayings of Mine, and DOES THEM, I will liken him unto a wise man, which built his house upon the ROCK. And everyone that hears these sayings of Mine and DOES NOT DO THEM, shall be likened unto a foolish man, who built his house upon the sand, and the rain descended, and the floods came, and the winds blew, and beat upon that house and it fell; and great was the fall of it.

The Law is important, but it is where it is found in a person's life that matters. The Law held outside of a person, either in trying to make the outside of the cup clean in our own strength or in pushing the Law far away in an attempt to annul or destroy it by replacing it with a false grace, both will result in the Lord Jesus saying, "Depart from Me, I never knew you." Oh, what a tragedy, a sadness to hear those words.

The wonderful news is that when you truly receive Yeshua into your heart, He cleans the inside of you so that the Holy Spirit can come in and write God's Law in your heart, and by the power of the Holy Spirit, Yeshua fulfills the Law in you perfectly. Galatians and other places in the Bible do not speak of the Law being abolished, only that the burden on people would be reduced until they learn more by the Holy Spirit and they begin to do what is in the Law supernaturally by the power of the Holy Spirit within them.

It is a matter of position. Where is the Law in your life? On the outside being performed. On the outside, as far away as possible, so there is license to do whatever you want based on false grace. Or is the Law written on the inside of you, in your heart, being fulfilled, even as it is revealed to you by the Holy Spirit through the daily reading of the Word of God?

This perfect Law written in our hearts will unravel like a scroll revealing more and more the heart of God. Yeshua took the burden off of our shoulders and makes it clear that those filled with the Holy Spirit will gravitate towards the teachings of the Word and will become more and more like Yeshua (our Jewish Messiah) with time as we mature in Him.

Like a tree needs years before it can bear fruit, so people, as new believers, need years of study in the Word of God before fruit appears. These are times of gathering in nourishment (the Word of God) and cannot be rushed. When the time of maturity comes, the fruit will naturally come without the tree's effort. It is just who the tree is.

Matthew 7:16-20 says,

> Ye shall know them by their fruits. Do men gather grapes from thorns or figs from thistles? Even so every good tree brings forth good fruit; but a corrupt tree brings forth evil fruit. A good tree CAN NOT bring forth evil fruit, neither can a corrupt tree bring forth good fruit. Every tree that does not

> bring forth good fruit is hewn down and cast into the fire. Wherefore by their fruits you shall know them.

The Law and Grace go together. They do not annul one another. It is a matter of position. Do you hold the Law on the outside of you for a show of self-righteousness? Do you hold the Law on the outside far away from you and say it has been annulled and done away with? Or do you have the Law written in your heart by Jesus, who washed the inside of you clean by His sacrifice on the cross, and now because you are clean on the inside, the Law has been written on your hearts, and Yeshua fulfills the Law in you perfectly by the power of the HOLY SPIRIT? Where is the Law in your life? Where is the grace and mercy that fulfills it? It is positional; it is to be on the inside of you, who you are, never annulled.

The fruit of the Law written in our hearts is renewal, eternal life, the righteousness of God in Yeshua HaMashiacH (Jesus, Messiah). We are washed clean both inside and out and made perfect by the blood of the Lamb.

Matthew 7:13-14 says,

> Enter in at the narrow gate, for wide is the gate, and broad is the way, that leads to destruction, and many there be which go in that way. Because straight is the gate, and narrow is the WAY, which leads unto life, and few there be that find it.

On the one side are those that say the Law must be obeyed in our own strength. On the other, there are those who say the Law has been done away with. Both are wrong. Both lead to destruction. The narrow WAY that leads to life is the Law written on our hearts, fulfilled by GRACE and Mercy in Yeshua Ha'MashiacH. We must know the Law, the prophets, the whole Word of God in order to know Him. This is our responsibility. If the Law is written in our hearts, we will want and earnestly desire to know it, as it is revealed more and more to us as we spend time in prayer and in His Word learning what the Holy Spirit will reveal to us.

The Old Covenant is the Law on the outside of us.

The New Covenant is the Law written on the inside of us, fulfilled perfectly by Yeshua through the power of the Holy Spirit!

Grace is not separate from the Law. It just takes the burden off your shoulders and places it on Yeshua, the King of your heart!

Yeshua fulfills the Law and the prophets within us!

> Then I will sprinkle clean water upon you, and you shall be clean from all your filthiness and from all your idols, I will cleanse you. A new heart also I will give to you, and a new spirit I will put within you, and I will take away the stony heart out of your flesh and I will give you a heart of flesh. And I will put my Spirit within you, and cause you to walk in my statutes, and you shall keep my judgments and do them. And you shall dwell in the land that I gave to your fathers and you shall be My people and I will be your God.
>
> Ezekiel 36:25-28

Isaiah 42:21 says, "The Lord YHVH is well pleased for His righteousness' sake; He will magnify the LAW and make it honorable."

Chapter Two

The Prophetic Word

The Pharisees and the Sadducees missed Yeshua the first time even though there were over a hundred prophecies in the Word of God that foretold of His coming. Yeshua fulfilled every one, but the "keepers" of the Law missed Him because they did not have the Holy Spirit to show them; they did not ask for YHVH's help.

Today, we have many more written prophecies about Yeshua's second coming than they had about His first. Yet many people do not know about them, or cannot understand what they mean, or just do not care. The Lord YHVH, ABBA Father, is calling us to understand, for Yeshua is coming again soon. Here, we will talk about prophecies related to ten prophetic events that have occurred recently or will in the very near future. By the prophetic Word, we can determine the times and the seasons of the twenty-first century. We will see that Israel has a lot to do with knowing we have entered into a new appointed time (mo'edim) that proves the time of Yeshua's (Jesus') return is very near.

ONE–A Nation Will Be Born in a Day

Isaiah 66:8-10 says,

> Who has heard such a thing? Who has seen such things? Shall the earth be made to give birth in one day? Or shall a nation be born at once? For as soon as Zion travailed, she brought forth her children. Shall I bring to the birth and not

cause delivery? says YHVH. "Shall I cause to bring forth, and shut the womb," says your God. Rejoice with Jerusalem and be glad with her, all you that love her. Rejoice for joy with her, all you that mourn for her.

This prophetic Word speaks of the day that Israel will be born again in the last days. The nation of Israel, wiped off the map in 70 AD by the Roman occupation and the people dispersed to the four corners of the earth, was reborn 1878 years later on May 14, 1948! We are the generation to see this rebirth. The people of Israel, the Jewish people, and all the remnant of people of the nations grafted into the House of Israel have been waiting for this day for almost 2000 years! This prophetic Word fulfilled marks a new time in History, and from that date on, May 14, 1948, we, as God's people, should be watching for the fulfillment of all other prophesies that foretell of Yeshua's second coming.

TWO–The People of Israel Will Be Gathered Back Again to the Nation of Israel

Many prophecies speak of this re-gathering of God's people to Israel. It is called "Aliyah" in the Hebrew tongue and means "To go up to God." It is a call to Return (Teshuvah) after almost 2000 years of not having a homeland, not having a place of refuge, a place to call their own. Here are some Scriptures that prophesy this physical return of the Jewish people to the land of re-born Israel.

Isaiah 11:11 says,

And it shall come to pass in that day, that YHVH shall set His hand again the second time to recover the remnant of His people, which shall be left, from Assyria, and from Egypt,

> and from Pathros, and from Cush and from Elam, and from Shinar and from Hamath, and from the islands of the sea. And He shall set up an ensign for the nations, *and shall assemble the outcasts of Israel, and gather together the dispersed of Judah from the four corners of the earth.*

Jeremiah 3:18 prophesies, "In those days, the house of Judah shall walk with the House of Israel, and they shall come together out of the land of the north to the land that I have given for an inheritance unto your fathers."

> Therefore, behold, the days come, says YHVH, that they shall no more say, YHVH lives that brought up the children of Israel out of the land of Egypt; But, the Lord YHVH lives, which brought up and which led the seed of the house of Israel out of the north country (Russia, etc.), and from all countries where I had driven them; and they shall dwell in their own land (Israel).
>
> Jeremiah 23:7-8

> Therefore thus says YHVH God, "*Now I will bring again the captivity of Jacob, and have mercy upon the whole House of Israel,* and will be jealous for My Holy Name. After that they have borne their shame, and all their trespasses whereby they have trespassed against Me, when they dwell safely in their land, and none made them afraid. *When I have brought them again from the people, and gathered them out of their enemies' lands, and I am sanctified in them in the sight of many nations*, then shall they know that I am YHVH, their God, which caused them to be led into captivity among the nations, *but I have gathered them unto their own land, and have left none of them any more there.* Neither will I hide My

FACE any more from them. For I have poured out My Spirit upon the House of Israel, says YHVH."

Ezekiel 39:25-29

For the children of Israel shall abide many days without a king, and without a prince, and without a sacrifice, and without an image, and without an ephod, and without teraphim. *afterward shall the children of Israel return and seek the Lord YHVH their God*, and David their king (when he is restored), and shall fear YHVH and His goodness in the latter days.

Hosea 3:4-5

For, behold, in those days, and in that time, *when I shall bring again the captivity of Judah and Jerusalem,* I will also gather all nations, and will bring them down into the valley of Jehoshaphat (means YHVH judges) and will plead with them there for my people and for my heritage Israel, whom they have scattered among the nations, and parted my land.

Joel 3:1-2

In that day I will raise up the tabernacle of David that is fallen, and repair the breaches thereof; and I will raise up his ruins, and I will build it as in the days of old. *And I will bring again the captivity of my people of Israel and they shall build the waste cities, and inhabit them; and they shall plant the vineyards, and drink the wine thereof; they shall make gardens, and eat the fruit of them.* And I will plant them upon their land, and they shall no more be pulled up out of their land which I have given them, says YHVH your God.

Amos 9:11,14-15

Obadiah 1:17: "But upon Mount Zion shall be deliverance and there shall be holiness; and the house of Jacob shall possess their possessions."

Micah 2:12: "*I will surely assemble, O Jacob, all of thee. I will surely gather the remnant of Israel. I will put them together as the sheep of Bozrah*, as the flock in the midst of the fold."

> But in the last days it shall come to pass, that the mountain of the House of YHVH shall be established in the top of the mountains, and it shall be exalted above the hills and people shall flow unto it. *And many nations shall come, and say Come, Let us go up to the mountain of YHVH and to the House of the God of Jacob*; and He will teach us His ways, and we will walk in His paths. For the LAW shall go forth of Zion, and the Word of YHVH from Jerusalem.
>
> Micah 4:1-2

Micah 5:3 says, "Therefore He will give them up until the time (moed'im) that she which travails has brought forth (1948); *then the remnant of his brethren (and sisters) shall return unto the children of Israel.*"

> The remnant of Israel shall not do iniquity, nor speak lies; neither shall a deceitful tongue be found in their mouth. For they shall feed and lie down, and none shall make them afraid. Sing, O daughter of Zion, shout O Israel, be glad and rejoice with all your heart, O daughter of Jerusalem… in that day, it shall be said to Jerusalem (Yerushalayim), Fear not, and to Zion, Let not your hands be slack. Behold at that time, I will undo all that afflict you, and will save her that halts and gather her that was driven out and I will get them praise and fame in every land where they have been put to shame. At

> that time, *I will bring you again, even in the time that I gather you, for I will make a name and a praise among all people of the earth, when I turn back your captivity before your eyes,* says YHVH.
>
> Zephaniah 3:13

> And I will strengthen the House of Judah, and I will save the House of Joseph, and *I will bring them again to place them;* for I have mercy upon them. And they shall be as though I had not cast them off; for I am YHVH, their God and will hear them.
>
> Zechariah 10:6

As I gathered some of these prophetic Words about Aliyah, or the Return of God's people to Israel in the last days, I recognize that there are many more, yet even the few that I have written, speak over and over again that in the last days, YHVH God will bring back His people Israel from the four corners of the earth after He has "birthed" the nation of Israel again in the last days. We see this prophecy of Aliyah happening for the past seventy years or more. Currently, as of 2020, approximately 7 million Jewish people have returned to Israel, with a total population of about 9 million in Israel, including Arabs and other people from other nations. This prophetic Word is being fulfilled before our very eyes. We are the generation who sees this, what others who *know* the Word of God have been waiting for, for close to 2000 years.

Charles Spurgeon, a British Reformed Baptist preacher of the nineteenth century, was quoted as saying back in 1855, on June 3 at New Park Street Chapel, Southward, the following:

> The hour is approaching, when the tribes shall go up to their own country; when Judea, so long a howling wilderness, shall once more blossom like the rose; when, if the temple itself be not restored, yet on Zion's hill shall be raised some Christian building, where the chants of solemn praise shall be heard as erst of the old Psalms of David were sung in the Tabernacle... *I think we do not attach sufficient importance to the restoration of the Jews. We do not think enough about it. But certainly, if there is anything promised in the Bible it is this. I imagine that you cannot read the Bible without seeing clearly that there is to be an actual restoration of the Children of Israel... For when the Jews are restored, the fullness of the Gentiles shall be gathered in*; and as soon as they return, then Jesus will come upon Mount Zion with his ancients gloriously, and the halcyon days of the millennium shall then dawn; we shall then know every man to be a brother and a friend; Christ shall rule with universal sway.[1]

Charles Spurgeon was one of the few that saw the day approaching when the prophecies of Israel's rebirth and the return of the Jewish people would be fulfilled. He did not see it physically himself, yet he understood about one hundred years before it happened that when we did see this, the return of Yeshua (Jesus) would occur soon thereafter, in the very generation that saw these prophecies fulfilled. We are this generation! Yet, many do not understand the prophetic Word or know it. Many missed Messiah the first time. We must wake up! We do not want to miss Him when He comes again, this time as the Lion of Judah.

THREE–The Nations Around Israel Will Be Gathered Against Her

Another prophetic Word given over 2500 years ago says in the last days after Israel has been born again as a nation, and millions have gathered back to their homeland, after 1878 years of exile, that the nations around her would gather against her.

Jeremiah 30:3-7 says,

> For, lo (behold), the days come, says YHVH, that I will bring again the captivity of My people Israel and Judah, says YHVH, and I will cause them to return to the land that I gave to their fathers, and they shall possess it. And these are the words YHVH spoke concerning Israel and concerning Judah, For thus says YHVH, "We have heard a voice of trembling, of fear, and not of peace. Ask ye now, and see whether a man does travail with child? Why do I see every man with his hands on his loins as a woman in travail, and all faces are turned into paleness? Alas! for that day is great, so that none is like it. *It is even the time of Jacob's trouble*; but he shall be saved out of it."

Joel 3:1-2 says,

> For behold, in those days, and in that time, when I shall bring again the captivity of Judah and Jerusalem, I will also gather all nations, and will bring them down in to the valley of Jehoshaphat (means YHVH judges) and will plead with them there for My people and for My heritage Israel, whom they have scattered among the nations, and parted my land.

Since the birth of Israel in May of 1948, Israel has faced war with its neighbors. On May 15, 1948, the day after Israel declared independence as a nation, five Arab nations attacked the newly born nation. Israel survived by YHVH's grace and promise and the intense bravery and fortitude of a small military force. In 1967, a war lasting six days broke out with nearly half a million Arab troops coming against Israel, again with the full intention of wiping Israel off the map. Israel not only survived the onslaught but took back a lot of territories given to her that were lost in the 1948 war. Israel regained the Golan Heights, the West Bank, Jerusalem, and the Sinai Peninsula. Again YHVH fought for the Israelis, and the nation became stronger. Other wars include the 1973 Yom Kippur War, 1982-1985 First Lebanon War, 1987-1993 First Palestinian Intifada, 2000-2005 Second Palestinian Intifada, 2006 Second Lebanon War, 2008 Operation Cast Lead, where Israel fought Hamas in the Gaza Strip after enduring three years of ongoing rocket attacks launched on Israeli citizens. In 2014, Operation Protective Edge was initiated to stop the constant barrage of rocket attacks from Hamas once again from Gaza, as well as to stop the breach of terror tunnels being dug in the area. These rocket attacks and the use of incendiary balloons to start fires in the land of Israel are an everyday onslaught[2] (Why Israel? The Jewish State's biblical Roots, Miraculous Rebirth, and Modern Trials, CUFI, 2019).

And just recently, in May 2021, the biggest war occurred between Hamas in the Gaza Strip and the Israelis since 2014; for eleven days, the Israeli Defense Force (IDF), through Operation Guardian of the Walls and the Iron Dome, protected Israel and her people as over 4000 rockets were hurled into her borders. This kind of warfare will continue and intensify until Yeshua returns to fight for Israel in the final battle in the Valley of Megiddo.

Conflict and war have been the norm for Israel since the first day of her existence. Many great books have been written on these conflicts and about the many times miraculous victories of Israel were won over her enemies. Yet, the conflict and threats of annihilation from surrounding nations have not stopped. Iran, Turkey, Syria, Lebanon, Yemen, and many others continue to threaten Israel, and the Israeli Defense Force is on constant alert for threats to the safety of the nation and her citizens. To find out more, a list of a few books on this subject is provided in the back of this book under resources. The point of this chapter, though, is to focus on the overall prophetic Word and see that it is coming to pass right in front of our eyes.

Amid peace treaties (also fulfilling Scripture), the war cry has not lessened. Israel knows they can never completely let down their guard. A nation the size of New Jersey, with the memory of the Holocaust forever etched in their hearts and minds, does not take lightly the threat of any nation, Iran or otherwise, who taunts them and promises their destruction. YHVH will always watch over Israel, though, even though the days ahead will be difficult for Israel and for every true believer in Yeshua *Ha'MashiacH* (Jesus, the Messiah).

Ezekiel 38:16-23 says,

> And you shall come up against My people of Israel, as a cloud to cover the land; it shall be in the LATTER DAYS, and I will bring you against my land, that the heathen may know me, when I shall be sanctified in you, O Gog, before their eyes. Thus says the Lord God, "Are you he of whom I have spoken in old time by My servants the prophets of Israel, which prophesied in those days many years that I would bring you against them? And it shall come to pass at the same time when Gog shall come against the land of Israel, says the Lord God, that My fury shall come up in My face. For

> in my jealousy and in the fire of my wrath have I spoken, Surely in that day there shall be a great shaking in the land of Israel; so that the fishes of the sea, and birds of the heaven, and the beasts of the field and all creeping things that creep upon the earth, and all the men that are upon the face of the earth, shall shake at my presence, and the mountains shall be thrown down, and the steep places shall fall and every wall shall fall to the ground. And I will call for a sword against him throughout all my mountains, says the Lord God; every man's sword shall be against his brother. And I will plead against him with pestilence and with blood; and I will rain upon him, and upon his bands, and upon the many people that are with him, an overflowing rain, and great hailstones, fire, and brimstone. Thus, will I magnify Myself and sanctify Myself; and I will be known in the eyes of many nations, and they shall know that I am YHVH."

This war of Ezekiel 38 is in the future, possibly the very near future. But it is for His glory that all nations of the earth shall know the God of Israel, the Holy one of Israel, YHVH. If you want proof that this prophecy is coming to pass in front of your eyes, just turn on the true news, or look in the newspapers like Jerusalem Post or World Israel News, or others. Yes, "the nations do rage, and the people imagine a vain thing. The kings of the earth set themselves up, and the rulers take counsel together against YHVH, and against His anointed, saying, 'Let us break their bands asunder, and cast away their cords from us.' He that sits in the heavens shall laugh. YHVH shall have them in derision. Then shall He speak unto them in His wrath, and distress them in His sore displeasure" (Psalm 2:1-5).

FOUR–A Peace Treaty Will Be Signed Between the Palestinians and the Israelis

Deep study of the Word of God reveals a peace treaty to be signed in the last days that will usher in the rise of the antichrist and the coalescence of the One World Government and One World Religion. The prophetic book of Daniel speaks of this treaty in Daniel 9:24-27 happening in the last days.

> Seventy weeks are determined upon Thy people and upon the Holy City, to finish the transgression, and to make an end of sins, and to make reconciliation for iniquity, and to bring in everlasting righteousness, and to seal up the vision and prophecy, and to anoint the most holy. Know therefore and understand, that from the going forth of the commandment to restore and build Jerusalem (during the time of Zerubbabel, Ezra and Nehemiah) unto the Messiah the Prince shall be seven weeks (7x7 = 49 years) and threescore and two weeks (62 x 7 = 434 years).
>
> Daniel 9:24-25

The sixty-nine weeks totals 483 years.

According to historians, the first temple was destroyed in 586 BC by the Babylonians, and approximately seventy years later, the Second Temple was completed in 515 BC as prophesied by Jeremiah in Jeremiah 29:10, "For thus says YHVH, That after seventy years be accomplished at Babylon I will visit you and perform My good word toward you in causing you to return to this place." Although the dates are approximate based on scholars understanding, the time between when Jerusalem was rebuilt, both the second Temple by Zerubabbel and Ezra (515 BC) and the walls of Jerusalem by Nehemiah (444 BC), until the time Jesus was born and fulfilled His time on the earth (thirty-one years, almost thirty-two) and the second temple is also destroyed, was the time period of that first sixty-nine weeks.

As I pondered dates and continued to research and ask the Holy Spirit, a thought, maybe just a theory, came up in my heart that I wish to share if only for another possibility in the understanding of this prophecy. If Nehemiah was given the decree to repair the damage done to the second temple and to build the walls of Jerusalem in 444 BC by King Artaxerxes, then 434 years later (the sixty-two weeks) would be 10 BC. For most scholars, the range of time for Jesus to be born was 6 to 4 BC. Because of the uncertainty of the exact date, moving Jesus' birth to 10 BC would line up the prophecy of Daniel perfectly. If according to the prophecy, Yeshua was born in 10 BC and He started His ministry on the earth at about age thirty, His Ministry could have started in 19 AD or 20 AD. Luke 3:23 says Jesus Himself began to be about thirty (meaning He was most likely still twenty-nine about to be thirty years old) when He was baptized by John and the dove, the Holy Spirit, descended upon Him. This would make His ministry started at about 19 AD.

Although many say Jesus ministered on the earth with miracles and wonders and teachings for three years because they count three Passovers, a good look at Scripture also leaves open that He ministered for a little more than two years because His ministry started a week or so before the first Passover counted. In John 2, Jesus is baptized, and three days later goes to a wedding in Cana (John 2:1), and they continued there for not many days (John 2:12). John 2:13 goes on to say, And the Jews' Passover was at hand, and Jesus went up (from Cana of Galilee) to Jerusalem. This was the first

Passover when He began publicly ministering to all the people in Israel. If this is the case, from the first Passover to the second Passover is one year, and from the second Passover to the third is another year. The first Passover He was introduced as the "Lamb of God who takes away the sins of the world" by John the Baptizer. The second one, Yeshua taught His disciples. The third one, Jesus Himself, died on the cross as the Lamb of God. It would then be a little over two years of ministry. He would have died in 21 AD if this is correct. If we add the seven times seven, forty-nine years of the second part of the Daniel 9 prophecy to 21 AD, we get the year 70 AD exactly, the very year the second temple was completely destroyed by the Romans. The gap between the sixty-two weeks and the seven weeks is the thirty-one thirty-two years of Jesus' life. This fits the Daniel 9 prophecy perfectly and is easy to understand, and I believe given by the Holy Spirit. It is a thought worth thinking about and would eliminate a lot of confusion to the alignment of years in the Daniel 9 prophetic Word. Yet, I leave it to each person to pray about and ask YHVH God to illuminate the truth. It is not a matter of salvation but of pondering, asking, and seeking for revelation in the Holy Spirit where we are still trying to fit the pieces together.

I came across an article recently that started with these words, "It's always a good thing to question established theories, as it allows ideas to be tested anew. A consensus cannot mean that the theory is correct but only that most of us have stopped thinking about the matter critically."[3] So, we think about these things…

The Scriptures go on to say, the street shall be built again, and the wall, even in troublous times (this speaks of the whole of the books of Ezra and Nehemiah) and even of the adding on to the second temple all the way through the time of King Herod. Daniel 9:26 says,

> And after threescore and two weeks shall Messiah be cut off (Yeshua was born, lived His life and was cut off about 31 AD or 21 AD if we acknowledge the possibility of Him being born in 10 BC) but not for Himself, and the people of the prince that shall come shall destroy the city and the sanctuary (70 AD); and the end thereof shall be with a flood, and unto the end of the war desolations are determined (the last days before the millennial age).

Between the sixty-two weeks and seven weeks, there is a short gap of time, the lifetime of Jesus on the earth. After the sixty-nine weeks, there is a huge gap in time before the final week. In Daniel 9:26, the end of the Scripture speaks, "and the end thereof shall be with a flood, and unto the end of the war desolations are determined." The flood alluded to here is also found in Revelation 12:15: "And the serpent cast out of his mouth water as a flood after the woman, that he might cause her to be carried away of the flood." It is an end-time prophetic word. This part of the Scripture refers to the final week or seven years. Daniel 9:27 goes on to say,

> And he shall confirm the covenant with many for one week (seven years), and in the midst of the week (three and a half years) he shall cause the sacrifice and oblation to cease, and for the overspreading of abominations he shall make it desolate, even until the consummation, and that determined shall be poured upon the desolate.

From 70 AD until now, it has been almost 2000 years. This last week will soon be upon us. Daniel sees a vision that shows him what will happen after the temple of YHVH is re-established and built and the walls of Jerusalem also, after the Babylonian captivity of Judah. Within 434 (62x7) years of this time period, Messiah would come and then be cut off (crucified for us). Then in forty-nine years (7x7) (70 AD), the burning and destroying of the city and the sanctuary (the second temple) would happen again. After this, a great leap in time occurs, which is the final week of history before Yeshua (Jesus) comes again. We are very near this time where this covenant for one week, or seven years, shall occur. The covenant leads to the desecration of the temple again (the third temple, which will be built in the near future) and the rise of the anti-christ to full power.

In Matthew 24:15-16, Jesus tells His disciples,

> When you therefore shall see this abomination of desolations spoken of by Daniel, the prophet, stand in the holy place (whoso reads this, let him understand): Then let them which be in Judaea flee into the mountains; let him which is on the housetop not come down to take anything out of his house; neither let him which is in the field return back to take his clothes. And woe unto them that are with child, and to them that give suck (nurse) in those days! But pray that your flight be not in the winter, neither on the sabbath day; for then shall be great tribulation, such as was not since the beginning of the world to this time, no, nor ever shall be. And except those days be shortened, there shall no flesh be saved, but for the elect's sake those days shall be shortened.

So that it is clear that these are the days when Jesus shall come again, He goes on to say in Matthew 24:23-30,

Then if any man shall say unto you, Behold, here is Christ, or there; believe it not. For there shall arise false Christs, and false prophets, and shall show great signs and wonders, insomuch that, if it were possible, they shall deceive the very elect. Behold I have told you before. Wherefore if they shall say unto you, Behold He is in the desert; go not forth. Behold He is in the secret chambers, believe it not. For as the lightening comes out of the east, and shines even unto the west, so shall the coming of the Son of man be (His second coming!).

Jesus is speaking these words of Himself. It did not occur back in 70 AD. Of course not, for He has not yet returned. It is in our very near future.

The verses then go on to speak of the tribulation of those days and the great sound of the trumpet as Yeshua calls His Bride to Him.

With the Word of God to give us Light, we see there will be a seven-year covenant made with the antichrist in the last days. The words of Jesus in the Book of Matthew tie the prophecy of Daniel's last week to the last days before the second coming of Jesus.

This covenant with many (nations) shall be confirmed for one week (seven years). Now that we know a peace treaty for seven years will be made between the antichrist and many nations, what will be included in this peace treaty? What will let us know this is the one? Based on a study from Jerusalem Prophecy College, the covenant that will usher in the last seven years before the second coming of Jesus must include five things:

1. Based on Matthew 24:15-16 and 21, Judaea, the west bank will be given to Palestinians for their own; it will be a two-state solution. This is where the danger arises in these passages for the Jewish people already living in that area. Palestinians are the only ones vying for a two-state solution.

They will turn on the Jews living near them after the abomination of desolation occurs, which will cause the Jewish people to flee for their lives, hence the warning in Matthew 24 given by Jesus.

2. Jews living in this new Palestinian "homeland" can stay there to live among the Palestinians if they choose to do so.

3. Jews will be allowed to build their temple on the Temple Mount without disturbing the mosque already there (Revelation 11:1-3).

4. The Temple Mount will come under a sharing agreement. Revelation 11:1-3 says,

   > And there was given unto me a reed like unto a rod, and the angel stood saying, Rise and measure the Temple of God, and the altar, and them that worship therein. But the court which is without the temple leave out, and measure it not, for it is given to the Gentiles and the Holy City shall they tread under foot for forty-two months (three and a half years). And I will give power unto My two witnesses and they shall prophesy a thousand two hundred and sixty days, clothed in sackcloth.

5. The control of Jerusalem and the Temple Mount will remain unresolved during the peace treaty, which will lead to the Battle of Armageddon at the end of those seven years for the fight for control.

Of course, we see peace treaties being made between Israel and her Arab neighbors right now (United Arab Emirates, Bahrain, Sudan, Morocco). This alone is unprecedented, yet these peace treaties are not the ones prophesied in the Bible. They do, however, set the stage for this final seven-year peace treaty with the

Palestinians, for the Palestinian Government knows they must take advantage of what is being offered in the Trump Peace Plan, or they will, in the end, lose all leverage to gain anything. Many other Arab nations (Sunni Muslims vs. Shi'ite Muslims) are seeing that the PLO and others who lead in Palestine are not really looking for peace and will not be satisfied unless they receive *all* of Israel and push the Jewish people "into the sea" again. This is not a position of making deals, and so many Arab nations who see the strength of Israel and the danger of nations like Iran (who is allied with proxies in Lebanon, Palestine, Syria, and Yemen, and others) are making peace with Israel instead of continuing to cater to a people that will not be satisfied unless Israel is destroyed. The Palestinian government is seeing that their ploy is exposed, and they need to "make peace" somehow, even temporarily, so they can survive and again have resources to fuel their plans. Otherwise, they will be left with nothing. This kind of pressure is what will lead to them finally signing this prophesied peace deal, although the change in US administrations may put this off for a while. Keep watching the news and reading the newspapers. Israel is front and center again on the world stage, as YHVH said it would be, in the last days, through the prophets of old and with Jesus' words as well.

A Quick Note: Who does the land belong to?

For more on the Covenants with Abraham, Isaac, and Jacob for the land of Israel, see Genesis 12:3, Genesis 15:7-21, Genesis 17:7-8, 15-16, Genesis 26:1-5, 24-25, Genesis 28:10-17, Genesis 32:24-28. I bring a reminder of these Scriptures because of many who would say the Palestinians are the true owners of this land. Based on scripture and history, this is just not true, although Jewish people have welcomed Palestinian people who really want to live in Israel peacefully. Here is a little history.

In 135 AD Emperor Hadrian renamed the land of Israel, Palestine.[4] He did this after the Romans defeated and dispersed the Jewish people from their homeland. Palestine is the Greek name for Philistine, the ancient enemies of Israel. It was a sort of "in your face" renaming of the land. During the last 1878 years, those opposed to YHVH and His people continued to call God's land of Israel, Palestine. Those who settled in the land were a mix of poor Jewish people and poor Arabs over the centuries. The Arabs of the land became known as the Palestinians. After World War II, the United Nations offered the land to both the Jewish and Arab populations. The Jewish people rejoiced to have a homeland once again. The Palestinians (the government of the Palestinian people) rejected the offer, for they wanted all the land to themselves and would not agree to share it officially with the Jewish people. There has been "war" ever since.

Palestine was never the true name of the land called Israel. YHVH allowed this for a time, the time of the Gentiles, until the time of the Gentiles be fulfilled. This Scripture is found in Luke 21:24-28,

> And they shall fall by the edge of the sword, and shall be led away captive into all nations, and Jerusalem shall be trodden down of the Gentiles until the times of the Gentiles be fulfilled. And there shall be signs in the sun, and in the moon, and in the stars; and upon the earth distress of nations with perplexity; the sea and the waves roaring; men's hearts failing them for looking after things which are coming on the earth; for the powers of heaven shall be shaken. And then

> shall they see the Son of man coming in a cloud with power and great glory. And when these things begin to come to pass, then look up and lift up your heads; for your redemptions draws nigh (near).

As YHVH God promised His people, the land of Israel would be reborn. Surely, it has. It has always belonged to the people descended from Abraham, Isaac, and Jacob, and all those grafted into the house of Israel from the nations since the first day YHVH God made the promise to Abraham, "In the same day YHVH God made a covenant with Abram saying, 'Unto your seed I have given this land, from the River of Egypt (Nile) to the great River Euphrates'" (Genesis 15:18). "And I will give unto you, and to your seed after you, the land wherein you are a stranger, all the land of Canaan, for an *everlasting* possession; and I will be their God" (Genesis 17:8). YHVH God will never change His mind and never goes back on His promises. The Jewish people have suffered much, and now they are home again. YHVH God's eyes are now focused on this nation in fulfillment of end-time prophecy.

FIVE–The Temple of the Jewish People Will Be Re-built on the Temple Mount

As part of the seven-year peace plan between the Palestinians and the Israelis, and many other nations, a temple for the Jewish people will be built on the Temple Mount. For over a thousand years, a Muslim mosque has stood there, although destroyed several times in history by earthquakes, once in 746 AD and another mosque destroyed in 1033 AD. As recently as 1927, a 6.5 magnitude earthquake rocked Jerusalem and surrounding areas, causing extensive damage, including the destruction of the foundation of the mosque on the Temple Mount. The current mosque, rebuilt once again, is the Al-Aqsa Mosque.[5] [6] [7]

The amount of information coming out every day on this "for-to-come" rebuilding of the Jewish temple is overwhelming. The Temple Institute has been preparing for decades for the day when permission to build the Jewish temple on the Temple Mount will be given. Every detail of the third temple for the worship of YHVH has been prepared and is ready to go; they only need the opening of the door to proceed, and the temple could be built in less than two years.

The promise of Amos 9:11-15 remains deep in the heart of the Jewish people and in all the remnant of the nations who long for restoration of God's temple and our Messiah to return.

> In that day, I will raise up the Tabernacle of David that is fallen, and close up the breaches thereof, and I will raise up his ruins and I will build it as in the days of old; that they may possess the remnant of Edom and of all the nations which are called by my name, says YHVH that does this. Behold the days come, says YHVH, that the plowman shall overtake the reaper, and the treader of grapes him that sows seed; and the mountains shall drop sweet wine, and all the hills shall melt. And I will bring again the captivity of MY people of Israel and they shall build the waste cities, and inhabit them and shall plant vineyards, and drink the wine thereof. They shall also make gardens, and eat the fruit of them. And I will plant them upon their land, and they shall no more be pulled up out of the land which I have given them, says YHVH.
>
> Amos 9:11-15

Once again, the temple of YHVH shall be built. First by human hands, "who serve unto the example and shadow of heavenly things, as Moses was admonished of God when he was about to make the tabernacle; for See, says He, that you make all things according to the pattern showed to you in the mount" (Hebrews 8:5). Then, at the end of this age, the true temple will be sanctified and built with living stones by God Himself, "a Minister of the sanctuary, and of the True Tabernacle, which YHVH pitched, and not man" (Hebrews 8:2).

There is heated contention over this, of course, but the Word of God says this will happen in the last days. Although this temple, being prepared by the Temple Institute, is not the one made without human hands, as spoken of in Hebrews 8:2 and other places (1 Peter 2:5), it will be built in fulfillment of Scripture, and it will be the place where the abomination of desolation occurs, and the antichrist proclaims himself to be God (Daniel 9:27).

Books, articles, videos abound on this topic. I write this only to bring awareness and understanding that this too has been prophesied, and so when we see this third temple being built in front of our eyes, we can be assured YHVH is on His throne in full control in these last days before the second coming of our Lord and Savior, Jesus (Yeshua) the Messiah, who will rule and reign from the true Tabernacle of David built by YHVH Himself. First Corinthians 3:16 says, "Do you not know that you are the Temple of God, and that the Spirit of God dwells in you?"

"And it shall come to pass in the last days, that the mountain of YHVH's House shall be established in the top of the mountains, and shall be exalted above the hills, and all nations shall flow unto it" (Isaiah 2:2).

"When He (YHVH) arises to shake terribly the earth. Cease

ye from man whose breath is in his nostrils; for wherein is he to be accounted of?" (Isaiah 2:21-22).

SIX–World War III and Peace?, Revelation 9 and Daniel 11

In World War I, approximately 9 million people were killed, with up to 30 million more wounded, taken prisoners, or missing.[8] In World War II, up to 75 million people died[9] with the horrific extermination of 6 million Jewish people based only on their ethnicity. Revelation 9 prophesies a coming World War III wherein one-third of the world's population will die in this war. With over 7 billion people in the world, this means more than 2 billion people will die. No one wants to focus on this upcoming war, and many believe it will not happen or cannot fathom so great a loss of human life. Yet, this war is prophesied to happen in the last days.

Revelation 9:12-21 says,

> One woe is past; and behold, there come two woes more hereafter. And the sixth angel sounded, and I heard a voice from the four horns of the golden altar which is before God, saying to the sixth angel which had the trumpet, Loose the four angels which are bound in the great River Euphrates. And the four angels were loosed, which were prepared for a day, and a month, and a year, for to slay the third part of men. And the number of the army of the horsemen were two hundred thousand thousand; and I heard the number of them. And thus, I saw the horses in the vision, and them that sat on them, having breastplates of fire, and of jacinth, and brimstone; and the heads of the horses were as the heads of lions, and out of their mouths issued fire and smoke and brimstone. By these three was the third part of men killed, by the fire,

> and by the smoke, and by the brimstone, which issued out of their mouths. For their power is in their mouth, and in their tails, for their tails were like unto serpents, and had heads, and with them they do hurt. And the rest of the men which were not killed by these plagues yet repented not of the works of their hands, that they should not worship devils, and idols of gold, and silver, and brass, and stone, and of wood, which neither can see, nor hear, nor walk. Neither did they repent of their murders, nor of their sorceries, nor of their fornication, nor of their thefts.

To break this down and rightly divide the Word of God, we must read it again and meditate on what this is saying.

First, it occurs at the sixth trumpet in the last days.

Second, this war starts in the area of the Euphrates River, which is in the Middle East. The Euphrates River runs through four nations: Turkey, Syria, Iraq, and Iran. The headwaters of the Euphrates start in Turkey. The river then runs through Syria to Iraq, and the last fifty miles or so run along the border between Iran and Iraq and empty into the Persian Gulf.

Third, the war will last a day, a month, and a year.

Fourth, it will result in the third part of men on the earth to be killed. This, of course, brings to mind the potential destruction of nuclear warheads.

Fifth, the army released upon God's people will be two hundred thousand, thousand or two hundred million. The nations of China or India currently have an army this numerous. The leader of the Chinese people boasted of an army with exactly 200 million in recent years[10]. The Muslim nations, with a focus on the Shi'ite

Muslims in Iran, Syria, Turkey, and other countries, also have a huge army of people.

Sixth, this war is different than Armaggedon (Har Megiddo). Armageddon is spoken of 7 chapters later in Revelation 16:16.

After World War III, the Word of God in Revelation 11 speaks of the temple being measured, which implies that it has already been built, either right before this war or right after this war. In one scenario, it could very well be that this horrific war will have all people around the world crying out for peace, and this will solidify the peace plan spoken of in Daniel 9 and Daniel 11:21-31 for the world will demand it between the Palestinians and Israelis and the other nations in the Middle East so that peace can finally truly be achieved in the Middle East, the place this war breaks out. As part of this peace plan, as spoken of earlier, the Israelis will demand that they also can build their Temple on the Temple Mount. A person will rise up to this demand and be instrumental in completing this peace plan. He will rise up "by flatteries," and after the league is made with him, "he will work deceitfully" (Daniel 11:21, 23).

Daniel 11:21-32 says,

> And in his estate, shall stand up a vile person, to whom they shall not give the honor of the kingdom, but he shall come peaceably, and obtain the kingdom by flatteries. And with the arms of a flood (speaks of nations) shall they be swept away from before him, and shall be broken, yes, also the prince of the covenant. And after the league made with him, he shall work deceitfully, for he shall come up, and shall become strong with a small number of people. He shall enter peaceably even upon the richest places of the province, and he shall do that which his fathers have not done nor his fa-

> thers' fathers; he shall scatter among them the prey, and spoil, and riches. Yes, and he shall forecast his devices against the strong holds, even for a time. And he shall stir up his power and his courage against the king of the south with a great army; and the king of the south (Iran?) shall be stirred up to battle with a very great and mighty army; but he shall not stand for they shall forecast devices against him. Yes, they that feed of the portion of his meat shall destroy him, and his army shall overflow, and many shall fall down slain. And both these kings' hearts shall be to do evil, and they shall speak lies at one table; but it shall not prosper, for yet the end shall be at the appointed time. Then he shall return into his land with great riches; and his heart shall be against the holy covenant, and he shall do exploits and return to his own land. At the TIME APPOINTED he shall return, and come toward the south, but it shall not be as the former, or as the latter. For the ships of Chittim (the Mediterranean islands) shall come against him; therefore, he shall be grieved, and return and have indignation against the holy covenant; so shall he do. He shall even return and have intelligence with them that forsake the holy covenant. And arms shall stand on his part, and they shall pollute the SANCTUARY of strength, and shall take away the daily sacrifice, and they shall place the abomination that makes desolate. And such that do wickedly against the COVENANT shall he corrupt by flatteries.

Second Thessalonians 2:9-12 says,

> Even him, whose coming is after the working of Satan with all power and signs and lying wonders, and with all deceivableness of unrighteousness in them that perish, because they received not the LOVE OF TRUTH, that they might be saved. And for this cause, God shall send them strong delusion, that they should believe a lie, that they all might be condemned who

> believed not THE TRUTH, but had pleasure in unrighteousness.

World War III will set the entire world on its head, upside down, shaken to its core. The world will be looking for a savior, someone, something to bring peace. The enemy of God, and of all God's people, has the answer for those who do not know YHVH. He is the antichrist, and he will deceive many in the last days.

Jeremiah 6:14-17 says,

> They have also healed the hurt of the daughter of MY people slightly, saying Peace, Peace, when there is no Peace. Were they ashamed when they had committed abomination? No, they were not at all ashamed, neither could they blush. Therefore, they shall fall among them that fall. At the time that I visit them, they shall be cast down, says YHVH. Thus says YHVH, Stand in the ways, and see, and ask for the old paths, where is the good way, and walk therein, and you shall find rest for your souls. But they said, We will not walk therein. Also, I set watchmen over you, saying, Hearken to the sound of the trumpet… But they said, we will not hearken.

Yet with this warning, YHVH says to those who love Him,

"But the people that do know their God shall be strong, and do exploits. And they that understand among the people shall instruct many" (Daniel 11:32-33).

First Thessalonians 5:1-6 says,

> But of the times and seasons, brethren (and sisters), you have no need that I write unto you. For yourselves know perfectly that the DAY OF THE LORD so comes as a thief in the night. For when they shall say, PEACE AND SAFETY, then sudden destruction comes upon them, as travail upon a woman with child,

> and they shall not escape. But you, brethren (and sisters) are not in darkness, that that day should overtake you as a thief. You are all children of Light, and the children of the day. We are not of the night, nor of darkness. Therefore, let us not sleep as do others; but let us watch and be sober.

SEVEN–The Time of the Gentiles, What does this mean?

In Luke Chapter 21, Jesus speaks to His disciples about the last days before His return. The disciples ask Him, "saying, Master, but when shall these things be? And what sign will there be when these things shall come to pass?" (Luke 21:7).

In Luke 21:20-24, Jesus goes on to explain,

> And when you shall see Jerusalem encompassed with armies, then know that the desolation thereof is near. And let them which are in Judaea flee to the mountains and let them which are in the midst of it depart out; and let not them that are in the countries enter thereinto. For these be the days of vengeance that all things which are written may be fulfilled. But woe unto them that are with child, and to them that give suck (nurse) in those days! For there shall be great distress in the land, and wrath upon this people. And they shall fall by the edge of the sword, and shall be led away captive into all the nations; *and Jerusalem shall be trodden down of the Gentiles, until the times of the Gentiles be fulfilled.*

In Daniel 8:13-17, the Word of God says,

> Then I heard one saint speaking, and another saint said unto that certain saint which spoke, How long shall be the vision concerning the daily sacrifice, and the transgression of desolation, to give both the sanctuary and *the host to be trodden*

> *under foot? And he said unto me, Unto 2300 days; then shall the sanctuary be cleansed.* And it came to pass, when I, even I Daniel, had seen the vision, and sought for the meaning, then, behold, there stood before me as the appearance of a man. And I heard a man's voice between the banks of Ulai, which called, and said, Gabriel, make this man to understand the vision. So, he came near where I stood, and when he came, I was afraid, and fell upon my face, but he said unto me Understand, O son of man. For at the time of the end shall be the vision.

Daniel, carried away to Babylon in approximately 605 BC, sees the vision but does not understand it. God commands Gabriel, the archangel, to explain to Daniel what this means and what shall be in the last days.

Continuing with the prophetic Word, Daniel 8:18-27 says,

> Now as he was speaking with me, I was in a deep sleep on my face toward the ground, but he touched me, and set me upright. And he said, Behold, I will make you to know what shall be in the last end of the indignation, for at the time appointed the end shall be. The ram which you saw having two horns are the kings of Media and Persia. And the rough goat is the King of Greece, and the horn that is between his eyes is the first king. Now that being broken, whereas four stood up for it, four kingdoms shall stand up out of the nation, but not in power. And in the latter time of their kingdom, when the transgressors are come to the full, a king of fierce countenance, and understanding dark sentences shall stand up. And his power shall be mighty, but not by his own power; and he shall destroy wonderfully, and shall prosper, and practice, and shall destroy the mighty and the holy people.

> And through his policy also, he shall cause craft to prosper in his hand, and he shall magnify himself in his heart and by peace, he shall destroy many. He shall also stand up against the Prince of princes; but he shall be broken without hand. And the vision of the evening and the morning which was told is true. Wherefore shut up the vision, for it shall be for many days. And I Daniel fainted, and was sick certain days; afterward, I rose up and did the king's business and I was astonished at the vision, but none understood it.

Daniel sees the future of a king of Greece that will take full power and become ruler of the known world at the time. Now looking back with twenty/twenty vision, we can see this prophecy was pointing to Alexander the Great, who came into power approximately 300 years later after Daniel has the vision. It goes on with great detail as the vision shows the "world government" that Alexander the Great will rule will break into four weaker kingdoms. World history proves this is exactly what happened. Alexander the Great's kingdom, after his death in Babylon, 323 BC, was given to his four generals, Cassander, Ptolemy, Antigonus, and Seleucus. The prophecy then jumps to a time when out of these Greek / Macedonian people (European today) will come one that will again rule the world and will have a "fierce countenance and understand dark sentences." This prophetic Word points to the very end of days when the antichrist will come into power, and he will use his promise of "peace" to gain ascendency. In the end, there is no peace through him, only war and destruction for many. Daniel sees all the way to the end of days, the times we are living in now, and he faints at what he sees and is "sick certain days" because of what he saw.

So what does this all have to do with the time of the Gentiles?

Luke 21 and Daniel 8 both share the phrases "transgression of desolation, the sanctuary/Jerusalem, and trodden under foot." Both are talking about the end of the age. Daniel goes on to say the vision spoken says this trampling of the sanctuary will last 2300 days, from the time of the first king of Grecia (Daniel 8:21) until the time the sanctuary is taken back into the control of the Jewish people. One morning, as I was in prayer, the Holy Spirit had me focus on these verses. I believe YHVH gave me a revelation of the last days upon us, drawing very near, as He spoke to me of the 2300 days as 2300 years. What is the beginning of this trampling? Daniel 8 starts with the first king of Grecia, Alexander the Great. When did he first go into Jerusalem to establish his authority–approximate date 332-333 BC. The Lord YHVH then asks me the question, "When was Jerusalem fully in the hands of the Jewish people again?" I realized that soon after the Greek rule, there was the Roman rule and the Jewish people never really had full authority in Jerusalem from the time of Alexander the Great all the way up to the Six-Day War that occurred in 1967. It was during this war that the Israeli people re-captured Jerusalem as their own for the first time in thousands of years. The Lord asks me to "do the math," so to speak, and find out the time period between when Alexander the Great first steps into Jerusalem to proclaim his authority (332-333 BC) and 1967; the number of years is exactly 2300! I feel YHVH was saying the time of the Gentiles trampling of Jerusalem was over in 1967, although the Israelis gave power over to the Jordanians at that time and kept the Dome of the Rock and the Al-Aqsa Mosque on the temple because of fear of the international community. Still, it was now in their authority what to do with Jerusalem, even if they chose to do what was wrong in the sight of YHVH.

It is another time that we are entering into or already have. Israel is the time clock, and non-believing Gentiles no longer have authority and rule over Jerusalem. The Jewish people are now in control of Jerusalem again. The 2300 days (years) are over. We have entered into the last days and new revelations for the times at hand.

The 2300 days can also have a double meaning, that there will be 2300 literal days from the time the temple is built after the peace plan until Yeshua returns to literally cleanse it with fire and the breath of His holiness. Two thousand three hundred days is approximately 6.3 years, so it could very well happen within the time of the seven-year peace plan, at the end of man's rule. The temple could be built very quickly after the Jewish people get permission through the coming peace plan. The sacrifices to take place there will again be under the Law, and the people will need to be corrected and see that Yeshua is the "Lamb of God" that takes away the sins of the world. Man and his sacrifices have no power to take away sin. The sanctuary will need to be cleansed of all unrighteousness when Jesus returns.

> Moreover, I will make a Covenant of Peace with them; it shall be an everlasting covenant with them and I will place them and multiply them, and will set My Sanctuary in the midst of them forevermore. My Tabernacle also shall be with them. Yes, I will be their God, and they shall be My People. And the nations shall know that I, YHVH, do sanctify Israel when MY SANCTUARY shall be in the midst of them forevermore.
>
> Ezekiel 37:26-28

The Gospel (*besorah*) has gone into all the world (all the Gentile nations) as commanded by YHVH to the Jewish disciples.

Holy Spirit power, the Revealer of Yeshua to the hearts of people, started in Jerusalem (Acts 1:8) and has gone around the world, "from Jerusalem, in all Judaea, and in Samaria, and unto the uttermost part of the earth." In the last days, the Gospel has come back to Jerusalem. The Jewish people will hear again of our Jewish Messiah. The time of the Gentiles is coming to a close. YHVH's eyes are now focused on Israel with laser-like attention, although of course, He sees all the other nations too! Yet, just as YHVH is watching Israel, we should be watching too.

Amos 9:13-15 says,

> Behold, the days come, says YHVH, that the plowman shall overtake the reaper, and the treader of grapes him that sows seed, and the mountains shall drop sweet wine, and the hills shall melt. And I will bring again the captivity of MY people Israel and they shall build the waste cities, and inhabit them, and shall plant vineyards, and drink the wine thereof; they shall also make gardens, and eat the fruit of them. And I will plant them upon their land, and they shall no more be pulled up out of their land which I have given them, says YHVH your God.

Many times, the Scriptures hold layers of meaning. It has gone full circle, the gospel, and we are back in Jerusalem, Israel. This is one such mystery that the Lord YHVH is revealing to His people today.

EIGHT–Rising, One New Man, The Bride of Yeshua

The time of the Gentiles has been long, but we are entering into a new time, a new period, a new thing that the Lord YHVH is doing.

"Behold, I will do a new thing. Now, it shall spring forth; shall you not know it? I will even make a way in the wilderness, and rivers in the desert" (Isaiah 43:19).

In Isaiah 44:21, God says,

> Remember these, O Jacob and Israel, for you are My servant. I have formed you. O Israel, you shall not be forgotten of Me. I have blotted out, as a thick cloud, your transgressions, and as a cloud, your sins. Return unto Me, for I have redeemed you. Sing, O ye heavens, for YHVH has done it. Shout, you lower parts of the earth. Break forth into singing, you mountains, O forest and every tree therein, for YHVH has redeemed Jacob, and glorified Himself in Israel.

The time of the Gentiles was a time of war and a time of grace when the gospel went into all the nations of the world through the Jewish people first and then handed over to believing Gentiles. The Jewish people during this time were cut off, and the Gentile nations took center stage, even as the Jewish temple was destroyed by the Romans in 70 AD; soon thereafter, the Jewish people were dispersed to the four corners of the earth in 135 AD by the Emperor Hadrian. And so, the time of the Gentiles continued in earnest for the next almost 1900 years.

Genesis 12:1-3 says,

> Now YHVH had said unto Abram, Get thee out of your country, and from your kindred, and from your father's house, unto a land that I will show you. And I will make of you a great nation, and I will bless you, and make your name great; and you shall be a blessing, and I will bless them that bless you, and curse him that curse you, and in you shall all the families of the earth be blessed.

In the last 2000 years, all nations have been blessed through the nation of Israel as the Word of God, our Jewish Messiah Yeshua (Jesus), and the gospel message (*besorah*) would come through her. The time period we are coming out of is marked by a hostile, fierce battle between those who worship the Greco-Roman gods and other pagan gods still, whether knowingly or not, and those who worship the one true God, the God of Abraham, Isaac, and Jacob, the God of Israel, the God of the Bible, YHVH, and the Word of God, who is Jesus.

When Jesus died on the cross, the grand rescue and taking back of territory started with each heart from the nations that came to know the true God and were rescued from enemy territory. This battle has continued for over 2000 years and will end at the Battle of Armageddon, when Jesus returns with the host of heaven and fells all His enemies with a Word. In the interim, between the ending of the time of the Gentiles trampling on Jerusalem (1967) and the Battle of Armageddon, is a time period I will call the Rising of the One New Man, the Bride of Messiah Yeshua–it is Jewish and Gentile believers in the God of Israel, Yeshua, our Messiah, that come together to form the army rising up for the last days! It is a powerful army in the Holy Spirit!

Ezekiel 37:9-14 says,

> Then said He unto me, Prophesy unto the wind, prophesy, son of man, and say to the wind, thus says YHVH God, Come from the four winds, O breath, and breathe upon these slain, that they may live. So, I prophesied as He commanded me, and the breath came into them, and they lived, and stood up on their feet, an exceeding great army. Then He said unto me, Son of man, these bones are the whole house of Israel.

> Behold, they say, "Our bones are dried, and our hope is lost. We are put off for our parts." Therefore, prophesy and say unto them, thus says YHVH God, "Behold, O My People, I will open your graves, and cause you to come up out of your graves, and bring you into the land of Israel (a prophecy already happening still). And you shall know that I am YHVH, when I have opened your graves, O My People, and brought you up out of your graves. And shall put MY Spirit in you, and you shall live, and I shall place you in your own land. Then shall you know that I, YHVH, have spoken it, and PERFORMED IT, says YHVH.

This prophetic Word spoken to Ezekiel speaks to these last days when Israel will be revived as a people. It speaks of the Holocaust when over 6 million Jewish people (and those Gentiles who tried to protect them) were murdered only because of who they were and that they believed in YHVH, the God of Israel. YHVH says they will arise in the last days and be gathered back to their land, Israel. They will arise a great army, the end of days army, for such a time as this.

We are to be grafted into the house of Israel. A remnant of God's people, throughout the generations and nations, has always known this and has understood the importance of our Jewish roots. They have not forgotten, and although there was blindness over the nation of Israel for a time, this blindness is falling away as we enter these days of the One New Man Rising. Romans 11:7-8 says,

> What then? Israel has not obtained that which he seeks for; but the election (those Jewish people of the Bible who believed in Jesus, for example all of His disciples, thousands at the first Pentecost, the Bereans etc.) has obtained it, and the rest were blinded. According as it is written, God has given them the spirit of slumber, eyes that they should not see,

and ears that they should not hear, unto this day.

Romans 11 goes on to say there will be a day when they awaken from their slumber!

> For if the casting away of them be the reconciling of the world, what shall the receiving of them be, but life from the dead? For if the first fruit be holy, the lump is also holy; and if the root be holy, so are the branches. And if some of the branches be broken off, and you, being a wild olive tree, were grafted in among them, and with them partake of the root and abundance of the olive tree, do not boast against the branches. But if you boast, you bear not the root, but the root bears you.
>
> Romans 11:15-18

This Scripture requires humility first to understand it. The Gentiles (all other nations) that have been blessed through Israel by receiving the gospel of Yeshua (Jesus) 2000 years ago as well as the whole Bible, written by Jewish people, need to understand where we came from, our Jewish roots, and never be so prideful as to say we have taken over, and they have been left behind. We are all sinners and have all rejected Jesus at some point in our lives until the Holy Spirit gave us the ability to see. We have been taught Replacement Theology which says the Jews rejected Jesus, so, therefore, Jesus rejected them. This is a lie from the pit of hell. We have only to read the scriptures to see that all our beloved heroes and heroines in the Bible were almost 100 percent Jewish. The Bible speaks of those from other nations being grafted in, such as Ruth, RacHab, and Cornelius, and these beautiful people represent us, but still, all the others represent where our Gospel came from, the Jewish people!

> You will say then, the branches were broken off, that I might be grafted in. Well; because of unbelief they were broken off, and you stand by faith. Be not haughty, but fear. For if God did not spare the natural branches, take heed lest He also not spare you. Behold, therefore the goodness and severity of God, on them severity (for a time), but toward you, goodness, if you continue in His goodness; otherwise you shall also be cut off. And they also, if they stop abiding in unbelief shall be grafted in; for God is able to graft them in again. For if you were cut out of the olive tree which is wild by nature (Gentiles) and were grafted in contrary to nature into a good olive tree, how much more shall these, which be the natural branches (the Jewish people), be grafted into their own olive tree?
>
> Romans 11:19-24

Romans 11:25 goes on to point to a mystery and to warn us, especially for the days we live in now as we see Israel back on the map and the people being gathered together again…

"For I would not, brethren (and sisters) that you should be ignorant of this mystery, lest you should be wise in your own conceits; that blindness in part is happened to Israel, until the fullness of the Gentiles be come in" (Romans 11:25).

This blindness of the Jewish people, in some mysterious way, has been for the benefit of the nations, for our benefit. Now we enter into a time where God is taking the blinders off, and we should all rejoice and run to our Jewish brothers and sisters to tell them what they told us 2000 years ago, "Jesus (Yeshua), our Jewish Messiah, loves you and is calling you Home, is calling us Home together."

Romans 11:26-27 says, "And so all Israel shall be saved. As it is written, There shall come out of Zion the Deliverer, and shall turn away ungodliness from Jacob. For this is MY Covenant unto them, when I shall take away their sins."

So what is the One New Man Arising, and is it in the Bible? Ephesians 2 is beautiful. Our salvation is a free gift, not anything we have earned more than anyone else. It was a personal awakening in each person by the Holy Spirit that brought us to the knowledge of Jesus our Messiah. The Jewish people brought us this message. In Ephesians 2:11 through 15, the Word of God says,

> Wherefore remember that you being in time past Gentiles in the flesh, who are called Uncircumcision (of the heart) by that which is called the Circumcision (separated from the world) in the flesh made by hands; that at that time you were without Messiah, being aliens from the commonwealth of Israel, and strangers from the covenants of promise, having no hope, and without God in the world; but now in Messiah Yeshua (Christ Jesus), you who were sometimes far off are made near by the blood of Messiah. For He is our peace, who has made both one, and has broken down the middle wall of partition between us, having abolished in His flesh the enmity, even the law of commandments contained in ordinances, for to make in Himself of the two, ONE NEW MAN, so making peace.

One New Man is born out of the two groups of people, the Jewish nation of Israel and the rest of the nations, the Gentiles. In the book of Acts, Peter and other Jewish disciples are called by God to go to the Gentiles and preach Jesus (Yeshua) to them also. At first, mostly ALL that followed Yeshua were Jewish. Peter obeys and is amazed to find that the Holy Spirit comes to the Gentiles as well.

> While Peter yet spoke these words, the Holy Spirit fell on all of them which heard the Word. And they of the circumcision which believed were astonished, as many as came with Peter, because on the Gentiles also was poured out the gift of the Holy Spirit. For they heard them speak with tongues, and magnify God.
>
> Acts 10:44-46

Paul, formerly Saul, a Jew of Tarsus, a city of Cilicia, was also called specifically to the Gentiles to preach the good news of Yeshua. Acts 9:13-16 says,

> Then Ananias answered YHVH, I have heard by many of this man, how much evil he has done to the saints (Jewish believers in Yeshua at this time) at Jerusalem, and here he has authority from the chief priests to bind all that call on Thy name. But the Lord said unto him, Go your way, for he is a chosen vessel unto Me, to bear My name before the Gentiles, and kings, and the children of Israel. For I will show him how great things he must suffer for My name's sake.

After about ten years from the first outpouring of the Holy Spirit on the Jewish disciples in Jerusalem, Peter goes to the house of Cornelius, and the birth of One New Man begins. Now both Jewish and Gentile people are receiving the gospel message of Jesus and being baptized with the Holy Spirit. It is an amazing time but short-lived. Within the next three to four hundred years, the attacks on the people of YHVH are fierce. Persecution, murder, torture became the norm for how the Roman Government deals with the believers in Yeshua. Finally, the story of Constantine seeing the sign of the cross before a war and the promise of winning that battle if he would bear the sign of the cross and winning it changes this particular emperor's heart, and the persecutions begin to lessen. He promises to make this religion the Law of the land but, with a very high price attached–the Jewish people, the Jewish customs, the Jewish holy days, and feasts must all be cut off. Sadly, the Gentile believers, in order to finally receive "peace," conceded to these demands more and more over time. This becomes the apostate church for the most part and has reigned for the past almost 2000 years, with always a remnant of people who truly know their Bibles and see through the false or shallow teachings. Yet, God has been merciful, and there is a mystery in all of this so that the power of God has still reached many to believe through the name of Jesus. Yet with the birth of Israel and the re-gathering of the Jewish people, YHVH, the God of Israel, the only true God of all the earth, is awakening the One New Man again, and this time, it is an army for the last days, a bride of troops, that will conquer and defeat the harlot of the last days, the false religious spirit which is still sadly very prevalent in the world and will continue to grow as the day of our Lord Yeshua draws near.

It is spiritual warfare, the fight against apostasy, the time to return to the purity of our roots, and to join once again with our Jewish brothers and sisters in the One New Man, that through the Holy Spirit, we are gathered as one.

> No longer strangers or foreigners in the household of God, and are built upon the foundation of the apostles and prophets, Jesus Messiah Himself being the chief cornerstone; in whom all the building fitly framed TOGETHER grows into an holy temple in YHVH; in whom you also are built TOGETHER for a habitation of God through the Spirit.
>
> Ephesians 2:19-22

The daughter of troops is to arise–Micah 5:1-3 says,

> Now gather yourself in troops, O daughter of troops. He has laid siege against us. They shall smite the Judge of Israel with a rod upon the cheek. But you, Bethlehem Ephratah, though you be little among the thousands of Judah, yet out of you shall He come forth unto me that is to be Ruler in Israel; whose goings forth have been from of old, from everlasting. Therefore, He will give them up (the Jewish people, the dispersion), until the time, that she which travails has brought forth (Isaiah 66:8), when the remnant of his brethren (and sisters) return unto the children of Israel.

We are to come out of her (Babylon, apostasy, replacement theology, dualism, lightweight or shallow teaching, the despising of true prophesying, the quenching of the Holy Spirit).

Revelation 18:4 "And I heard another voice from heaven, saying, Come out of her, MY PEOPLE, that you be not partakers of her sins, and you receive not of her plagues."

We must arise, O daughter of Zion, the bride of Jesus (Yeshua). We must arise TOGETHER.

NINE–One World Government, One World Religion

In all of history, we have seen this before, this one-world government, one-world religion but on a much smaller scale than what is coming soon upon the earth. In the book of Daniel, King Nebuchadnezzar of Babylon has a dream about a statue with a golden head, silver arms and breast, bronze belly and thighs, iron legs, and his feet part of iron and part of clay. King Nebuchadnezzar wakes up one morning highly agitated and disturbed. He has this dream but can not remember it, but knows it is highly significant. He summons all of his magicians, astrologers, and sorcerers, and Chaldeans to tell him the dream and interpret it. None of them can do it. The king is ready to have them all executed. But Daniel… Daniel finds out what has happened as they pound on his door to take him also to be executed. He asks for permission to talk with the king. It is granted. He asks the king for time to know the dream and interpret it. It is granted. Daniel prays with his three friends, Hananiah, Mishael, and Azariah, also known as Shadrach, Meshach, and Abednego. YHVH, the God of Israel, reveals the secret to Daniel that very night in a night vision. Daniel goes back into the presence of the king and says,

> The secret which the king has demanded the wise men, the astrologers, the magicians, the soothsayers cannot show to the king; but there is a God in heaven that reveals secrets, and makes known to the king Nebuchadnezzar what shall be in the latter days. As for you, O king, your thoughts came into your mind upon your bed, what should come to pass hereafter, and He that reveals secrets makes known to you what shall come to pass.
>
> Daniel 2:27-29

Daniel goes on to say, "This secret is not revealed to me for any wisdom that I have more than any living, but for their sakes it shall be made known the interpretation to the king, and that you may know the thoughts of your heart," (Daniel 2:30). Daniel gives YHVH, the God of Israel, all the glory and then tells the king that he dreamed of a huge statue, "a great image." "This great image, whose brightness was excellent, stood before you and the form thereof was terrible" (Daniel 2:31). Daniel goes on to tell the king that each of these metals in the statue represents world kingdoms that shall go to the end of time when a large stone from heaven "made without human hands" shall crush all the other kingdoms and then set up His rule forever in all the earth.

After careful study of the Word and history, the full interpretation of who these kingdoms will be is made known to us in our day–the golden head is the kingdom of Nebuchadnezzar, the kingdom of Babylon, which Daniel reveals to the king. The silver arms and breast are the Medes and the Persians, King Darius and King Cyrus, ruling together that begin to rule right after King Belshazzar is taken down by King Darius (Daniel 5:30-31). The third kingdom is the Greek Kingdom starting with Alexander the Great, which Daniel foretells in Daniel 8:19-22. The fourth kingdom is the Romans, who ruled during the time of Yeshua. The fifth kingdom and the last of human government, the feet and toes of the statue, is a mix of iron (Romans) with clay. This last kingdom is a mix of two powers, the original Roman power with the religious aspect of the Roman power, and is called the Holy Roman Empire.

It started in 803 AD when Charlemagne, the Roman Emperor, was crowned king by the Pope Leo III of Rome. These two powers, the political and the religious, became as one. The Holy Roman Empire has been resurrected on November 3, 2009,[11] and is now, in the last days, the world power that continues to grow as the final one-world government and one-world religion. There is much evidence for this as we see the United Nations, World Health Organization, Council on Foreign Relations, World Bank, and other entities with worldwide influence and power. The development of 5G technology and other tracking devices makes it very clear that these organizations now have the ability to implement their power on people who do not understand the times we are living in.

But there is good news for those who watch and know the Word of God. In the last part of Nebuchadnezzar's dream, he sees a stone cut without human hands, which smote the image upon his feet that were of iron and clay and broke them into pieces. Then was the iron, the clay, the brass, the silver, and the gold broken into pieces together, and became like the chaff of the summer threshing floors and the wind carried them away, that no place was found for them and the stone that smote the image became a great mountain and filled the whole earth (Daniel 2:34-35). This stone is the "chief cornerstone." It is Jesus, Yeshua, when He comes back again to destroy all man-made government. This Stone will grow to fill the whole earth. It is the final, and forever rule of Yeshua from the throne of David and "the earth shall be filled with the knowledge of the glory of YHVH, as the waters cover the sea" (Habakkuk 2:14).

This prophetic Word given to Nebuchadnezzar in a dream and interpreted by Daniel was revealed around 600 BC, 2600 years ago! It is a vision of all of history "in a nutshell." It speaks of all the world governments that will come upon the earth until the final one, which will mix one-world government with a one-world religion. We can see in the news this is happening already. End Time Ministries with Irvin Baxter and Dave Robbins explains this vision of Nebuchadnezzar in great detail. The Jerusalem Prophecy College with End Time Ministries covers all of this so well that I will only give highlights to show we are at the place that this final one-world government and religion is upon us. We need to be ready and understanding.

In the last book of the Bible, Revelation, God reveals to John on the Island of Patmos what the final days before His second coming will be like. Chapter 13 of Revelation specifically deals with the last One-World Government and the One-World Religion. Here is what John sees:

> And I stood upon the sand of the sea, and saw a beast rise up out of the sea, having seven heads and ten horns, and upon his horns ten crowns, and upon his heads the name of blasphemy. And the beast which I saw was like unto a leopard, and his feet were as the feet of a bear, and his mouth as the mouth of a lion, and the dragon gave him power, and his seat, and his great authority.
>
> Revelation 13:1-2

This passage speaks of the one-world government rising up. It alludes to the passages in Daniel Chapter 7, which also speak of these particular beasts or kingdoms rising up in the last days. Now each of these four beasts in Daniel 7 has come together as one beast in Revelation 13. Again, from research from End Times Ministries, each of the beasts spoken of here represents a kingdom–the leopard, Germany, the bear, Russia, the lion, Great Britain, and the dragon, from the European Union. Each of these beasts is a national symbol for the nation it represents, even as the bald eagle represents the United States.

Revelation 13:5-8 goes on to say that this beast was given unto him a mouth speaking great things and blasphemies, and power was given unto him to continue forty-two months (or three and a half years).

> And he opened his mouth in blasphemy against God, to blaspheme His Name, and His tabernacle, and them that dwell in heaven. And it was given unto him to make war with the

> saints (kedoshim, holy ones) and to overcome them; and power was given him over all kindreds, and tongues, and nations. And all that dwell upon the earth shall worship him, whose names are not written in the Book of Life of the Lamb slain from the foundation of the world.
>
> Revelation 13:6-8

In this one-world government, we see the nations spoken of 2000 years ago in the book of Revelation (written about 95 AD) on the world stage today.

John, the disciple that Jesus loves (John 21:7), then goes on to write about another vision.

> And I beheld another beast coming up out of the earth; and he had two horns like a lamb, and he spoke as a dragon. And he exercises all the power of the first beast before him, and causes the earth and them which dwell therein to worship the first beast. And he does great wonders, so that he makes fire come down from heaven on the earth in the sight of men. And deceives them that dwell on the earth by means of those miracles which he had power to do in the sight of the beast, saying to them that dwell on the earth, that they should make an image to the beast, which had the wound by a sword, and did live. And he had power to give life unto the image of the beast, that the image of the beast should both speak, and cause that as many as would not worship the image of the beast should be killed.
>
> Revelation 13:11-15

This vision is of the one-world religion that shall give credence to the one-world government, just as Pope Leo III gave his "blessing" upon Charlemagne. It is a religion that says all religions are equal and valid, and any belief that says otherwise is "hate" speech and must be dealt with. According to this view, all religions lead to god (interfaithism) and will be invited and even commanded to worship the beast.

John 14:6 is where Jesus (Yeshua) proclaims, "I am the Way, the Truth, and the Life. No one comes to the Father, except through Me." Yeshua specifically says He is the only way. Under this one-world religion, this kind of speech will not be tolerated. All eyes will be upon this first beast, and he will proclaim himself to be god. He will make an image of himself, and just like the days of Daniel, when all were commanded to bow before the statue of Nebuchadnezzar or be thrown into the fire, this antichrist will proclaim himself to be the christ, to be the savior, and he will proclaim this from the sanctuary of the re-built temple on the Temple Mount. In Matthew 24:14-15, Jesus says, "And this gospel of the kingdom shall be preached in all the world for a witness, and then the end shall come." When you, therefore, shall see the abomination of desolation spoken of by Daniel the prophet (Daniel 9:27), stand in the holy place (whoso reads, let him understand), then let him who reads which be in Judaea flee into the mountains…

How do we know the true from the false? By knowing and reading and meditating and praying the Word of God and asking the Holy Spirit to teach us and give us discernment. Just knowing where Jesus says He will return will help many to see that this antichrist who proclaims himself to be god in the middle of the sanctuary in Jerusalem is not the Messiah, for Yeshua Messiah said Himself that when He returns the second time, He will come back to the place from which He departed, the Mount of Olives. Zechariah

14 says that when all nations gather themselves against Jerusalem, and all looks hopeless, He will come again to fight for His people.

> Then shall the Lord go forth and fight against those nations, as when He fought in the day of battle. And His feet shall stand that day on the Mount of Olives, which is before Jerusalem on the east, and the Mount of Olives shall cleave in the midst thereof toward the east and toward the west, and there shall be a very great valley; and half of the mountain shall remove to the north, and half of it toward the south.
>
> Zechariah 14:3-4

He will come again in great power, and all will see Him. "For as the lightning comes out of the east, and shines even unto the west, so shall also the coming of the Son of man be" Matthew 24:27.

> And when they shall see the Son of man coming in a cloud with power and great glory. And when these things begin to come to pass, then look up, and lift up your heads… for your Redemption, (your Salvation, your Yeshua) draws near.
>
> Luke 21:28

Yeshua (Jesus in Greek) literally means salvation in the Hebrew language. Our Messiah would have been called Yeshua as He walked throughout Israel, for that is the name given unto Him. Oh, what a beautiful, powerful name!

TEN–A Great Falling Away and the Outpouring of the Holy Spirit

The days we are entering into are both dark and light, in increasing measure. At the beginning of 2020, the Lord YHVH impressed upon me the Burden of Dumah in Isaiah 21, which says:

"The Burden of Dumah. He calls to me out of Seir, Watchman, What of the night? Watchman, what of the night? The watchman said, 'The morning comes, but also the night. If you will inquire, inquire. Return, Come'" (Isaiah 21:11-12).

The Lord YHVH was speaking of a time where we must watch intently as the darkness and evil of this world continue to grow, but also, at the same time, YHVH is doing something marvelous in His Bride. He will provide an abundance of Holy Spirit power to walk through these days of darkness, and His House, His people, will shine brighter as the dark grows darker.

In 2 Thessalonians 2:1-12, it says,

> Now we beseech you brethren (and sisters), by the coming of our Lord Jesus Messiah, and by our gathering together unto Him, that you be not soon shaken in mind, or be troubled, neither by spirit, nor by word, nor by letter as from us, as that the day of Messiah is at hand. Let no man deceive you by any means, *for that day shall not come, except there come a falling away first, and that man of sin (the antichrist) be revealed*, the son of perdition, who opposes and exalts himself above all that is called God, or that is worshipped, so that he as God sits in the temple of God, showing himself that he is God. Do you not remember that when I was yet with you, I told you of these things? And now you know what withholds that he might be revealed in his time. For the mystery of iniquity does already work, only he that now restrains will restrain, until he be taken out of the way. And then shall that Wicked be revealed, whom YHVH shall consume with the

> spirit of his mouth, and shall destroy with the brightness of His Coming, even him (antichrist) whose coming after the working of Satan with all power and signs and lying wonders, and with all deceivableness of unrighteousness in them that perish; *because they received not the love of the truth*, that they might be saved. And for this cause, God shall send them strong delusion, that they should believe a lie, that they all might be damned *who believed not the truth* but had pleasure in unrighteousness.

This passage of Scripture gives a clear warning of the times we are living in. Many who do not know the Scriptures, who do not know the prophetic Word of God, will be swept away in this powerful delusion. People will receive what they have reaped. But God has given us a warning because He loves us, and He does not want any to perish. In 2 Peter 3:1-9, God's Word says,

> Beloved, I now write unto you; in both which I stir up your pure minds by way of remembrance; that you may be mindful of the words which were spoken of by the holy prophets, and of the commandment of us the apostles of the Lord and Savior, knowing this first, *that there shall come in the last days scoffers (mockers), walking after their own lusts, and saying, Where is the promise of His coming?* For since the fathers fell asleep, all things continue as they were from the beginning of creation. For this they willingly are ignorant of, that by the Word of God the heavens were of old, and the earth standing out of the water and in the water, whereby the world that then was, being overflowed with water, perished, but the heavens and the earth, which are now, by the same word are kept in store, *reserved unto fire*, against the day of judgement and perdition of ungodly men. But beloved, be not ignorant of this one thing, that one day is with the Lord YHVH as a thousand

> years, and a thousand years as one day. *The Lord YHVH is not slack concerning His promise, as some men count slackness, but as longsuffering to us-ward, not willing that any should perish, but that all should come to repentance.*

Again, the Lord YHVH gives warning through Peter that in the last days, there will be a rise in the number of people who mock and make fun of those bringing the warning that if we do not look for Him through His Word and heed the signs of His coming, we will miss Him altogether, just as they did the first time. The prophetic Word is extremely important in our day, even as false prophets will arise and deceive many who do not know the Word of God for themselves. We must go deep in the Word of God and ask the Holy Spirit to help us understand passages of Scripture that have been mostly ignored in our day. For God says, the love of man will grow cold, even as His appearing draws nearer.

Matthew 24:11-13 says, "And many false prophets shall rise, and shall deceive many. And because iniquity shall abound, the love of many shall grow cold. But he that shall endure unto the end, the same shall be saved."

The wonderful news for those who love God and His Word is that even in the midst of all this darkness and delusion, those who hold on to YHVH and spend time with Him each day in His Word, by the Holy Spirit, will be directed to passages of Scripture that will awaken us to TRUTH and increase our love for the TRUTH. We will not be lost if we hold tight to the teachings of the Word of God by the Holy Spirit, from Genesis to Revelation.

> In everything give thanks, for this is the will of God in Messiah Yeshua concerning you. Quench not the spirit. Despise not prophesying. Prove all things. Hold fast to that which is

> good. Abstain from all appearance of evil. And the very God of peace sanctify you wholly; and I pray God that your whole spirit and soul and body be preserved blameless unto the coming of our Lord Yeshua Messiah (Jesus Christ). Faithful is He who has called you, who will also do it.
>
> 1 Thessalonians 5:18-24

As the dark grows darker and the love of many grows cold and scoffers and mockers abound, the Lord YHVH promises His people that He will bring upon His people a great outpouring of His Holy Spirit.

> And it shall come to pass, in the last days, says God, I will pour out My Spirit upon all flesh, and your sons and your daughters shall prophesy, and your young men shall see visions, and your old men shall dream dreams; and on My servants and on My handmaidens, I will pour out in those days of My Spirit, *and they shall prophesy.*
>
> Acts 2:17-18

There is an army rising up. But first, we must be cleansed from all unrighteousness, all false teaching and apostasy, all complacency, all self-righteousness and pride, all shallowness. We must return to the God of Abraham, Isaac, and Jacob. We must return to the God of Israel. We must *return* to the roots of our faith to draw deep from the waters of God's Word. We must understand the appointed times of God (mo'edim). We must understand there is a heavenly host also here to help us.

With just these ten prophesies being highlighted, we can see we are approaching the time when Yeshua returns again. It is an exciting time, yet also perilous. But YHVH God has not left us alone; in fact, YHVH Yeshua is with us always through His Holy Spirit, and He has His heavenly host all around us. Some can see into this heavenly realm more than others, but the Bible makes it clear the angels have always been with us throughout history, and they are with us now as we are called to Return to the God of Israel and make our way Home to the Promised Land even as Yeshua's (Jesus') return to earth is very near.

A TIME TO RETURN

In closing of this chapter, a few stories of the Bible come to mind about returning to YHVH (Hosea), returning to the Promised Land (Jacob), returning to His Word (Nehemiah), returning to our Jewish Roots (Ezekiel), and seeing in this *return* (Elisha), we are not alone.

In Genesis 32, Jacob is about to face his brother Esau for the first time since he fled from home. He had deceived his father Isaac to give him the blessing of the firstborn that belonged to Esau, his twin brother. Earlier in the story, Esau had sold it to Jacob for a bowl of pottage or stew. Jacob had to flee his homeland, for Esau was very angry when he found out what Jacob had done. After about twenty years of being gone, Jacob was afraid that his brother may still be angry at him for stealing his birthright, but he was told by God that he must leave Laban, his uncle, and return to the land of his father. Because of what God had told him, Jacob *returns*. "And Jacob went on his way, and the angels of God met him. And when Jacob saw them, he said, 'This is God's host, and he called the name of that place MacHanaim,'" which in the Hebrew means double camp (Genesis 32:1-2). Jacob goes on to divide his own, by now huge family, "people that was with him" into two companies for fear if Esau attacks one company, the other might escape. "Then Jacob was greatly afraid and distressed; and he divided the people that was with him, and the flocks, and herds, and the camels, into two bands" (Genesis 32:7).

Before meeting his brother Esau again, Jacob, in agony of spirit, cries out to the Lord YHVH,

> And Jacob said, O God of my father Abraham, and God of my father Isaac, the Lord YHVH which said return unto your country, and to your kindred, and I will deal well with you. I am not worthy of the least of all the mercies, and of all the truth, which You have showed unto Your servant; for with my staff, I passed over this Jordan; and now I am become two bands. Deliver me, I pray you, from the hand of my brother, from the hand of Esau; for I fear him, lest he will come and smite me, and the mother with the children. And You said, I will surely do thee good, and make thy seed as the sand of the sea, which cannot be numbered for multitude. And he lodged there that same night; and took of that which came to his hand a present for Esau his brother.
>
> Genesis 32:9-13

In the Word of God, there are types and shadows of the things which will happen in the last days (Isaiah 46:10). This story gives us a few clues about the days we are living in. One, it is a call to *return* to the Promised and and to the God of Abraham, Isaac and Jacob; the appointed time is now. Two, it speaks of the angels that are with us to help us go back Home as we face obstacles, and potential enemies. It shows there is a human "army" of two camps and an angelic "army" of two camps. It shows that God will deal well with those who are called to return to Him and obey. It shows we must return in humility and that the call out of the land of Israel was only to bring back many more in the final Return. We see a picture of Jacob leaving the Promised Land only to come back to Israel with a large family with him. Israel and all that are grafted in, we are that family, two bands.

In the book of Nehemiah, Nehemiah was called by God to *return* to rebuild the walls of Jerusalem. The temple of God, built by Solomon, had been burned down by the Babylonians in 586 BC. Seventy years later (516 BC), as prophesied by Jeremiah, the people of the God of Israel were allowed to go back to rebuild their city. Ezra with Zerubabbel is the first to start rebuilding the second temple. Nehemiah, in 444 BC, with the blessing of King Artaxerxes, goes back to Jerusalem to see what had been built and the disrepair and what still needed to be done to repair the walls around the city of Jerusalem. In Nehemiah 2:13-17, it says,

> And I (Nehemiah) went out by night by the gate of the valley, even before the dragon well, and to the Dung Gate, and viewed the walls of Jerusalem, which were broken down, and the gates, also, were consumed with fire. Then I went on to the gate of the fountain, and to the king's pool, but there was no place for the beast that was under me to pass. Then I went up in the night by the brook, and viewed the wall, and turned back, and entered by the gate of the valley, and so returned. And the officials knew not where I went, or what I did; neither had I as yet told it to the Jews, nor to the priests, nor to the nobles, nor to the rulers, nor to the rest that did the work. Then I said unto them, you see the distress that we are in, how Jerusalem lies waste, and the gates thereof are burned with fire; Come, and let us build up the wall of Jerusalem, that we be no more a reproach.

Nehemiah, in this part of the story, assesses the situation and finds that as he approaches the Dung Gate, there is so much rubbish, trash, rubble that he and the donkey that he rides cannot pass through to get to the Fountain Gate. It is a picture of the state of God's house. There is so much rubble, so much false teaching, so much complacency and pride, so much forgetfulness of our roots and the depth of our faith that we cannot get to the fountain of life. The Holy Spirit, in many churches, has departed, and many in the churches have not even noticed. It is a time for assessment, a time for repair, a time to clean up the mess of false and shallow teaching and apostasy. It is time to *return* to rebuild God's house of prayer.

In the book of 2 Kings, Chapter 6, Elisha is walking with his servant. The king of Syria is coming after Elisha, for it was told this king that fought with Israel that all his plans were revealed supernaturally to Elisha and therefore thwarted by the king of Israel. The king of Syria finds out where Elisha is and sends his troops in to surround the city of Dothan so they can kill Elisha. The Word of God says in 2 Kings 6:12-17,

> And one of his servants said, None, my lord O king (Syria); but Elisha the prophet that is in Israel, tells the king of Israel the words that you speak in your bed chamber. And he (the king of Syria) said, Go and spy where he is, that I may send and fetch him. And it was told him, saying, Behold, he is in Dothan. Therefore, he sent there horses, and chariots, and a great host, and they came by night, and compassed the city about. And when the servant of the man of God was risen early, and gone forth, behold, a host surrounded the city both with horses and chariots. And his servant said unto him, Alas, my master! What shall we do? And he (Elisha) answered, Fear not (al tirah), for they that be with us are more than they

> that are with them. And Elisha prayed, and said, Lord YHVH, I pray, open his eyes that he may see. And YHVH opened the eyes of the young man and he saw; and behold, the mountain was full of horses and chariots of fire round about Elisha.

Elisha has no worries. He could see into the heavenly realm. He knew God was all around him and was fighting for him. We also will need to see this way and know, not just in our minds, that there exists a heavenly host to help us, but know it in the depths of our hearts so that we can "see," however God shows us, into this realm and not be afraid for the days ahead. Just as Jacob saw the host of angels and called the place MacHanaim (מחנים), before he faced his brother, and just as Elisha saw the host of heavenly angels encamped around him, we also will NOT be able to go further without first stopping at the place of MacHanaim (the hosts of angels, the two camps).

In the book of Ezekiel, the prophet Ezekiel is told to prophesy to dry bones. He prophesies, and the dry bones come together, bone to bone, "but there was no life in them." This speaks of the return physically of the people of Israel, but yet there is no life in them. Ezekiel 37:9-14 says,

> Then said He unto me, *Prophesy unto the wind, prophesy, son of man, and say to the wind, Thus says YHVH God, Come from the four winds, O breath, and breathe upon these slain, that they may live. So, I prophesied as he commanded me, and the breath came into them, and they lived and stood upon their feet, an exceeding great army. Then He said unto me, Son of man, these bones are the whole house of Israel (we are grafted in with understanding*); behold they say, Our bones are dried, and our hope is lost. We are cut off from our part. (This is the time after the Jewish dispersion from their land

> during the Roman reign and also refers to the Holocaust). Therefore, prophesy and say unto them, Thus says YHVH God, Behold, O my people, I will open your graves, and cause you to come up out of your graves, and bring you into the land of Israel. And you shall know that I am YHVH, when I have opened your graves, O My people, and brought you up out of your graves. *And shall put My spirit in you, and you shall live, and I shall place you in your own land. Then shall you know that I the Lord have spoken it, and performed it, says YHVH.*

Oh, the plans of our God! He is now gathering His people back to the land of Israel physically and awakening them spiritually to the truth of their Jewish Messiah, our Jewish Messiah. Many of the Jewish people have had a blindness on them for almost 2000 years, and now the blinders are being removed, so they can see. They are being awakened spiritually again! And those of us gathered from the nations, the Remnant, are being joined together with them as a *Great Army.* Ezekiel 37:19 goes on to say,

> Say unto them, Thus says YHVH God, Behold, I will take the stick of Joseph (Gentile remnant), which is the hand of Ephraim, and the tribes of Israel, his companions, and will put them with him, even with the stick of Judah, and make them one stick, and they shall be one in mine hand.

Two bands into One.

God's House, since the day we were separated from our Jewish brothers and sisters, exchanging Truth for safety, in the days of Constantine, has been a house of dry bones, a mostly apostate house, which has led to the persecution of our Jewish brothers and sisters increasingly since the days of the Council of Nicaea and the

Council of Laodicea. The last persecution, on a worldwide scale of the Jewish people during the days of the Holocaust of World War II, shows how deep the hatred goes towards God's chosen people; the ones who first received the Word of God on Mount Sinai through Moses, who wrote, by inspiration of the Holy Spirit, the whole Word of God, both Old and New, and through Mary (Miriam), a Jewish handmaiden, birthed our Jewish Messiah, Yeshua, the Savior of the world. We are in the days where those who understand the times must see that we are to be reunited with our Jewish brothers and sisters in love and humility and repentance, and Return, for therein lies the power of God to build His tabernacle, the true Tabernacle of David from His Bride.

In closing of this chapter, Song of Solomon 6:13 says, "Return, return, O Shulamite; return, return, that we may look upon you. What will you see in the Shulamite? As it were, the company of two armies." The Jewish and Gentiles believers together, the angelic host and the army of YHVH on earth, together, His Bride.

We are called to separation and to be cleansed by the washing of the water of His Word (Ephesians 5:26) presented as a spotless bride, blameless. The process will be difficult at times, and many will fall away. This will be painful but necessary.

> Little children, it is the last time, and as you have heard, the antichrist will come, even now are there many antichrists (both in the Gentile nations and in the Jewish nation), whereby we know that it is the last time. They went out from us, for if they had been of us, they would no doubt have continued with us; but they went out, that they might be made manifest that they were not all of us.
>
> 1 John 2:18-20

It is a time of separation, a time of cleansing of the House of God first, and then the greatest outpouring of God's Holy Spirit, the latter rain, in these latter days shall come upon the true House of God, His people. And we must know the appointed time.

We pray,

> Come, let us return unto YHVH, for He has torn, and He will heal us; He has smitten, and He will bind us up. After two days, He will revive us. In the third day, He will raise us up, and we shall live in His sight. Then we shall know, if we follow on to know YHVH, His going forth is prepared as the morning; and He shall come unto us as the rain, and the latter and former rain unto the earth.
>
> Hosea 6:1-3

It is a call to Return, for then He will revive us with His Holy Spirit power. The time is now for it is the third day.

Chapter Three

As in the Days of Noah...

As God's people, we must know the appointed times. God's Word is filled with the prophetic for both Yeshua's first coming and His second coming. In Matthew 24, Jesus tells us many things that will happen in the last days before His return, and one of them is these days will be similar to the days of Noah before the world-wide flood came.

Matthew 24:37-39 says,

> But as the days of Noah were so shall the coming of the Son of man be. For as the days that were before the flood, they were eating and drinking, marrying and giving in marriage, until the day that Noah entered into the ark. And knew not until the flood came, and took them all away; so shall also the coming of the Son of man be.

One morning in my prayer time back in 2018, the Lord YHVH prompted me through the Holy Spirit to look again at the story of Noah in the book of Genesis to find out more about what Jesus meant when He said these last days would be like the days of Noah.

Genesis Chapter 6 is where the story begins. It speaks of a time where men began to "multiply on the earth and daughters were born unto them." Of course, sons were also born to men, but the passage focuses on the daughters and the corruption between heav-en and earth that happens between the daughters of men and the sons of God. This is a profound mystery, difficult to comprehend, yet somehow, because the daughters and sons of Adam were now born in sin because of the fall in Eden, the mixing of heaven and earth by the daughters of men and the sons of God was prohibited until the Messiah Jesus would come and make people "perfected" by His blood that was spilled to cover our iniquities and set us free from evil. Until the sin issue was dealt with, eternal could not mix with mortal. This was a complete abomination to the Lord. This mixing of the two produced profound evil, and YHVH was grieved in His Spirit that He even made man. God plans to destroy mankind, but there is hope in two words. But Noah…

But Noah found grace in the eyes of YHVH, and Noah walked with God, even as the earth was corrupt before God, and the earth was filled with violence (Genesis 6:8, 9 and 11). "And God said to Noah, The end of all flesh is come before Me, for the earth is filled with violence through them, and behold, I will destroy them with the earth. Make an ark of gopher wood" (Genesis 6:13). God goes on to tell Noah all the details of how this ark should be built and what will happen as soon as the ark is completed.

> And behold, I, even I, do bring a flood of waters upon the earth, to destroy all flesh, wherein is the breath of life, from under heaven, and everything that is in the earth shall die. But with you, I will establish My Covenant, and you shall come into the ark, you and your sons, and your wife and your sons' wives with you.
>
> Genesis 6:17-18

Then, as many of us know, God tells Noah to bring in the animals, two by two and some by sevens.

This part of the story is familiar to most of us. We can easily see the parallels of the days of Noah and the increased corruption, evil, and violence upon the earth in these days that we live in. So, these days will be similar to the days of Noah in respect to the dark gets darker, and evil abounds. Yet the Lord YHVH wants to show us more.

Looking closer, we see that the building of this ark was quite an undertaking. From the Word of God, we can understand that it took Noah and his family about one hundred years to build this enormous "boat." The Lord YHVH speaks to Noah about this ark when he is 500 years old. In Genesis 5:32, it says, "And Noah was five hundred years old and Noah begat Shem, Ham, and Japheth." In Genesis 6:10, it again says, "And Noah begat three sons, Shem, Ham, and Japheth." Soon thereafter, God speaks to Noah about building the ark. In Genesis 7:6, the Word of God says, "And Noah was six hundred years old when the flood of waters was upon the earth." During this time of about a hundred years, Noah and his family continued to warn the people of the day. Yet, they only mocked them.

The same will happen with the true prophetic Word today. In many places, it will be mocked. Again in 2 Peter 3:3, "knowing this first, that there shall come in the last days scoffers, mockers, walking after their own lusts." And saying, "Where is the promise of His coming? For since the fathers fell asleep, all things continue as they were from the beginning of creation" (2 Peter 3:4).

Without knowing prophecy, many will not see the signs of the birth of Israel, the gathering together of His people from the four corners of the earth, the nations gathered against Israel, the coming seven-year peace plan between the Palestinians and the Israelis, the birth of globalism, and ecumenism and universalism in religion that we have spoken of previously in the last chapter and many other prophecies spoken of in Isaiah, Jeremiah, Ezekiel, Daniel, Amos, Hosea, and all of the prophetic books. They will see things are going on as they always have (or will hope things will get back to "normal") and will not be able to interpret and understand the times. Yes, they will say, based on Matthew 24, rumors of wars, and earthquakes, and false prophets–just as it has always been, even when Jesus was here the first time. What is the difference now? How can we tell? We cannot know the day or the hour. And the response of those who carry the prophetic Word in their hearts will be, and should be, "Yes, this is true, but we can know the time and the season, and we are commanded to do so."

Jesus spoke to the Pharisees of His day, reprimanding them for not being able to see that He was the Messiah because they did not know the prophetic Word. He says to them, "You hypocrites, you can discern the face of the sky and of the earth, but how is it that you do not discern this time?" (Luke 12:56). He calls to us today to know the times because He loves us and does not want anyone to perish...

Back to the story of Noah. In Genesis 7:11-12, it says,

> In the six hundredth year of Noah's life, in the second month, the seventeenth day of the month, the same day were *all the fountains of the great deep broken up, and the windows of heaven were opened.* And the rain was upon the earth forty days and forty nights.

We see here that the fountains of the earth came together with the outpour of rain from heaven. Heaven and earth touched, meld-ed together, to cleanse the earth once again from all evil. It rained for forty days and forty nights. The number forty is found 146 times in the Bible and is a number used to indicate testing or trial. We see that later in the Bible, Moses was sent into the wilderness for forty years before being called to lead the children of Israel out of Egypt, the children of Israel were tested for forty years in the wilderness before going into the Promised Land, Jesus Himself fasted for forty days in the wilderness before starting His public ministry. Forty days and nights, the earth was tested and cleansed to start again.

Still, there is much more to this story. Genesis 7:18 says, "And the waters prevailed, and were increased greatly upon the earth, and the ark went upon the face of the waters." Genesis 7:23 says,

> And every living substance was destroyed which was upon the face of the ground, both man, and cattle, and the creeping things, and the birds of heaven and they were destroyed from the earth; and only Noah remained alive, and they that were with him in the ark.

The Lord speaks that just as in the days of Noah, the waters prevailed, so in these last days, the nations, signified by waters, shall prevail over the earth. It is a one-world government, and only those in the ark (in Jesus) will remain, will be protected from the coming destruction.

Revelation 12:15-16 says,

> And the serpent cast out of his mouth water as a flood after the woman (this is Israel, God's Bride, including all of us grafted in), that he might cause her to be carried away after the flood. And the earth helped the woman, and the earth opened her mouth, and swallowed up the flood which the dragon cast out of his mouth.

Just so you can see, the waters are nations interpreted so by the Bible itself, Revelation 17:1,15 says,

> And there came one of the seven angels which had the seven vials, and talked with me saying unto me, Come, here. I will show you the judgement of the great whore (the one world religion) that sits upon many waters. And he says unto me, The waters which you saw, where the whore sits, are peoples, and multitudes, and nations and tongues.

This is warfare, and YHVH God will have the last word. Isaiah 58:19 says, "So shall they fear the name of YHVH from the west, and His glory from the rising of the sun, When the enemy shall come in like a flood, the Spirit of YHVH shall lift up a standard against him."

It is amazing to see that Satan always uses a mimic of what the God of all creation is doing. YHVH God used a flood of waters to cleanse the earth of evil in the beginning. Satan will try to use a flood of nations to conquer and destroy goodness and God's people in the last days. But the earth shall open up and swallow these nations. This could very well mean a great earthquake will happen, which will destroy many of those who come against Israel and all God's people.

Yet, there is more to this story. After the forty days, Genesis 7:24 says, "the waters prevailed upon the earth 150 days." Noah and his family, for five more months, wait in the ark for something to change. Then after 150 days, God remembers Noah (like He ever forgot!). Genesis 8:1-4 says,

> And God remembered Noah, and every living thing, and all the animals that were with him in the ark, and God made a wind to pass over the earth. The fountains also of the deep

> and the windows of heaven were stopped, and the rain from heaven was restrained… And the ark rested in the seventh month, on the seventeenth day of the month, upon the mountain of Ararat.

The day the ark rested was on the seventh month, the seventeenth day. What is the significance of that, if any? In Leviticus 23, YHVH speaks to the children of His appointed holy days. All of these holy days are commanded to be kept for a very special reason; they are shadows and types of what is to come, appointed times to keep His people looking for Him to appear as Savior first (the spring holy days), and then King of kings (the fall holy days). The feasts or holy days of the Lord are important today, but for the story of Noah, the seventh month, the seventeenth day falls right in the middle of when God ordains the Feast of Tabernacles for the children of Israel, once this nation is called out of Egypt about 1000 years later, through Moses.[12] The Feast of Tabernacles is a celebration pointing to the day when Jesus returns "to tabernacle with us" forever, Imanuel (Hebrew spelling), God is with us. In this seventh month, the seventeenth day, the Mount Ararat gives a place for the ark to rest, and for Noah and his family to feel hope for a new day. The Feast of Tabernacles was given to the people of Israel to remember there will be a day for Messiah to return, to give hope, and then REST forevermore in His second coming. These are just windows of looking into a much bigger subject, yet still fascinating as we look to the layers of mystery and beauty in God's Word.

The actual revelation of a day back in 2018 came as I meditated on the next part of this story.

> And it came to pass at the end of forty days, that Noah opened

> the window of the ark which he had made, and *he sent forth a raven*, which went forth to and fro, until the waters were dried up from off the earth. Also, *he sent a dove* from him, to see if the waters were abated from off the face of the ground; but the dove found no rest for the sole of her foot, and she returned unto him into the ark, for the waters were on the face of the whole earth. Then he put forth his hand, and took her, and pulled her in unto him into the ark. *And he stayed yet other seven days; and again, he sent forth the dove* out of the ark; and the dove came into him in the evening; and lo, in her mouth was an olive leaf plucked off, so Noah knew the waters were abated from off the earth. *And he stayed yet other seven days, and sent forth the dove*, which returned not again unto him anymore.
>
> Genesis 8:6-12

The Lord YHVH speaks by His Spirit to rivet my eyes upon the birds being released in each time period. The first bird Noah releases is the raven, and then in three consecutive sets of seven days, he releases a dove. YHVH speaks that each of these birds represents a time period for all of history! I look closer. At the end of forty days, after the rains had stopped and the cleansing of the earth occurred, the raven is released. "And it came to pass at the end of forty days, that Noah opened the window of the ark which he had made, and he sent forth a raven, which went forth to and fro, until the waters were dried up from off the earth." The raven, I hear in my spirit, is the time period of man "when everyone did what was right in their own eyes." The raven flies back and forth, as he pleases, and does what he wants throughout all the time periods, "until the waters were dried from off the earth." The raven represents when God was silent for a time; it was the time period when He let man do what he wanted, and there was no Holy Spirit to guide people to righteousness. "And God saw that the wickedness of man was great in the earth." This represents all the time of Noah before and after until God begins to speak again directly to man. It also represents all of the appointed times, as there will always be people that will refuse the gift of the next bird, the dove, which represents God's Holy Spirit.

The next time period, represented by the first dove, a symbol of the Holy Spirit, starts when God calls to Abram in Genesis 12:1 about the year 2000 BC. Now the Lord YHVH said unto Abram, "Get out of your country, and from your kindred, and from your father's house, and unto a land I will show you." God is once again speaking directly to humans; the first one is Abram, and calling a people unto Himself, separated from the world. Again, this time period is about 2000 BC when Abram is called.

From this calling, the nation of Israel is born. Abraham begat Isaac and Isaac begat Jacob. In Genesis 32, as we recall, Jacob is renamed Israel, and the rest of the Tanakh or as it is also called the Old Testament, is devoted to telling the story of this Chosen people; the Israelites, the Jewish people, are being set apart from the rest of the world and their gods, and to point to the only true God, the God of Israel. In this time period, we find the roots of our faith.

The people try to live by the Law of God given to them on Mt. Sinai through Moses but find over the next 2000 years that keeping the Law perfectly is impossible in their own strength. The only ones who can keep the Law are the ones that God pours out His Holy Spirit on them. These are far, and few between but are all the heroes and heroines we love in the Old Testament, Abraham, Sarah, Gideon, Deborah, Isaiah, Jeremiah, Ezekiel, the list goes on.

They are anointed individually with the Holy Spirit to lead the people, but once the leader anointed with the Holy Spirit dies, or the Spirit is lifted from them (for example, King Saul), the people find themselves doing wrong again. There is no "corporate" outpouring of the Holy Spirit in this 2000 years "under the Law." The people try, but *NO ONE* can keep the Law in their own strength, as YHVH teaches us this through His chosen people. God then moves to *the* remedy.

The next dove sent out, still finding no place for the sole of her foot to rest, comes back with an olive branch in her mouth. The Lord YHVH speaks this dove represents when Yeshua was born unto people. The dove has an olive *branch* in her mouth. This is significant and speaks directly of Jesus. Let us look at some Scriptures.

Isaiah 11:1-2 says,

> And there shall come forth a rod out of the stem of Jesse (King David's father), and a BRANCH shall grow out of his roots. And the Spirit of the Lord YHVH shall rest upon Him, the Spirit of wisdom and understanding, the Spirit of counsel and might, the Spirit of knowledge and of the fear of YHVH.

Jeremiah 33:15-16 says,

> In those days, and at that time, I will cause the BRANCH of righteousness to grow up unto David, and He shall execute judgement and righteousness in the land. In those days shall Judah be saved, and Jerusalem shall dwell safely, and this is the name wherewith she shall be called, The Lord our righteousness.

We see in this verse the people called to be separated from the world will now find their righteousness not in their own works but in the Lord YHVH.

Zechariah 3:8 says,

> Hear now, O Joshua the high priest, you and your fellows that sit before you, for they are men wondered at; for, behold, I will bring forth My Servant, the BRANCH. For Behold, the stone that I have laid before Joshua, upon one stone shall be seven eyes. Behold, I will engrave the inscription thereof, says YHVH of hosts, and I will remove the iniquity of that land (Israel) in one day.

This speaks of Yeshua, the Branch, coming back the second time to remove iniquity from His people completely, yet it speaks of Jesus as the *branch.*

Just one more verse to show how the dove with the branch truly represents Yeshua, although there are still others.

> And speak unto him, saying, Thus speaks YHVH of hosts saying, Behold the man whose name is The Branch; and He shall grow up out of His place and He shall build the temple of YHVH. Even He shall build the Temple of YHVH, and He shall bear the glory, and shall sit and rule upon his throne, and He shall be a priest upon His throne; *and the counsel of peace shall be between them both.*
>
> Zechariah 6:12-13

Yeshua is the bridge between the Jewish people and the nations, "between them Both."

This verse also speaks of when Yeshua will build the final temple of God, the one built "without human hands."

We also know that when Jesus first starts His ministry, a dove descends upon Him, and YHVH says, "this is My Son, in whom I am well pleased." We enter a time when Yeshua dies for the people to forgive them and cleanse them of their sin. Those who receive Jesus as their Savior are then ready to receive a greater outpouring of the Holy Spirit at the time of Pentecost or in the Hebrew, Shavuot. In Acts 2:2-4, it says,

> And suddenly there came a sound from heaven as of a rushing mighty wind, and it filled all the house where they (the disciples of Jesus) were sitting. And they were ALL filled with the Holy Spirit, and began to speak with other tongues, as the Spirit gave them utterance.

These Jewish disciples *all* were filled with the Holy Spirit, and they spoke in other languages.

YHVH is showing that He is about to send the Jewish people that believed in Yeshua unto all the nations with the Gospel (*besorah*) of Jesus. In Acts Chapter 2, verses 38, 39, and 41 says,

> Then Peter said unto them, Repent, and be baptized every one of you in the name of Jesus Messiah for the remission of sins, and you shall receive the gift of the Holy Spirit. For the promise is unto you and to your children (the Jewish people) and to all that are afar off (the Gentile people who will be grafted in), even as many as YHVH God shall call. Then they that gladly received His Word were baptized, and the same day there were added unto them about three thousand souls.

About ten years later, Peter is commanded to preach unto the first Gentiles to also receive the Holy Spirit. He goes to Cornelius' house. Acts 10:34-35 says, "Then Peter opened his mouth, and said, 'Of a truth I perceive that God is no respecter of persons, but in every nation, he that fears Him, and works righteousness is accepted with Him.'" Peter speaks many other words through the Holy Spirit, and–

> While Peter yet spoke these words, the Holy Spirit fell on ALL them which heard the Word. And they of the circumcision (the Jewish people) which believed were astonished, as many as came with Peter, because that on the Gentiles also was poured out the gift of the Holy Spirit. For they heard them speak with tongues, and magnify God.
>
> Acts 10:44-46

This marks a whole new 2000 year period where God's people, His House, go into all the nations preaching the Good News of Yeshua. All that receive this Word and believe in their hearts that Jesus is Lord and Savior receive the Holy Spirit. It is an outpouring of the "sign of the dove."

Once again, for the third time, Noah releases the dove after another seven-day period, "which returned not again unto him any-more." Again, this represents another 2000 years from Yeshua's first coming and the outpouring of the Holy Spirit to the current day. The last dove represents the millennial period we are entering into now.

According to Answers in Genesis, the founder Ken Ham, and other biblical scholars of the book of Genesis, the world is about 6000 years old, starting in about 4004 BC. [13] So, according to this understanding, the raven represents the time without God when men did "whatever was right in their own eyes" and did not have the Holy Spirit at all (except for Noah and his family) in the first

2000 years (from around 4000-2000 BC). The next bird, the first dove, represents the time of Abram, the Law through Moses, and the separation of a people unto the God of Abraham, Isaac, and Jacob (Israel), from 2000 BC to the day of Pentecost (21 AD-31 AD). The second dove represents the time of the Holy Spirit outpouring unto *all* that believe in the atoning work of Yeshua. The Holy Spirit gives the power to keep the Law of God that was not available to all during the Old Testament. This time period is from approximately the first outpouring of the Holy Spirit detailed in Acts 2 to current times, the twenty-first century. The third dove is the time we are entering into now when the dove flies out of the ark and finds *rest* in all the earth, for Jesus has returned to rule and reign from the throne of David, as prophesied. It is the seventh millennial period and will start soon when Yeshua comes back again, and we, His people, have finally found a place for the sole of our foot to rest. We, His people, will change in the twinkling of an eye, and we will no longer need to return to the ark because the ark has taken over the whole world, and we are with Him, ruling and reigning on the earth! The Holy Spirit is now not just inside us but all around us and fills the whole earth with His glory! It is a time of *rest*, the Sabbath day, the seventh day in all the earth.

Second Peter 3:8 says, "But beloved be not ignorant of this one thing, that ONE DAY is with the Lord YHVH as a thousand years, and a thousand years as one day."

Three 2000 year periods equals 6000 years or six days, according to this Scripture. We are entering into the seventh day, the day of *rest*, the millennial kingdom.

Psalm 90:4, "For a thousand years in Your sight are but as yesterday when it is past, and as a watch in the night."

Habbakuk 2:14, "For the earth shall be filled with the knowledge of the glory of YHVH as the waters cover the sea."

In all the Bible, we see the ark over and over again. The ark represents a place of refuge and hiding during dark and difficult times. It represents Jesus, Yeshua. The ark is found in the story of Noah; in Moses as a baby; in Moses with the Ten Commandments; in the carrying of the ark by Joshua across the Jordan; in the story of David and shekinah glory; in the tomb of Jesus, the two cherubim over the mercy seat! In the ark, in Yeshua, we are covered and protected by the waters of destruction, whether physical or spiritual forces. When Yeshua comes again as the Lion of Judah, the darkness will be overcome. We will not need to hide in the ark. We will live with Him openly and freely in His glory!

One final note, in these days, as in the days of Noah, YHVH invites us to enter into His rest, into His ark of safety, until these dark days be finished. Hebrews 4:1-11 says,

> Let us therefore fear, unless a promise being left us of entering into His REST, any of you should seem to come short of it (miss it). For unto us was the gospel preached, as well as unto them; but the Word preached did not profit them, not being mixed with the faith in them that heard it. For we which have believed do enter into REST, as He said, As I have sworn in My wrath, if they shall enter into My Rest, although the works were finished from the foundation of the world. For He spoke in a certain place of the SEVENTH DAY (significant) on this wise, And God did Rest the seventh day from all His works. And in this place again, If they shall enter into MY Rest. Seeing therefore it remains that some must enter in, and they to whom it was first preached entered not in because of unbelief. Again, He limits a CERTAIN DAY, saying in David,

> Today, AFTER SO LONG A TIME, as if is said, TODAY, if you will hear His Voice, harden not your hearts. For if Jesus had given them REST (His first coming), then would He not afterward have spoken of another day. There remains therefore a REST to the People of GOD. For he that is entered into His Rest, he also has ceased from His own works, as God did from His. Let us labor therefore to enter into that REST, lest any man fall after the same manner of unbelief.

YHVH, Father, ABBA invites all that have heard the Gospel of Yeshua to not only hear the Word but to take it in, receive it, so that the Holy Spirit will confirm that it has been made personal, and He will seal the Word in your heart. Seal it, write it upon your heart, the Word of God, all of it. The Rest spoken of in the Scriptures is the Holy Spirit. For without the Holy Spirit, all of our works profit nothing. We enter His rest when the Word falls on good soil, the Holy Spirit is received, and we become abundant in good works that God, the Father, has given us to do. Our eyes are on Him, Yeshua, not on the world around us, not on impressing people, not on making a name for ourselves, not on becoming famous or well-liked, but by "every Word that proceeds out of the mouth of God." It is so good to enter into His rest, for He gives us everything we need in order to accomplish His will by the power of the Holy Spirit. Enter into the ark, He beckons us, for these days are like the days of Noah…נח

Oh, and by the way, Noah's name in Hebrew is NoacH (נוח, נח pronounced NoaKH). It means *REST*.

Chapter Four

Where We Are in Time, The Feasts of YHVH

In the book of Leviticus, YHVH God speaks to Moses and tells him to speak unto the children of Israel concerning the feasts of the Lord, the special times God wanted the children of Israel to turn away from the busyness of their everyday lives to stop and remember Him. The Lord YHVH speaks to Moses of a sabbath rest that must be kept every week on the seventh day and seven other feasts or holy convocations that point to Him. The first three feasts are to be kept in the spring and are closely tied together: It is the Feast of Passover, the Feast of Unleavened Bread, and the Feast of First Fruits. The fourth feast, Shavuot, is to be kept in the summer, fifty days after the first sabbath day of the spring feasts. The last three holy convocations, the Feast of Trumpets, the Day of Atonement, and the Feast of Tabernacles, are to be kept in the Fall, starting in the seventh month of the Jewish calendar. These appointed times are times of reflection, repentance, and also celebration. Yet, they are more than that. These appointed times (moed'im) are shadows of things to come. They all point to Jesus the Messiah, and they are reminders of the appointed times of prophecy.

Leviticus 23 begins,

> And YHVH spoke unto Moses saying, Speak unto the children of Israel, and say unto them, Concerning the feasts of the Lord, which you shall proclaim to be holy convocations,

even these are My Feasts. "Six days shall work be done, but on the SEVENTH day is the Sabbath of REST, a holy convocation; you shall do no work therein; it is the Sabbath of the Lord in all your dwellings."

Leviticus 23:1-3

Leviticus 23:4-6 goes on to say,

These are the feasts of the Lord YHVH, even holy convocations, which you shall proclaim in their seasons. In the fourteenth day of the first month (Jewish month, Nisan, which can fall in March or April of the Gregorian calendar), at evening, is the Lord's PASSOVER. And on the fifteenth day of the same month is the FEAST OF UNLEAVENED BREAD unto the Lord; seven days you must eat unleavened bread (flat bread without yeast).

In Leviticus 23:9-10, the Lord then goes on to tell the children of Israel of the sacrifice of first fruits. "Speak unto the children of Israel, and say unto them, When you come into the land which I give unto you, and shall reap the harvest thereof, then you shall bring a sheaf of the FIRST FRUITS of your harvest."

These three feasts unto the Lord YHVH, the Passover, the Feast of Unleavened Bread, and the Feast of First Fruits are the spring feasts of the Lord, and they have spiritual significance in what they symbolize every time the Jewish people held these feasts.

In Leviticus 23:15-16, YHVH speaks of a summer holy convocation unto Him.

And you shall count unto the next Sabbath, from the day that you brought the sheaf of the wave offering, seven sab-

> baths shall be complete (forty-nine days after the beginning of Passover); even unto the next day shall you number fifty days, and you shall offer a new meat offering unto YHVH.

This celebration is called Shavuot, the feast during the summer harvest. It usually occurs in May or June of each year in the Jewish month of Sivan.

The last three feasts unto the Lord occur in the fall or autumn. The first is spoken of in Leviticus 23:23-25,

> And the Lord YHVH spoke unto Moses, saying, Speak unto the children of Israel, saying, In the seventh month, (Jewish month of Tishrei, which is usually in our months of September or October), in the first day of the month, shall you have a sabbath, a memorial of blowing of trumpets (shofars), a holy convocation. You shall do no service work that day; but you shall offer an offering made by fire unto YHVH.

This is the Feast of Trumpets. Yom te'ruah, or Rosh ha'shanah are two other names given to this holy day.

The second fall holy day is the Day of Atonement.

> And the Lord spoke unto Moses saying, Also, on the tenth day of this seventh month, there shall be a DAY OF ATONEMENT; it shall be a holy convocation unto you, and you shall afflict your souls (fast), and offer an offering made by fire unto YHVH... It shall be unto you a sabbath of REST, and you shall afflict your souls (fast, pray, repent); in the ninth day of the month at evening, from evening (ninth) unto evening (tenth), shall you celebrate your sabbath.
>
> Leviticus 23:26-28, 32

The third fall holy convocation is the Feast of Tabernacles.

Leviticus 23:33-37, 39,

> And the Lord YHVH spoke unto Moses, saying, Speak unto the children of Israel, saying, The fifteenth day of this seventh month shall be the FEAST OF TABERNACLES, for seven days unto the Lord. On the first day shall be a holy convocation; you shall do no service work therein. Seven days you shall offer an offering made by fire unto the Lord; on the eighth day shall be a holy convocation unto you; and you shall offer an offering made by fire unto the Lord; it is a SOLEMN assembly; and you shall do no service work therein. These are the feasts of the Lord YHVH, which you shall proclaim to be Holy Convocations, to offer an offering made by fire… Also, in the fifteenth day of the seventh month, when you have gathered in the fruit of the land, you shall keep a feast unto the Lord seven days; on the first day shall be a sabbath, and on the eighth day shall be a sabbath.

This last feast onto YHVH shall be a total of seven days and then an eighth day to complete the celebration. It is a harvest of fall fruits.

Altogether, besides the sabbath that we are given to keep each week to enter into His *rest*, there are seven feasts commanded by the Lord. Three occur at the same time, within the same week, in the spring season; one occurs in the summer, and the last three in the fall season. In each of these seasons, there is a harvest: first fruits in the spring, summer harvest at Shavuot, and the fall fruits to be gathered in, or fall harvest during the month of Tishrei, in September or October of the Gregorian calendar. It is a beautiful picture! YHVH God will first send out the good news through our Messiah in the spring of all history; these first fruits, first believers (mostly all Jewish in the beginning) will take the Gospel message to the nations and gather in the summer harvest (the past 2000 years), and once the time of the Gentiles is fulfilled, the final fall harvest will be gathered in, Jewish and Gentile believers together. This is where we are in time. God is about to gather the final fall harvest, His bride, before Yeshua's return to the earth.

Let's look at each of these holy convocations one at a time to see what they really mean. The Lord speaks of these holy days as shadows and types of what is to come, through Paul in the book of Colossians. So, what is he speaking of in Colossians 2:16-17 when he says, "Let no one therefore judge you in meat, or in drink, or in respect of a holyday, or of the new moon or of the sabbath days, which are a shadow of things to come; but the substance is of Yeshua." He is saying, when you celebrate these days, commanded in Leviticus, do not let anyone judge you for doing so, for these are a shadow of things to come, and all these feasts point to Messiah. The Word of God is not saying, "Do not keep these holy days," for Jesus kept every one of them Himself; instead, He is saying, "Let no one judge you for doing them for the substance of them is Me!" They all point to *Me*! They are holy and to be remembered because they keep our eyes on Jesus and on the prophetic Word of God.

So, what does this have to do with us today? Why keep these feasts? Why honor these days? What is YHVH saying to us through these feasts, even today?

When I returned from Israel back in 2018, the Holy Spirit awakened in me a fire, an urgency for the soon return of Jesus. I knew very little about the feasts of God and felt no need to keep them, but something began to change. One morning in late summer of 2018, I felt the Lord Jesus speak to me through the Holy Spirit that He wanted me to bring the Feast of Trumpets to Culpeper,

VA, the place where my family and I have lived for almost fifteen years. I know I protested a bit since I barely knew what a Feast of Trumpets was and definitely had no idea how to bring it to Culpeper. The Lord was gentle yet persistent. This is what He wanted. So, I prayed, and each day, the Lord Jesus gave me instructions on how to bring this to my hometown. I delved in and learned as much as I could about this holy day. I made invitations, invited a band to play, made a PowerPoint from what I had learned with praise and worship and teaching on Israel and all the feasts and how they too pointed to a timeline, all of the HIStory of God. I was fascinated, and maybe a bit overwhelmed, but God made it happen. I followed His instructions, and every obstacle that stood in the way was removed. That night, on Sept. 10, 2018, over sixty people came out from churches in the community, and we celebrated with prayer, teaching, praising, and dancing. The shofars blew, the Israeli flags waved, and the people rejoiced. It was beautiful! I knew something very special had happened in my hometown. No one felt they were under the *Law* in keeping this feast. We were celebrating the soon return of Yeshua! I wanted to know more. I hope you will too.

The Spring Holy Days (3) Passover, Feast of Unleavened Bread, and First Fruits

Briefly, the three spring feasts, Passover, the Feast of Unleavened Bread, and the Feast of First Fruits, pointed to the day when the Messiah Jesus would come the first time. Many of us know that Jesus is called The Lamb of God who takes away the sins of the world (John 1:14). Passover celebrates the days when Israel was commanded before leaving Egypt to put the blood of the lamb on their doorposts so that the angel of death would "pass over" them.

The blood of these lambs pointed to the day when the Lamb of God would take away the sins of all those who believed, and death would have no more power over the children of God; they would have eternal life with YHVH forevermore. We celebrate this day with a Passover Seder (seder means "in order"), and we retell the story of Moses, by the hand of YHVH, leading the Israelites out of Egypt, out of slavery to follow the one true God. It reminds us that we have been released from slavery to sin by Yeshua (Jesus) once and for all. It is a wonderful time as the Messianic Seder retells the story with Jesus in mind every step of the way.

The Feast of Unleavened Bread

The Feast of Unleavened Bread reminds us that the sin of our lives has been swept clean, and there is a process, after we are saved, to come into a mature understanding of God's Word. For this week, all leaven and leavening ingredients are taken out of the house for a week, symbolizing in the natural the cleansing of sin from our lives because of the blood of Jesus. It is a challenge not to eat such things as leavened bread, waffles, muffins, or cakes for a week, but it is a good reminder of the children of Israel needing to leave quickly from Egypt and that they had no time to let their bread rise. They needed to make flatbread for provision, for they were to leave the next day. Jesus later teaches that leaven symbolizes sin and needs to be cleansed. In Matthew 16:6, Jesus says unto His disciples, "Take heed and beware of the leaven of the Pharisees and the Saducees." At first, the Jewish disciples do not understand what Jesus is teaching but then as He explains, "Then they understood how He bade them not beware of the leaven of bread, but of the doctrine of the Pharisees and of the Saducees (man-made religion)" (Matthew 16:12).

As we have celebrated Passover (with a Passover seder that retells the story of the Exodus, the deliverance of the children of Israel from Egypt) and the week of Unleavened Bread in our family, it is a great reminder for all of us, from generation to generation, what Jesus did on the cross for us, and that He took the leaven (the sin) out of our lives. The leaven being taken out of the house for a week reminds us that sin being taken out of our life, although fully forgiven at the cross, takes time to mature into a deep understanding of His Word as we spend time with YHVH through the power of the Holy Spirit.

The Feast of First Fruits

The Feast of First Fruits is the giving our lives over to Yeshua completely; the first believers were the first fruits of Yeshua's sacrifice. The prophetic fulfillment of these feasts has already occurred. This part of the telling of history from Leviticus 23 happened when Jesus came to the earth to take away our sins and bring Salvation to a dying world. The first fruit believers, His Jewish disciples, were then later commanded in the Book of Acts to take the Gospel to all the nations, into all the world, starting with Cornelius' house. But first, they would need to be baptized in the Holy Spirit.

SUMMER HOLY DAY, Shavuot (1)

Fifty days after Passover, after Jesus was crucified as the Lamb of God, the first fruit disciples were baptized by the Holy Spirit and sealed with the Holy Spirit of promise (Ephesians 1:13). The summer feast, Shavuot, or Pentecost (as we call it), celebrated by reading the Book of Ruth each year, signified the time when the Holy Spirit would be poured out to all believers in Jesus, first to the Jewish people (in Acts 2) and then to the Gentile people who are grafted in (Acts 10 and forward). It is a great summer harvest, both physically and spiritually. We remember the days when Jesus told His disciples that they should not depart from Jerusalem but wait for the promise of the Father, which says He, you have heard of Me. "And He said unto them, But you shall receive power, after the Holy Spirit is come upon you; and you shall be witnesses unto me both in Jerusalem, and in all Judaea, and in Samaria, and unto the uttermost part of the earth" (Acts 1:4 and 8).

Soon thereafter, many Jewish people were added to those who believed in Jesus. In Acts 2:36-41, it says,

> Therefore let all the House of Israel know assuredly, that God has made that same Jesus, whom you have crucified, both Lord and Messiah. Now when they heard this they were pricked in their heart, and said unto Peter and to the rest of the apostles, Men and brethren, what shall we do? Then Peter said unto them, Repent, and be baptized every one of you in the name of Yeshua Messiah for the forgiveness of sins, and you shall receive the Holy Spirit. For the promise is unto you and unto your children, and to all that are afar off (Gentiles that they would be sent to later), even as many as YHVH our God shall call. And with many other words did he testify and exhort, saying, Save yourselves from this untoward generation. Then they that gladly received His W ord were baptized, and the same day there were added unto them about three thousand souls (all Jewish, my friends. Please see this).

In Acts 2:47 it says, and the Lord added to the ha'edah daily such as should be saved. Ha'edah is interpreted as church by the Greek interpreters, yet it really means congregation. The Gentile Church was not born yet. These all were Jewish people. The birth and connection of Jewish and Gentile believers together happen in Acts 10.

This giving of the Holy Spirit has continued throughout the last 2000 years as the former rain; Shavuot points to the summer harvest of all God's people that would come to know Jesus (Yeshua) in the following years because of the preaching of the Word by the first fruit harvest. Yet even a greater harvest and a later day rain, the outpouring of God's Holy Spirit is coming in our day!

Fall Holy Days (3), Feast of Trumpets, Day of Atonement, and Feast of Tabernacles

The last three feasts signify the days ahead, which believers in this last generation watch for with anticipation, even as the second coming of Jesus draws near. These feasts have not happened yet in the spiritual realm; yet, we look earnestly for their arrival.

The Feast of Trumpets, (also known as Yom Te'RuacH or Rosh Ha'Shana)

The Feast of Trumpets, which we celebrated in Culpeper, and is celebrated in many places around the world today both by Jewish and Messianic Jewish believers and Gentile believers grafted in, points to the day when the trumpet will be blown, and the Lord Yeshua will call His Bride home. It is a joyful sound to those who know Him. With the greater outpouring of the Holy Spirit, this last harvest will be greater than we can imagine. It points to the calling Home of His people.

First Corinthians 15:51-54 says,

> Behold, I show you a MYSTERY; we shall not all sleep, but we shall all be changed. In a moment, in the twinkling of an eye, at the last Trump, for the TRUMPET will sound, and the dead shall be raised incorruptible, and we shall be changed. For this corruptible must put on incorruption, and this mortal must put on immortality. So when this corruptible shall have put on incorruption, and this mortal shall have put on immortality, then shall be brought to pass the saying that is written, Death is swallowed up in Victory.

Matthew 24:31 says, "And He shall send His angels with a great sound of a TRUMPET and they shall gather together His elect from the four winds, from one end of heaven to the other."

With the celebration of the Feast of Trumpets every year, we are reminded that Jesus, our Messiah, not only came the first time as our Passover Lamb, but He will come again as the Lion of Judah. We are reminded to keep watch and to prepare for this day. The Feast of Trumpets or Rosh Ha'Shana (the New Year) is the celebration of the new beginning.

Yet, the shofar call of the Feast of Trumpets is also a warning call and relates to the Day of Atonement. The bride must be prepared, sanctified, and filled with Holy Spirit oil before she is taken Home. It leads into the observance of the Day of Atonement.

The Day of Atonement

The Day of Atonement is a call to repentance. It is the time period we are in right now, between the call to repent and re-dedicate ourselves to YHVH, the God of Israel, and the time when the shofar trumpet will call us Home. We are being called to be still and know that I am God (Psalm 46:10). YHVH wants us to know Him and to repent and heal the breaches in His House. We will not be able to go back to the way we have always done things. We must first repent and be cleansed, and God is giving us warning and reproof in these days.

We have much to repent of. The "Church," in many places, has been shallow in its teachings or, worse, false. Many are taught that the "Church" has replaced Israel and the Jewish people. This false and evil teaching is called Replacement Theology and perpetuates anti-semitism in the hearts of many. Maybe it is not taught outright, but it is there, underlying so much of the teaching we hear in our "churches." This is a terrible breach that must be healed in these last days. We must return to the God of Israel, for there is no other. We must repent of the false teaching of Replacement Theology and the teaching of Dualism, the belief that Jewish people do not need Jesus or if they are saved at all, they will be saved another way. This again is a lie from the pit of hell. Jesus is our Jewish Messiah. He preached mostly only to the Jewish people while on the earth, where many believed Him and many (mostly the religious leaders of Israel) did not. He then commanded His Jewish disciples to preach the whole Word and the Gospel message to the nations around them and then unto the whole world. Again, the Jewish people gave us the Word of God, gave us our Messiah Jesus, and preached the Gospel to all the Gentile nations so that we would know too and receive the Holy Spirit. We are to understand that it was only the Jewish religious leaders who were not willing to give up their prestige, power and wealth, that conspired against Jesus, much like the religious system of our world today. We are also now commanded to go back to the Jewish people in this day when the spirit of slumber is being removed and bring them back Home, not only physically but spiritually. We have done much damage to our Jewish brothers and sisters in the name of Christ, for one, the Holocaust. In these days of rising antisemitism, we, as the Gentile house of God, must make a concerted effort, lift up an audible voice that stands with the Jewish people and stands against the ancient and persistent hatred of antisemitism.

Many are the breaches in the House of God. So, why do I make such a big deal out of this particular *breach*? It is because this breach cuts at the root of our faith. It is whether we truly know Jesus or we do not. If we preach or learn from a false foundation, all other teachings of truth will ultimately fail. The foundation of our faith must be solid ground. Correcting this breach will bring truth to all other matters, including the stand for *life*, the stand for marriage according to God's principles, the stand for honesty, for liberty, for the healing of the nations, for the building of the true Kingdom of God. We must do it His Way, not ours, for without the Holy Spirit, "the heart is deceitful, who can know it?"

The prophetic Word must also be taught "rightly dividing the Word of Truth." This is a breach, a gaping hole, in many churches, where the pastor and leaders will not teach the prophetic Word pointing to the soon return of Jesus, either because they do not understand it or because they feel it is not important. Because of the absence of solid teaching on the thousands of Scriptures that point, not only to Jesus coming the first time as the Lamb of God but also His coming again as the Lion of Judah, much false prophecy has crept into the House of God and is deceiving many. Where there is a vacuum, a black hole, in the teaching of God's Word, the enemy will fill it. Some preachers will debunk this false prophecy but still refuse to understand and teach the true prophetic Word, which is necessary to prepare God's people for the days ahead and to show clearly that YHVH God is in full control of all time, from beginning to end. Without the prophetic Word being taught, the people lack knowledge and understanding. The scriptures say, "For lack of knowledge, My people perish" (Hosea 4:6).

Acts 2:17 says,

> And it shall come to pass in THE LAST DAYS, says God, I will pour out My Spirit upon all flesh; and your sons and YOUR DAUGHTERS shall prophesy, and your young men shall see visions, and your old men shall dream dreams; and on My servants and on My HANDMAIDENS I will pour out in those days of My Spirit; and they shall prophesy.

Many other false teachings are entering into the church added to these two huge, long-standing breaches (anti-semitism and despising prophecy), which have made the House of God weak and ineffective. We must repent. We must change our way of thinking. We must stop building our own kingdoms, our own popularity, our own comfort, and teach the whole Word of God, understanding the Jewish roots of our faith (where we've been) so that we can understand the prophetic Word (where we are going). If we continue to teach shallow behaviorism and cheap grace, many people will be lost in the days ahead to the great deception coming. A warning is given to the leaders of God's House in these days: Those who teach antisemitism through Replacement Theology or dualism, or teach "we can not know the day or hour," so, therefore, ignore prophecy completely will be held to account. Repentance must be deep in the House of God and it will start with the pastors and leaders.

Isaiah 30:1-14 was a warning to the children of Israel who relied on the power of men to save them, walking in the spirit of Saul and not David. We are given the same warning. A short portion of this passage says,

> That this is a rebellious people, lying children, children that will not hear the law of the Lord, which say to the seers, See not, and to the prophets, Prophesy not unto us right things; speak unto us smooth things; prophesy deceits; Get you out of the way, turn aside out of the path, cause the *Holy One of Israel* to cease from before us. Wherefore thus says the Holy One of Israel, Because you despise this word, and trust in oppression and perverseness, and stay there, therefore this iniquity shall be to you as a BREACH ready to fall, swelling out in a high wall, whose breaking comes suddenly at an instant. And He shall break it as the breaking of the potters' vessel that is broken in pieces. He shall not spare, so that there shall not be found in the bursting of it a sherd to take fire from the hearth, or to take water with it out of the cistern.

A warning is a loving way for God to say, "I love you. Get back to the truth of my Word; look to the Holy Spirit to teach you. Do not focus on man and his ways."

Feast of Tabernacles

The last feast commanded by the Lord YHVH is the Feast of Tabernacles. It is a great celebration! Again, Leviticus 23:33-39 is where this feast is commanded and described in the Bible. On the 15th of Tishrei (Sept. or Oct.) shall be the Feast of Tabernacles. The people are to keep this feast for seven days and then an eighth day. The people are told to build booths, or temporary shelters, where they will eat all their meals together and remember the days when YHVH God brought them out of Egypt.

We have celebrated the Feast of Tabernacles for the past few years by building a sukkah (temporary shelter) on our back deck. The temporary shelter covers our picnic table where we eat our meals, as many as we can, in the sukkah. Each night, my family lights candles and brings the meal to the picnic table. Yes, it is a bit cold, and we sometimes wear coats or jackets to dinner, yet it is a wonderful time to remember that our God YHVH delivered the Israelites and all those grafted into them from the hands of the Egyptians thousands of years ago, and He will deliver His people from all enemies today. We read Scriptures that the Holy Spirit puts in our hearts to read. Some of the Scriptures we read are about other places in the Bible where the people of God celebrated the Feast of Tabernacles.

The Feast of Tabernacles celebration is recorded in the Bible in many places. In Deuteronomy 31:10-13,

> Moses commanded them saying, At the end of every seven years, in the solemnity of the year of release, in the *Feast of Tabernacles*, when all Israel is come to appear before YHVH thy God in the place which He shall choose, you shall read this Law before all Israel in their hearing. Gather the people together, men, and women, and children and the stranger that is within your gates, that they may hear, and that they may learn, and fear YHVH your God, and observe to do all the

> Words of this Law, and that their children, which have not known any thing may hear, and learn to fear YHVH your God, as long as you live in the land where you go over to Jordan to possess it.

In Deuteronomy 16:12, it says,

> You shall remember that you were a slave in Egypt; and you shall observe and do these statues. You shall observe the *Feast of Tabernacles* seven days, after that you have gathered in you grain and your wine. And you shall rejoice in your feast, you, and your son, and your daughter, and your manservant and your maidservant, and the Levite, the stranger, and the fatherless, and the widow that are within your gates. Seven days you shall keep a solemn feast unto YHVH your God in the place which YHVH God shall choose; because the Lord thy God shall bless you in all your increase, and in all the works of your hands, therefore you shall surely rejoice.

So, in part, the Feast of Tabernacles is a time to read God's Word and teach the people of all that YHVH God has said. Without passing the Word of God to the next generation and knowing it intimately ourselves, it is lost, and the people of God scattered. Also, God commands us to rejoice. The Word of God should be taught with joy, not with a somber disposition. God's Word is a lamp unto our feet and a light unto our path!

In 2 Chronicles 6:40-42, upon completion of the first building of God's temple, King Solomon finishes his prayer unto God, saying,

> Now, my God, let, I beseech You, let Your eyes be open, and let Your ears be attentive unto the prayer that is made in this place. Now therefore arise, O YHVH God, into Your resting

> place, You and the ARK of your strength (alludes to Yeshua), let your priests, O YHVH God, be clothed with Salvation (Yeshua), and let your saints rejoice in goodness. O YHVH God, turn not away the face of Your anointed; remember the mercies of David Your servant.

Soon thereafter, Solomon begins a celebration of the dedication of the first Temple of God and observes the Feast of Tabernacles. Second Chronicles 7:8-10 says,

> Also, at the same time Solomon kept the feast seven days, and all Israel with him, a very great congregation, from the entering in of Hamath unto the river of Egypt. And in the eighth day they made a solemn assembly, for they kept the dedication of the altar seven days, and the feast seven days. And on the twenty-third day of the seventh month he sent the people away into their tents, glad and merry in heart for the goodness that YHVH had showed unto David, and to Solomon, and to Israel His people.

With the beginning of the building of the second Temple of God, again, there is a Feast of Tabernacles celebration in Ezra 3:1-6.

> And when the seventh month was come, and the children of Israel were in the cities, the people gathered themselves together as ONE MAN to Jerusalem… They kept the Feast of Tabernacles, as it is written… From the first day of the seventh month, they began to offer burnt offerings unto YHVH. But the foundation (Yeshua) of the Temple of YHVH was not yet laid.

In the book of Nehemiah, when the second temple is complete as well as the walls and gates of Jerusalem rebuilt, it is recorded again that the people of God celebrated the Feast of Tabernacles and built booths of "olive branches, and pine branches, and myrtle branches, and palm branches, and branches of thick trees, to make booths, as it is written." "Also day by day, from the first day unto the last day, he (Ezra) read in the Book of the Law of God. And they kept the feast seven days; and on the eighth day was solemn assembly, according to the manner" (Nehemiah 8:8-18).

After the first temple was burnt down by the Babylonians, the people of God had lost much of their understanding of the Word of God, for there was no one to read it to them and help them to understand it. When once again Ezra and Nehemiah are commissioned to rebuild the temple and rebuild the walls of Jerusalem seventy years after being in captivity in Babylon, the people are re-educated on how to keep God's Word and the priests how to minister in the temple. It is a time of sorrow as they realize how far they have been from God, yet they are told to celebrate with great joy, for YHVH God is bringing them out of captivity again. This time, they are coming out of Babylonian captivity.

In John 7:37-38, we see Jesus Himself celebrating the great Feast of Tabernacles. The Jewish people have kept the feasts faithfully, as the circumstances of history allowed, and so in the days of Jesus, we see Him keeping all the feasts as well. John 7:37-38 says, In the last day, that great day of the feast, Jesus stood and cried, saying, "If any man thirst, let him come unto Me, and drink. He that believes in Me, as the Scripture has said, out of his belly shall flow rivers of living water." This great feast is the Feast of Tabernacles. To explain what Yeshua is referring to, during the Feast of Tabernacles in Israel, the priests would take water from the pool of Siloam, carry it up the Pilgrimage Road (as it is today called), go up the southern steps of the Temple Mount, go through the gates to the temple and pour out the water around the altar. Jesus proclaimed that He was better than this cleansing water; He was the living water, which later we understood is the living water that cleanses us from all our sin and the living water that fills us with Holy Spirit power. The water the priests used to cleanse the altar was water that could only cleanse the physical; Jesus proclaimed that He was the living water that cleansed all sin forever.

The Feast of Tabernacles is a celebration of the final release from captivity; it is a celebration of God's Word and His goodness to His people who love Him and obey Him. It is a celebration of *Imanu'el* (Imanu means "with us" in Hebrew, and El means God, so the word Imanu'el, as many may know, means God is with us in English). The Feast of Tabernacles, God is with us! It points to the day when Jesus, our Messiah, will come to be with us forever. It points to His second coming and the day of rest (the seventh millennial) and then unto forever (the eighth day)! It is a picture of the end of this age, where we live in temporary houses (our mortal bodies) and points to the day when we will *rest* in Yeshua forever in immortality!

It is an awesome celebration of the fulfillment of the end of this age and a new day beginning! Zechariah 14:16 says when Jesus rules and reigns on this earth in the seventh millennial age and builds His third temple built without human hands (Hebrews 8:2), all nations will be required to come and celebrate together. What will we celebrate?

Zechariah 14:16 says, "And it shall come to pass that every one that is left of all the nations which came against Jerusalem shall even go up from year to year to worship the King, the Lord of hosts, and to keep the Feast of Tabernacles."

Isaiah 25:6-7 says,

> And in this mountain shall YHVH tsava'ot (the Lord of hosts) make unto all people a feast of fat (rich, abundant) things, a feast of wines on the lees, of fat things full of marrow, of wines on the lees well refined. And He will destroy in this mountain the face of the covering cast over all people, and the vail that is spread over all nations.

We shall celebrate the Feast of Tabernacles! We will finally see Him face to face and not through a glass darkly. It will be a holy, joyful, exuberant celebration!

With all this revelation as to how the holy days point to Jesus in every way, we should keep the Leviticus 23 holy days as best we can. The holy days, the Sabbath, the feasts of the Lord YHVH, commanded in Leviticus 23, are important for us today to remember and to look forward. But still, the question remains: Isn't keeping these feasts putting ourselves back under the Law? Doesn't it say in Romans 8:1-2, "There is therefore now no condemnation to them which are in Christ (Messiah) Jesus, who walk not after the flesh, but after the Spirit. For the Law of the Spirit of life in Messiah Jesus has made me free from the Law of sin and death." This beautiful passage is so often interpreted that the Law has no more bearing on our lives now that Jesus has come and died on the cross, and shed His blood for us, and washed us clean of all our sins, and made us brand new creations. Yet, look again. The passage says the Law of the Spirit of life in Messiah Jesus is now how we walk, not under the old Law. This new Law of Spirit and life is now written in our hearts. Jesus did not come to abolish the Law but to have it written on our hearts, on the inside, and with the help of the Holy Spirit, now we can be made perfect as God Himself, Yeshua (Jesus) fulfills the Law (and the prophets) for us, inside us. We are now joyful participants of the Law of YHVH instead of condemned slaves to it. We now, with Yeshua, have the ability to keep it! Holy Spirit power! We are never condemned. We are only taught to keep it as we spend more and more time with God. He has it written in our hearts. He unveils His words and wonders written there as we come before Him each day. Again, as we spoke of in chapter one, now the Law is no longer outside us, to be feared, to be abused, to be ignored, to be paraded in self-righteousness; it is now inside us, to be treasured, revered, honored, and kept.

Remember, keeping the Law is not something *we do* to please Yeshua. It is what Yeshua does in us through the Holy Spirit to please the Father. His yoke is easy, and His burden is light, for Jesus carries it for us as we obey Him! What a *revelation! All to His glory!*

So the holy days were commanded for a reason. They not only reminded the children of Israel to set aside special times to remember YHVH in their busy lives but also pointed to the days ahead when they would be fulfilled spiritually through our Messiah, Jesus. The holy days were shadows of things to come. They instruct us, as did the statue of Nebuchadnezzar, as do the days of Noah, of the days to come. They open our eyes to all of history and tell us that YHVH God is in full control.

For more information on the holy days and sabbath, an informative book titled *The Feasts of Adonai, Why Christians Should look at the Biblical Feasts,* written by Valerie Moody, is a great place to start. What an adventure for those who will look further! God does not expect us to keep these holy days with fear or condemnation but rather out of a deep love for Him and a deeper understanding of His Word. You will be greatly blessed in the trying. Each year I get a little better at understanding, even though when I first started keeping them, it was a bit (to say the least) intimidating. Yet, I felt Abba's smile with every effort and His help as He furthered my understanding and the understanding of my family members. We all celebrate together now, however imperfectly, for we are not under Law but under the Holy Spirit who guides us.

Chapter Five

Where We Are in Time: The Third Day, the Sabbath Rest

When Jesus walked upon the earth, He came to bring light, healing, and compassion on the many lost sheep of His house, but He also came with a passion to cleanse His Father's house from all corruption. John 2:13-17 says,

> And the Jews' Passover was at hand, and Jesus went up to Jerusalem, and found in the temple those that sold oxen and sheep and doves, and the changers of money sitting (in the temple!) and when He had made a whip of small cords, he drove them all out of the temple, and the sheep, and the oxen; and poured out the changers' money, and overthrew the tables. And He said unto them that sold doves, Take these things out of here, and do not make my Father's house a house of merchandise. And His disciples remembered that it was written, The zeal of Thine House has eaten Me up.

The Jewish leaders that were profiting nicely from the selling of sacrifices in the temple were angry at Jesus for disrupting the status quo and the lucrative business they had set up. They challenged Him with these words, "Then answered the Jews and said unto Him, What sign do you show us, seeing you do these things?" (John 2:18). In other words, what right do you think you have to do this? Who do you think you are?

> Yeshua answered them and said, "Destroy this Temple, and in three days, I will raise it up." Then the Jews (rulers, sellers, etc.) responded, "Forty-six years was this temple in the making, and will you raise it up in THREE DAYS?" But He spoke of the Temple of His Body. When therefore He was risen from the dead, His disciples remembered that He had said this unto them; and they believed the scripture, and the Word which Jesus had said.
>
> John 2:19-22

Jesus says unto them He will rebuild the temple in three days. This passage has layers of meaning. Jesus, here, is speaking of His physical resurrection from the dead, but He is speaking of even more. He is saying that, on the third day, He will raise up His temple made without human hands, the true believers in Him, after they go through two days of suffering, dispersion, death, and hopelessness. This third day speaks of the day we are entering into now.

In 2 Peter 3:8, as was written before, it says, "But beloved, be not ignorant of this one thing, that one day is with the Lord as a thousand years, and a thousand years as one day."

Psalm 90:4 is closely related and says, "For a thousand years in Your sight are but as yesterday when it is past, and as a watch in the night."

Yeshua, as fully God and fully man, can see all of history. He knows that in 70 AD, only a few decades after He dies and rises again and returns to the Father, that the temple in Jerusalem will once again be destroyed. He knows that from this time, His people, the Jewish people and all those who are grafted into them, will suffer greatly at the hands of those who do not put their faith and hope in Jesus. The Jewish believers in Jesus will take the gospel message (*besorah*) to the Gentile nations, and for the next 2000 years, His body, Jewish and Gentile believers together will be persecuted, cut off, murdered, and suffer greatly. It is His body. It is His temple made without human hands. He knows that after all the suffering and persecution, after two days (2000 years), and on the third day, the temple that is being built without human hands, the living stones (2 Peter 2:5) will be completed. It will be more glorious than anyone can imagine.

Let's look at a few more scriptures to validate this prophetic picture. Mark 14:55-58 says,

> And the chief priests and all the council were seeking witnesses against Jesus to put Him to death and found none. For many bare false witness against Him but their witness did not agree together. And there arose certain witnesses…saying We heard Him say, I will destroy this Temple that is made with hands, and within THREE DAYS, I will build another made without hands.

These witnesses, trying to accuse Jesus of lies and blasphemy, only proclaimed the truth of His Word again. They just did not understand what He was saying at all. Their hearts were hardened.

Through the power of the Holy Spirit, we can see this temple is the spiritual temple that Jesus will complete in these last days. He is putting on the final finishing touches before He comes again. Hebrews 8:1-2 says,

> Now of these things which we have spoken, this is the sum; we have a High priest, who is set on the right hand of the throne of the Majesty of the heavens; a Minister of the Sanctuary, and of the TRUE TABERNACLE, which the Lord pitched,

AND NOT MAN.

In the Book of Haggai the Lord YHVH, through the prophet Haggai, says to the people that have just built the second temple, back in the day of Ezra and Nehemiah, He says to them to look to the future when I build My house, the true third temple, built without human hands. Haggai is told to speak to the people during the Feast of Tabernacles. He exhorts them to keep working on the building of God's temple no matter how it looks now, even when the second temple, at first, was so much less glorious than the first temple of Solomon. YHVH promises that the third temple, the next one that is truly His, will be built without human hands. We know that satan will mimic this temple, and this is where the abomination of desolation will occur, yet God has a plan of redemption in all of this.

God, through Haggai, speaks to Zerubbabel, the son of Shealtiel, the Governor of Judah, and to Joshua, the son of Jehozadak, the High Priest, and to the *remnant* of the people, saying,

> Who is left among you that saw this house in her first glory? And how do you see it now? Is it not in your eyes in comparison to it as nothing? Yet now, (here comes the encouragement) be strong, O Zerubbabel says YHVH, and be strong, O Joshua, son of Jehozadak, the High Priest, and be strong, all you people, and work; for I am with you says YHVH tsava'ot (The Lord of hosts). According to the Word that I covenanted with you when you came out of Egypt, so My Spirit remains strong among you. Fear not. For thus says YHVH tsava'ot, Yet once, it is a little while, and I will shake the heavens and the earth, and the sea, and the dry land (signifying the last days). And I will shake the nations, and the desire of all nations shall come, and I will fill this house with glory, says YHVH

> tsava'ot. The silver is Mine and the gold is Mine, says YHVH tsava'ot.
>
> Haggai 2:2-8

Further, He says in Haggai 2:9, "The glory of this latter house shall be greater than the former, says the Lord of hosts; And in this place, I will give peace, says YHVH tsava'ot." King Herod built up the second temple and did make it more glorious in the days of Jesus, yet it was destroyed and burnt to the ground in 70 AD. Jesus was speaking of something way more than this second temple.

YHVH God has a plan. Jesus sees all of history and proclaims that He sees His body (His people) being torn down in the next two thousand years, yet on the third day, the temple of God will be finished. This latter glorious house is being built by God Himself, and He includes all those who love Him in the building of His house.

First Corinthians 3:9 says, "For we are laborers TOGETHER with God. You are God's husbandry; You are God's BUILDING!" (Exclamation added).

It goes on to say in 1 Corinthians 3:10-15,

> According to the grace of God which is given unto me, as a wise master builder, I have laid the foundation and another builds thereon. For another Foundation can no man lay than that is laid which is JESUS MESSIAH (Christ). Now if any man builds upon this foundation gold, silver, precious stones, (or) wood, hay, stubble; every man's (person's) work shall be made manifest; for THE DAY shall declare it, because it shall be revealed by fire. And the fire shall try every man's work of what sort it is. If any man's work abides which he has built thereon, he shall receive a reward. If any man's work shall be

> burned, he shall suffer loss, but he, himself, shall be saved, yet so as by fire.

We are called to build the Kingdom of God, the temple of God, right alongside Jesus through the power of the Holy Spirit.

First Corinthians 3:16-17 again reminds us that we are the House of God, the Temple of God. "Do you not know that you are the Temple of God, and that the Spirit of God dwells in you? If any man defiles the Temple of God, he, himself, shall be destroyed by God; for the Temple of God is holy, which Temple you are."

First Peter 2:4-5 speaks again of this holy living temple,

> To Whom, coming as a living stone (Jesus) rejected indeed of men, but chosen of God, and precious. You also, as living stones, are built up a SPIRITUAL HOUSE, a holy priesthood, to offer up spiritual sacrifices, acceptable to God by Jesus Christ (Yeshua ha'MashiacH).

God calls us out of darkness into His marvelous light, first to the Jewish people and then the Gentiles through the Jewish disciples. First Peter 2:9-10 is one of my favorite Bible passages. It says,

> But you are a CHOSEN GENERATION, a royal priesthood, a holy nation (Israel), a peculiar people, that you should show forth the praises of Him who has called you of darkness into His marvelous Light; which in times past were not a people, but are now the people of God...

Just as the seven days of all of history start from the beginning of time 4004 BC until now over 6000 years later, awakening us to see we are about to enter into the seventh millennial period of *rest*, the third day alerts us that from the time Jesus walked on this earth, over 2000 years ago, we have entered into the third day. We know within the beginning of this Day, the seventh Day from creation or the third Day from the rising of our Messiah Yeshua from the dead, we are entering into a new age, a new millennial age; we are soon to enter into His Rest and will abide in His Tabernacle forever.

The Sabbath rest is a reminder of this seventh day on a weekly basis. It is a reminder of all of history. The week itself shows us that YHVH had always planned six days for man to rule the earth (6000 years), and then on the seventh day, all those who love YHVH would enter into His rest (His seventh day). Here, I would like to segue or move into an explanation of the importance of a day of rest that God has commanded us to observe from the beginning of the nation of Israel, a nation set aside for Him.

Sabbath is the shadow of things to come. Each week, as we celebrate Sabbath or Shabbat, we honor the God of Israel by setting aside a day to remember His promised *rest*. In the increasing unrest in the world, we need even more to be hearing the voice of YHVH God to help us to know what to do, where to go, when to go, and when to be still. We need to hear His voice and the only way to do that is from a place of rest, where we are still and listening before Him.

In Isaiah 30:15, the Lord God, the Holy One of Israel, says, "In returning and rest shall you be saved; in quietness and in confidence shall be your strength; sadly, it ends with the words, 'and you would not.'"

God calls us to be still and come away with Him, but many will not do this. Busyness and piling on more activity are the norm for many when God calls us to "Be still and know that I am God"

(Psalm 46:10).

We see Jesus, many times, going away by Himself (and sometimes with a few disciples) to pray and be with the Father. "And when He had sent the multitudes away, He went up into a mountain apart to pray; and when the evening was come, He was there alone" (Matthew 14:23). "And He withdrew Himself into the wilderness, and prayed" (Luke 5:16). "And it came to pass about eight days after these sayings, He took Peter and John, and James, and went up into a mountain to pray" (Luke 9:28). Yeshua knew He, even as fully God and fully man, needed to pray to the Father and be in His presence by the power of the Holy Spirit. How much more do we need this daily time with our God?

The Sabbath was commanded not to burden people but as a gift to us so that we would take a weekly day off from all the activities, burdens, and distractions of this world and make sure we are getting a fresh start each week as we come before the Lord YHVH and receive instruction for the following six days. This was so necessary back when it was first commanded and even more so today as the distractions and messages of both good and evil are all around us, coming at us from every direction through television, radio, smartphones, newspapers, magazines, books, and more. We are surrounded by voices, many of them not speaking the truth.

A few of the Scriptures on Sabbath include:

Exodus 20:8-11,

> Remember the Sabbath day, to keep it holy. Six days you shall labor, and do all your work. But the seventh day is the Sabbath of YHVH thy God; in it you shall do no work, you, your son, nor your daughter, your manservant, nor they maid-

> servant nor your cattle, nor the stranger that is within your gates.

Everyone has a day off.

Ezekiel 20:19-20 says, "I am YHVH your God; walk in My statutes, and keep My judgments, and do them; and hallow My Sabbaths; and they shall be a sign between me and you, that you may know that I am YHVH your God."

It is a covenant sign between YHVH and His people.

Isaiah 58:13-14,

> If you refrain from trampling the Sabbath, from pursuing your own affairs on My Holy Day; if you call the Shabbat a delight, YHVH's holy day, honorable; and shall honor Him, not doing your own ways, nor finding thine own pleasure, nor speaking your own words; then you shall delight yourself in YHVH; and I will cause you to ride upon the high places of the earth, and feed you with the heritage of Jacob your father; for the mouth of YHVH has spoken it.

God delights in us when we delight ourselves in His Sabbath rest.

Hebrews 4:9-11,

> There remains therefore a Rest to the people of God. For he that is entered into His rest, he also has ceased from his own works, as God did from His. Let us labor therefore to enter into that Rest, unless any man fall after the same example of unbelief.

We need this time with God so that our faith is built up each week and we don't lose sight of Him.

About two years ago, my family and I started celebrating Shabbat (the Sabbath) each Friday night as the sun goes down. We light two candles for our table and make dinner together. We set the table and add olive oil, fresh bread, salad, grape juice, wine, matzoh, and whatever has been prepared for dinner, and we sit before the table together as a family. We play lively worship music before the meal as we are preparing. We pray together; we lift up Hebrew blessings on the wine and bread and take "communion" as we read Jesus' words in Luke or Matthew that He spoke before He died on the cross for our sins. We remember Him. We eat together and then sometimes will read a psalm or other portion of the Bible after the meal. This is a good start to Shabbat. Some will take the next twenty-four hours, the best we can, and give it to prayer, reading God's Word, and relaxing and resting. It has become a pillar in our family; when all of us are moving so fast that it can be difficult for all to be in the same room together very often, it is a time to stop, to rest. It is a day set aside for YHVH. Shabbat ends Saturday night as the sun goes down. Again, we have read from the Feasts of Adonai book for support for when we first started this family time. It has been a blessing for our family, a time set aside to remember together, our Mighty God, who loves us.

Again, on a deeper level, this Sabbath rest signifies the seventh millennial when Jesus will return the second time, and He will be with us forever. We will rest in Him and completely leave behind our own works. Shabbat reminds us of this day and helps us to lift our heads for our Redemption draws near. Yet, resting does not mean there is nothing to do. In the millennial Kingdom, we will be assigned our roles and our duties to rule and reign beside the King of kings, and Lord of lords, Yeshua, our Messiah. It will be a glorious time! We will work; it will be so exciting, yet we will work from the power of the Holy Spirit, from a place of rest; joy will be the result!

Shabbat is also a time to get our instructions for the work God wants us to do in the following week. We rest, we hear Him speak to us, we are refreshed in our soul and spirit to start anew. His ways are perfect. He is preparing us for the day of true Rest when He comes again on this seventh Day (seventh millennial). As 1 Corinthians 2:9-10 says,

> No eye has seen, nor ear has heard, neither has it entered into the heart of man, the things that God has prepared for them that love Him. But God has revealed them unto us by His Spirit; for the Spirit searches all things, yes, the deep things of God.

So, we remember to *rest*. For without *rest*, in the physical, we become exhausted; and without *rest* in the spiritual, we are lost in our purpose. The third day and the seventh day are the same; they speak of entering into that rest, the time when Yeshua will put the final touches on the house of God being built not by human hands but by God Himself. We are the Temple of God, that Tabernacle of David. Honoring the Sabbath or Shabbat reminds us every week, we are entering the seventh millennial of rest; we are entering that Third Day Yeshua spoke of when He was on the earth and said to the Jewish rulers, "Destroy this temple, and in three *days I will raise it up*" (John 2:19).

Amos 9:11 says, "In that day *I will raise up the tabernacle of David* that is fallen, and close up the breaches (repair the damage) thereof; and I will raise up his ruins, and I will build it as in the days of old." Again, in Acts 15, this prophetic verse is declared by Simeon, after Barnabas and Paul have just spoken about all the miracles and wonders God has wrought unto the Gentiles by them (the Jewish disciples). Simeon declares how God at first did visit the Gentiles, to take out of them a people for His name (a Remnant). He goes on to say,

> And to this agree the words of the prophets; as it is written, After this I will RETURN, and will build again the tabernacle of David, which is fallen down; and I will build again the ruins thereof and I will set it up; that the remnant of people might seek after YHVH, and all the Gentiles, upon whom My Name is called, says YHVH, who does all these things. Known unto God are all His works from the beginning of the world.
>
> Acts 15:14-18

These past 2000 years were the time when the Jewish disciples (the first fruits) were sent into all the world to gather in the remnant of the Gentile nations to be grafted into the House of God.

What a time we are living in! We are on the precipice of this third day! Hosea 6:1-2 again reminds us, "Come, and let us return unto YHVH; for He has torn, and He will heal us; He has smitten, and He will bind us up. After two days He will revive us; in THE THIRD DAY, He will raise us up, and we will live in His sight." HalleluYah!

Chapter Six

God's Heart, Ruth and the Nation and People of Israel

We have gone full circle, even though we are only in the middle of this book. YHVH speaks to me this morning as I walk along my long driveway in the cold, brisk air, this chapter is the heartbeat of the Greatest Story ever told, that is why it is "hidden" in the middle, in the center, at the core of this book.

"Behold, the days come, says YHVH, that the plowman will overtake the reaper, and the treader of grapes will overtake him that sows seed; and the mountains shall drop sweet wine, and all the hills shall melt" (Amos 9:13). I used to ponder this verse. What does it mean? I hear the Holy Spirit say it means we have come full circle. The story is coming to a close, and a new thing is about to begin.

In Acts chapter one, Jesus spoke to His Jewish followers, apostles, disciples before ascending into heaven that they should not depart from Jerusalem but wait for the promise of the Father, which said Jesus, "You have heard of this promise from Me." The disciples asked Yeshua, "Will at this time, the kingdom of Israel be restored?" Jesus replied that the generation He was speaking to would not see all these things come to pass, but something must happen first. He then goes on to tell them,

> "It is not for you to know times or seasons that the Father has fixed by His own authority. But you will receive power when the Holy Spirit has come upon you, and you will be My witnesses in Jerusalem and in all Judea and Samaria, and to the end of the earth."
>
> Acts 1:4-8

Jesus speaks to this generation that once the former rain, the first great outpouring of the Holy Spirit occurs, these first fruit Jewish believers in Jesus would have a great mission. They were to go into all the world and preach Yeshua! These Jewish followers, disciples, apostles would bring the Messiah to the Gentile nations. Jesus does not tell them that it will be another 2000 years before this is accomplished, and then the end will come of this age. He tells them they will be empowered to do the work given to them.

The Jewish believers wait, and fifty days from Passover, at Shavuot, or Pentecost, they receive Holy Spirit power and begin speaking in the tongues of all the nations around them. This is God's picture of what they are to do. They will speak to the nations. Little did they know, in order to do this, they would be dispersed to the nations, first after much persecution and destruction of their temple and nation. They would be scattered, as a people, to the four corners of the earth.

In Matthew 24, after Jesus tells His disciples that their temple will be destroyed and "There shall not be left here one stone upon another, that shall not be thrown down" (Matthew 24:2). The disciples ask, "When shall the sign of Your coming again be?" Jesus goes on to answer that there will be antichrists coming in His Name, wars, rumors of wars, pestilences, earthquakes, all the beginning of sorrows. False prophets will arise, and the love of many will grow cold. And then Jesus says, "And this gospel of the Kingdom shall be preached in all the world for a witness unto the nations; and then shall the end come."

The Gospel has gone full circle around the world. There are a few pockets of people that have not received the Word in their language, but the gap is filling fast with the technology of the twenty-first century. Yes, the Gospel has gone around the world and has returned to Jerusalem! We are the generation to see this. It has gone full circle… and then the end of this age will come.

YHVH God's heart has always been for all nations, but He chose Abraham, Isaac, and Jacob to birth the nation of Israel, a chosen people, to be set apart from all other nations, to carry the Word of God, protect it, bring forth our Jewish Messiah through Mary (Miriam) and through them, bring the Gospel to the whole world. It would cost Israel everything for a time, but God has a beautiful plan! Through Israel's loss, the whole world would be blessed. If this is the case, how much more will we be blessed the day the Jewish people return to their Messiah Jesus in great numbers. It is happening now! Romans 11 explains this in detail.

Yet, let's take a look at the Book of Ruth. In this story, by the Holy Spirit, I see the whole story of God's plan for humankind in just four short chapters, the whole timeclock of God's plan of redemption. It is a story of famine, loss, bitterness, struggle, return, trust, and ultimately deep love and redemption. It is a beautiful story, but there is much more than what is on the surface, much more than what first meets the eye. Let's dive in and see spiritually what this story speaks to us for today.

The story of Ruth begins with "a famine in the land" of Israel. Because of this famine, some families leave the land to find provisions for their families. The story focuses on a particular family from Bethlehem-Judah, who departs Israel to the neighboring nation of Moab (modern-day Jordan). Elimelech, his wife Naomi, and their two sons Mahlon and Chilion leave for Moab. After settling there, Elimelech dies. The Bible does not say why or how soon and then goes right on to say Naomi and her two sons continue to live in Moab after his death. Mahlon and Chilion take wives from the land of Moab, the name of one Orpah and the other Ruth. After ten years being in the land, both, yes, both of her sons also die! Naomi is bereft of all that she held dear. She has lost everything in Moab and hears soon after that Israel is no longer in famine. She decides to go back home, to *return*. In bitterness of spirit, she tells her two daughters-in-law to return to their own families. She can give them nothing. Orpah decides to return, but Ruth has a whole different spirit.

Naomi says to Ruth, "Behold thy sister-in-law is gone back unto her people, and unto her gods; you return after your sister-in-law." Here is Ruth's answer.

> Intreat me not to leave you, or to return from following after you; for wherever you go, I will go; and wherever you stay, I will stay. Your people shall be my people, and your God is my God. Where you die, I will die and there I will be buried. YHVH do so to me, and more so, if anything but death part you and me.
>
> Ruth 1:16-17

Naomi sees there is no deterring Ruth. She has decided that she belongs with Naomi and her people. Naomi is so downcast about all her loss that she decides to re-name herself Mara, which means bitterness. She and Ruth *return* to the land of Israel together. In all her loss, she has gained the prize of Ruth, a heart from a nation outside of Israel now fully devoted to Naomi and her people and her God.

"So, Naomi returned, and Ruth the Moabitess, her daughter in law, with her, which returned out of the country of Moab; and they came to Bethlehem in the beginning of the barley harvest" (Ruth 1:22).

After the return, the story of struggle and trust begins. Ruth goes out into the fields of barley to see if she can reap the few grains left behind by the harvesters. She "happens" to find a field belonging to a man named Boaz, who so "happens" to be the kindred of Elimelech, Naomi's former husband. Boaz notices Ruth very soon after she comes out to the fields to harvest. He asks who she is, and the reapers answer, she is the Moabite woman that has come back with Naomi. Boaz pours favor on Ruth and tells his workers to let her continue to reap and also to make sure she gets plenty to take back to Naomi. He then meets with Ruth and tells her she is welcome to stay in his fields, and he will make sure she is protected. She is overwhelmed by his mercy and grace upon her and "bows herself to the ground" in front of him. She speaks to him, "Why have I found grace in your eyes, that you should take knowledge of me, seeing I am a foreigner?" And Boaz answers her, "All that you have done for your mother-in-law since the death of your husband has been fully told to me, and how you left your father and mother and your native land and came to a people that you did not know before" (Ruth 2:10-11).

Ruth had left everything to be grafted into the house of Israel, and it was noticed. In Luke 18:28-30, Peter says to Jesus, Behold, we have left all, and followed You. Jesus answers, "Truly, I say unto you, There is no one who has left house, or parents, or brethren, or wife, or children, for the kingdom of God's sake, who shall not receive many times more in this present time, and in the world to come life everlasting."

Boaz sees Ruth's trust in the unknown days ahead as she follows the God of Israel and is faithful to Naomi. He rewards her with the provision she needs, but so much more is coming! Boaz says to her, "YHVH recompense your work, and a full reward be given to you of the Lord God of Israel, under whose wings you have come to trust" (Ruth 2:12). Ruth is again overwhelmed by his kindness in that he would bring comfort to her in this new land, even though she was not born there. Boaz invites her to eat with them at mealtime. He again commands his reapers to allow ample barley grain to fall for Ruth. She harvests plenty, and when she returns, Naomi notices the abundance.

Ruth 2:19-20 relays the conversation between Naomi and Ruth when she returns home. And her mother-in-law said unto her, "Where have you gleaned today? And where did you go? Blessed be he that did take notice of you." And Ruth showed Naomi all that she had harvested, and said "the man's name with whom I wrought today is Boaz." At the name of Boaz, Naomi gets excited. She says, "Blessed be he of YHVH who has not left off kindness to the living and to the dead." Then she says, "the man is a near of kin unto us, one of our next kinsman." She tells Ruth, Boaz is our Kinsman Redeemer. If he so chooses, Boaz will change everything!

Ruth goes on to tell Naomi that Boaz wants me to stay in his fields until the end of all the harvest. Naomi says this is very good. So, Ruth kept fast by the maidens of Boaz to glean unto the end of the barley harvest and of the wheat harvest; and dwelt with her mother-in-law (Ruth 2:23).

Ruth is now a full-time harvester of both barley and wheat. She represents the daughter of God who goes out to reap the harvest of both Jewish people and of the latter harvest of all the nations. It is a beautiful picture. Ruth is brought into the family of the God of Israel, and then she is commissioned to harvest. She will harvest with the other reapers until the full harvest of both the early barley and then the later wheat has been gleaned, the first fruits of the Jewish people (barley), and the later Shavuot harvest (wheat) of the nations.

We have seen famine, loss, bitterness, and now the struggle and the trust in the God of Israel that "all things will work together for good, to those who love Him and are Called according to His purpose" (Romans 8:28).

Yet, the second half of the story gets even better!

Naomi asks Ruth, "My daughter, shall I not seek REST for you, that it may be well with you?" (Ruth 3:1). Rest, Naomi seeks Rest for her daughter-in-law, a place of inheritance, a place where she will be grafted into the house of Israel forever, not only by her will to be with God's people but further by a strong covenant, a marriage covenant.

Naomi comes up with a plan. She has a bit of a matchmaker in her, and Ruth is ready to obey Naomi no matter if she understands or not what Naomi is saying. Naomi says, "Is not Boaz of our kindred, with whose maidens you were with? Behold, he winnows barley tonight in the threshing floor" (Ruth 3:2).

It seems a threshing floor is a place where a lot happens in the Bible. It is the place where Gideon asks for a sign to confirm he will have victory over the Midianites and the Amalekites and the people of the east that were gathered against Israel in the Valley of Jezreel (Judges 6:33-37). King David is called to purchase the threshing floor of Araunah by the prophet Gad; it is purchased to stop YHVH's anger against the people of Israel for David's sin. David purchases this threshing floor for fifty shekels of silver and builds an altar unto YHVH there and offered peace offerings and burnt offerings; then the Lord's anger was turned away (2 Samuel 24). This threshing floor of Araunah is on Mount Moriah, where Isaac was almost sacrificed. It is today the site of the Temple Mount in Jerusalem. David purchased this for the Israelite people 3000 years ago! And in the Book of Ruth, the threshing floor is the site where Boaz knows Ruth loves him and is the beginning of a covenant of marriage between the two. It is a testing ground, a place where the barley and the wheat grains are harvested and separated from the chaff.

So this is the plan. Naomi says,

> Wash yourself and anoint yourself and put on your most beautiful garment upon you, and get down to the threshing floor, but do not make yourself known to Boaz, until he has finished eating and drinking. And when he lies down, you shall mark or remember where it is where he lied down, and you shall go in, and uncover his feet and lay down by his feet;

after that, he will tell you what you are to do.

Ruth 3:3-4

Ruth may not have understood this protocol or this strange way of doing things, but she is more than willing to obey Naomi. She says unto Naomi, "All that you say unto me, I will do." (Ruth 3:5). And she did. Ruth went to the threshing floor, and when Boaz had eaten and drunk his wine, he was merry in heart and went to lie down at the end of the heap of grain, and she came out softly, for she was hidden, and uncovered his feet and laid down at his feet (Ruth 3:6-7).

What a picture of submission. To come before her Kinsman Redeemer, in full humility, and lay at His feet. It is a picture of our submission to Yeshua, our Messiah. We bow at His feet in full submission to His majesty and glory because we know how much He loves us.

Here's where it gets a bit comical. Laughter is good medicine. So it came to pass at midnight, that Boaz was startled and turned himself and behold, a woman lay at his feet (Ruth 3:8). Where is the exclamation point at the end of this verse?! "And he said, Who are you? And she answered, I am Ruth, thine handmaid; spread your skirt (kanafeka, your wings, in the Hebrew) over your handmaid for you are a near kinsman redeemer" (Ruth 3:9). Ruth asks Boaz to cover her with his tallit, the holy shawl also worn by Yeshua, that when touched by the woman with the issue, brought her healing (Luke 8:43-48). Boaz is delighted. He wants to cover her with protection under his wings, so to speak. He has already thought of her but probably in his mind felt he was too old for her and that she would not turn her eye to him in that way. We see this in his next statement. "And he said, Blessed be you of YHVH, my daughter; for you have showed more kindness in the latter end than at the beginning, inasmuch as you did not follow young men, whether poor or rich" (Ruth 3:10). Could it be that Ruth has turned her eye and heart to a much deeper love? She does not see outward appearances, but she sees the heart and the intense strength and passion of Boaz. She has chosen wisely, for this love will bring a rich reward. It speaks of our hearts turning to YHVH God and turning away from the glitter and false promises of the world. It speaks of the Gentile remnant who will be grafted in by an intimate covenant of marriage. It speaks of those who will turn away from false worship of the gods of this world and turn to the God of Israel. There is such treasure in this beautiful story but can only be uncovered when we see the God of Israel, redeeming His people, in covenant love, to the Jewish people first and then to the remnant of the nations grafted in, covered by His wings.

"And now, my daughter, fear not (al tirah in the Hebrew); I will do to you all that you request; for all the city of my people knows that you are a virtuous woman" (Ruth 3:11). He says essentially that he loves her too, but in the next statement, he says there is one matter that must be taken care of first. He must ask for her from someone closer in relation to her. "And now it is true that I am your near kinsman, howbeit there is a kinsman nearer than I." Boaz must go and see if this near kinsman will give her to him, even though this other kinsman has the first right to her. This brings to my heart a picture of Yeshua asking the Father for His bride. In John 10:29, Jesus says of his sheep, "My Father, which gave them to ME, is greater than all; and no one is able to pluck them out of my hand." He also calls her a virtuous woman (אשת חיל, eshet cHayil, woman of strength), which is the bride of Yeshua (Revelation 12), as compared to the woman called "Mystery Babylon the Great, the Mother of Harlots and Abominations of the Earth" written about in Revelation 17.

Boaz tells Ruth to,

> Tarry this night, and it shall be in the morning, that if he will perform unto you the part of kinsman, well; let him do the kinsman's part; but if he will not do the kinsman's part to you, then I WILL do the part of the kinsman to you, as YHVH lives, lie down until morning.
>
> Ruth 3:12-13

Psalm 126 reminds me of this waiting. It says,

> When YHVH turned again the captivity of Zion, we were like them that dream. Then was our mouth filled with laughter, and our tongue with singing. Then said they among the nations, YHVH has done great things for them (the Jewish people). YHVH has done great things for us (the Gentiles grafted in), whereof we are glad. Turn again our captivity, O YHVH, as the streams in the Negev. They that sow in tears shall reap in joy. He that goes forth and weeps, bearing precious seed, shall doubtless come again with rejoicing, bringing his sheaves with him.

The psalm reminds me that this life is like a dream, yet we have work to do. There is a harvest to sow, to grow, to reap. It is hard work, but those who do YHVH's work, sowing in tears, shall reap a great harvest as we keep our eyes on Him and await His return. Ruth also harvested and waited among the maidens of Boaz during the time of barley harvest and wheat harvest (Ruth 2:23). And she lay down until morning (Ruth 3:13).

We await until the morning comes…

"And she lay at his feet until the morning; and she rose up before one could know another (rose up very early while it was still dark). And he said, Let it not be known that a woman came to the threshing floor" (Ruth 3:14).

This is powerful. It is an army rising up, a woman on the threshing floor. Let it be quiet for a while until the bride is prepared with her armor.

Micah 4:13 says, "Arise and thresh, O daughter of Zion; for I will make your horn iron, and I will make your hoofs brass; and you shall beat in pieces many people, and I will consecrate their gain unto YHVH and their substance unto YHVH of the whole earth."

Micah 5:1-4 goes on to say,

> Now gather yourself in troops, O daughter of troops; he has laid siege against us. They shall smite the judge of Israel, with a rod upon the cheek. But you Bethlehem, Ephratah, though you be little among the thousands of Judah, yet out of you shall come unto me that is to be Ruler of Israel (Yeshua); whose goings forth have been from of old, from everlasting. Therefore, He will give them up (the Jewish people as a nation) until the time that she which travails has brought forth (Israel is born again in 1948); then the REMNANT of his brethren shall RETURN unto the children of Israel. And he (Israel) shall stand and feed in the strength of YHVH, in the majesty of the name of YHVH his God; and they shall abide; for now, He shall be great unto the ends of the earth.

"Also, he said, Bring the vail that you had upon you, and hold it. And when she held it, he measured six measures of barley, and laid it on her; and she went into the city" (Ruth 3:15).

The veil that had hidden Ruth now is the veil used to carry provision for the work she will need to do until she is revealed as the bride. The bride will have all she needs from the Kinsman Redeemer to build YHVH's house and to protect the work being done.

"And when she came to her mother-in-law," Naomi said, "Who are you, my daughter?" And Ruth told her all that Boaz had done to her (Ruth 3:16).

Naomi doesn't even recognize Ruth when she returns. She is elated and filled with joy. Her Kinsman Redeemer has filled her with provision and strength and has confirmed his love for her. She is sealed with the Holy Spirit, sealed with the promise that Boaz will come back for her. For the Bride of Messiah Yeshua, Ephesians 1:13-14 says,

> In whom you also trusted after you heard the Word of Truth, the gospel of Salvation, in whom also after that you believed, you were sealed with the Holy Spirit of promise, which is the earnest of our inheritance, until the redemption of the purchased possession, unto the praise of His glory.

Like Ruth, we are sealed with the promise of His return. We just have to wait for all the "business" to be completed.

And she said, "These six measures of barley he gave to me; for he said to me, Do not go empty to your mother-in-law," (Ruth 3:17). In other words, here is ample evidence that I love you, and I am about to make you mine. Naomi will understand. Show her the six measures of barley.

Jeremiah 32:11-15 are Scriptures that YHVH has shown me before I left for Israel in 2018; I did not know what He meant at the time. I am understanding more as the years go by, and I continue to hold unto His Word and promises. It says,

> So, I (Jeremiah) took the evidence of the purchase, both that which was sealed according to the law and custom, and that which was open. And I gave the evidence of the purchase unto Baruch... And I charged Baruch before them saying, Thus says YHVH tsava'ot, the God of Israel, take these evidences, this evidence of the purchase, both which is sealed, and this evidence that is open; and put them in an earthen vessel, that they may continue many days. For thus says YHVH tsava'ot, the God of Israel, houses and fields and vineyards shall be possessed again in this land.

We have an inheritance. It is sealed by the Holy Spirit in earthen vessels (the people of God). We see in part, for half of the evidence is in the open, and the other part is sealed until the day we receive our inheritance in full. Ruth had the evidence that the covenant was about to take place, but she only could see part of the picture at that time.

"Then said Naomi, 'Sit still, my daughter, until you know how the matter will turn out; for the man WILL NOT REST until he has FINISHED this matter today'" (Ruth 3:18).

She needed to wait a little longer, knowing Boaz was laser beam focused on settling the matter that very day and would let them know soon.

When Jesus went to the cross, He was laser beam focused and intent on getting to Jerusalem for the Passover. He knew the price for the bride was He, Himself, becoming the Passover Lamb.

When the matter was *finished* and the price paid in full, here is what He said as He gave up His Spirit to God the Father and died on the cross–"It is FINISHED" (John 19:30). We, then, received the promise in part, the sealing of the Holy Spirit. Yet we wait for the open fulfillment of this covenant of love, even as He prepares us, Jewish and Gentile believers together, His Bride, for the great day, the marriage supper of the Lamb.

Revelation 10:7 says, "But in the days of the seventh angel, when He shall begin to sound, the MYSTERY of GOD should be FINISHED, as He has declared to His servants, the prophets."

YHVH God is putting the finishing touches on His tabernacle made without human hands, His Bride, in preparation for His second coming. We are so near to His return.

So as the story of Ruth closes in the last chapter, we see Boaz at the gate, waiting for the other closer kinsman to come so that he can talk with him about Ruth. Boaz represents Yeshua in many ways, our *Goel* (גואל), the Hebrew word for Kinsman Redeemer. Yet, Boaz also represents the nation of Israel and the faithful Jewish people. It is God's plan. "All nations shall be blessed through Israel." Ruth symbolizes the remnant of nations, those who leave all to follow the God of Israel and to love His people that He first separated from the world, that through them He would bring the Word of God, our Jewish Messiah, and the Holy Spirit to all nations.

Ruth chapter 4:1 says, "Then went Boaz up to the gate, and sat down there; and behold, the kinsman of whom Boaz spoke came by; unto whom he said, Ho, such a one! Turn aside and sit down here. And he turned aside and sat down."

Boaz also asks ten other men of the elders of the city to come and join them so they can be witnesses of the conversation. Boaz begins to explain that Naomi, who has returned from the land of Moab, wants to sell her land, which was our brother's Elimelech's. Boaz then tells this near Kinsman Redeemer that it is his for the buying if he wants it. The man says he will buy it. Then Boaz says, yes, but it comes with a prize; her name is Ruth. Boaz says, "The day you buy the land from Naomi, you must also buy it from Ruth, the Moabitess," and redeem her also.

This changes everything, for the man has no interest in Ruth, only the land. He responds, "I cannot redeem it for myself," for this will mess up my own inheritance. This man does not want to be involved with marrying an outsider. He tells Boaz, "I give you the right to redeem the land and the Moabite woman."

"Now this was the manner in former time in Israel concerning redeeming and concerning the changing (of ownership, responsibility), for to confirm all things; a man plucked off his shoe and gave it to his neighbor and this was a TESTIMONY in Israel" (Ruth 4:7).

Boaz, surely, is delighted. He plucks off his shoe (maybe for this is holy ground) and gave it to the man to confirm that the exchange had been made. Boaz goes on to tell the other ten elders, and all the people that are watching, listening, "You are witnesses this day, that I have bought all that was Elimelech's, and all that was Chilion's and Mahlon's of the hand of Naomi" (Ruth 4:9).

Now here is the best part. "Also, Ruth, the Moabitess, the wife of Mahlon, I have purchased to be my wife, to raise up the name of the dead upon his inheritance, that the name be not cut off from among his brethren, and from the gate of his place; you all are witnesses this day" (Ruth 4:10).

A quick study of Hebrew names will show that something very significant has happened here. God is in the details. The name ElimelecH means *My God is King*. The name is beautiful, but ElimelecH, in taking his family out of Israel, brings his family into dangerous territory, not so much physically but spiritually. Naomi (means pleasant) and his two sons Mahlon (means sickly) and Chilion (means failing or annihilation), go with ElimelecH to a strange land with strange gods. ElimelecH dies soon thereafter. Maybe this was the judgement of YHVH for taking his family away from the true God and surrounding them with temptation to move away from Him. The two sons, after ElimelecH dies, marry Moabite women. Naomi must have been a strong teacher of the true God YHVH even in the midst of so much strangeness and confusion. By the names given to the sons, they also follow after their father's lead and continue in the way of those around them. Maybe this is the reason for their names, Mahlon (sickly) and Chilion (failing). The Bible uses names to tell a deeper story. I see Mahlon and Chilion both leading the family further away from the true God; they represent the Jewish people who will fall into temptation by the nations around them and move away from the true God of Israel, either because of the temptation or because the peer pressure is too strong for them. The judgment on them is also death. Naomi is left alone with her two daughters-in-law. They both have seen her strong adherence to the God of Israel even in the midst of this new Moabite culture. Ruth decides somewhere along the way that the God of Naomi is her God as well and renounces all other worship of any other gods. Orpah loves Naomi, but not with the ability to leave all to follow her back to the land of Israel to serve the God of Israel. Ruth is the treasure in all of this sorrow. Ruth, a gentile woman, has a complete change of heart and gives her whole life to Naomi's God and Naomi's people. All this to say, Boaz's name means strength. Ruth goes from sickly Mahlon, who will not lead in truth, to strong Boaz, who will lead her into the promises of the only true God, the God of Israel!

The people confirm the exchange that Boaz is now the rightful Kinsman Redeemer!

> And all the people that were in the gate, and the elders, said, We are witnesses. YHVH make the woman that is come into your house like Rachel and like Leah, which two did BUILD the house of Israel, and do worthily in Ephratah, and be famous in Bethlehem. And let your house be like the house of Pharez, whom Tamar bare unto Judah, of the seed which YHVH shall give to you of this young woman.
>
> Ruth 4:11-12

Wow! What a blessing spoken over Boaz and Ruth. Not only do the people confirm themselves as witnesses but then speak the prophetic words that will set the course for this union of Boaz to Ruth, Jewish to the Gentile believer in the God of Israel. They say of Ruth, the Moabite, the Gentile, make her like Rachel and Leah. Make her a builder of God's House. Leah and Rachel were the two wives of Jacob, with two other concubines, that birthed the twelve sons, the twelve tribes of Israel! Make Ruth the same. Make her one that will continue to build on the foundation that has already been started. Prophetically, they speak of Ephratah, and Bethlehem, where Yeshua will be born over a thousand years later (1100 to 1300 years later)!

It is a beautiful picture of the Gentile world being grafted in and becoming ever so much as treasured as the original chosen people to build God's House, to build His tabernacle. These Gentile people, like Ruth, will love the people of Israel (the Jewish people) and the God of Israel. "Your people shall be my people, and your God, my God" (Ruth 1:16).

"So Boaz took Ruth, and she was his wife; and when he went unto her, YHVH gave her conception, and she birthed a son" (Ruth 4:13). Ruth is not the only one blessed, but Naomi also.

> And the women said unto Naomi, Blessed be YHVH which has not left you this day without a Kinsman Redeemer, that his name may be famous in Israel. And he shall be unto you a restorer of life, and a nourisher of your old age; for your daughter in law, which loves you, which is better to you than seven sons, has born him.
>
> Ruth 4:14-17

The people again prophesy, this time over Naomi. They say, essentially, all the sorrow you went through in a strange land was for a purpose. You have brought back a Gentile woman that loves you more than seven sons. You are no longer in a covenant of weakness, but now, through YHVH's amazing plan and mercy, you are covenanted into strength and even to the very line of the coming Messiah! The Gentile woman and her love for your people and your God is the link that will lead you into a strong covenant with the God of Israel and the coming Messiah when you return again to the land of Israel. Through her and the Jewish people that know their God, you will see Messiah, and your bitterness will disappear.

> And Naomi took the child, and laid it in her bosom, and be-

> came a nurse unto it. And the women, her neighbors, once again prophesy over this little one. There is a son born to Naomi; and they called his name Obed; he is the father of Jesse, the father of David.
>
> Ruth 4:17

Yes, King David!

This union of Boaz to Ruth leads to King David and ultimately to King Jesus! Ruth has truly been grafted in!

> Now these are the generations of Pharez, born from Tamar and Judah. Pharez begat Hezron, and Hezron begat Ram, and Ram begat Amminadab, and Amminadab begat Nahshon and Nahshon begat Salmon, and Salmon begat Boaz, and Boaz begat Obed, and Obed begat Jesse, and Jesse begat David.
>
> Ruth 4:18-22

Again, as stated earlier, this is a story of famine, loss, bitterness, return, struggle, trust, and ultimately deep love and redemption. But it is not just a story of Naomi, Ruth, and Boaz. It is the story of Israel, the story of the God of Israel; it is the story of all redemption and the story God has written from the beginning of time.

It starts with a famine, not just of food, but a famine of the Word of God. In Amos 8:11, YHVH God says, "Behold, the days come, … that I will send a famine in the land, not a famine of bread, nor a thirst for water, but of hearing the words of YHVH."

This famine of God's Word leads to loss. Without God's Word, Elimelech led them into a dangerous place. It reflects the people of Israel that turned away from God's Word and, because of this, experience great loss. They lose YHVH's protection and are dispersed to the four corners of the earth. Yet, there is always a remnant that carries His Word faithfully (Naomi). In the dispersion, because of death and loss, the people experience bitterness. Naomi changes her name to Mara (bitterness), just as the Jewish people, over the past almost 2000 years dispersion have experienced great loss and bitterness (e.g., destruction of the first temple, second temple, captivity, persecution by Nero, Hitler, and so much more). In the midst of all this bitterness, there are always those who hold on through intense struggle to the belief in the God of Israel. Naomi does, and she returns even in her bitterness. The people of Israel, through the past almost 2000 years, have maintained their identity as set apart unto the God of Israel. They also are returning! It has been an intense fight for survival.

Yet, in all this loss, bitterness, and struggle, something beautiful has happened. Naomi returns with Ruth. The nation of Israel, the first Jewish believers in Yeshua, have spread the Gospel (*besorah*) of Messiah, to all the nations. They have, in their dispersion, a great mystery of God, brought back the remnant of the nations, those that have abandoned all (apostasy, secularism, worldliness) to follow the God of Israel. "Your people are my people, and your God is my God" (Ruth 1:16). All the pain of the Jewish people was to determine who would stay with God and who would go after the gods of the nations. Who, like Naomi, would represent the true God of Israel, even in the midst of paganism? Who would bring back the treasure of the nations, the remnant of the peoples? In the end, the spirit of Ruth in this world will turn to bless the Naomis that suffered so much to bring us Home and to graft us into the true and only God, the God of Israel. Naomi's name, which was changed to Mara, was changed again to Naomi.

Boaz married Ruth to redeem not only Ruth but Naomi as well. Both Naomi and Ruth went from weak leadership that led to pagan worship to strong leadership that leads to the God of Israel. Ruth is the story that shows both Jewish and Gentile believers will build the true Kingdom of God together.

What does this mean for us today? Ruth, representing the Holy Spirit-filled Gentile believers in Yeshua today, will work to heal the breach between Jewish people and Gentile people. The Jewish people have lost much in order to bring the Gentiles into covenant relation with the only true God. We are to turn again to our Jewish brothers and sisters. As Ruth, with immense love for them and humility, we are to bring those who have become bitter because of the loss, mostly by the hands of Gentile unbelievers or apostate believers, back into the House of God, and lead them straight to our Messiah, their Messiah, Yeshua! They brought us the truth, with tremendous loss, and in their bitterness, we are to turn around and bring them love and truth and graft those who became lost in the dispersion back Home both physically and spiritually. We must build trust first. We did not *ever* take over. It is time to repair the damage done. This is the story of Ruth. Famine, loss, bitterness, struggle, *return*, trust, covenant love, and redemption.

"For your Maker is your HUSBAND; YHVH tsava'ot (the Lord of hosts) is His Name; and your REDEEMER the Holy One of Israel; The God of the whole earth shall He be called" (Isaiah 54:5).

Other Verses That Speak of YHVH God, Yeshua, as our Kinsman Redeemer in the Bible:

Job 19:25 "For I know that my Kinsman Redeemer lives, and

that He shall stand at the latter day upon the earth."

Psalm 19:14 "Let the words of my mouth and the meditation of my heart be acceptable in Your sight, O YHVH, my Rock, and my Redeemer."

Psalm 78:35 "And they remembered that God was their Rock, and the high God their Redeemer."

Isaiah 41:14 "Fear not, thou worm Jacob, and you men of Israel; I will help you, says YHVH, and your Redeemer, the Holy One of Israel."

Isaiah 43:14, 15 "Thus says YHVH, your Redeemer, the Holy One of Israel; For your sake, I have sent to Babylon, and have brought down their nobles, and the Chaldeans, whose cry is in the ships. I am YHVH, your Holy One, the creator of Israel, your King."

Isaiah 44:6: "Thus says YHVH the King of Israel, and His Redeemer, YHVH tsavaot (the Lord of hosts); I am the first, and I am the last; and beside Me there is no God."

Isaiah 48:17-18 says,

> Thus says YHVH, your Redeemer, the Holy One of Israel; I am YHVH your God, which teaches you to profit, which leads you by the way that you should go. O that you had hearkened to My commandments! Then had your peace been as a river, and your righteousness as the waves of the sea.

Isaiah 49:6-8, 26 says,

> *And He said it is a light thing that you should be My servant to raise up the tribes of Jacob, and to restore the preserved of Israel; I will also give you for a light to the Gentiles, that you may be My Salvation unto the ends of the earth.* Thus says YHVH, *the Redeemer of Israel,* and His Holy One, to Him whom man despises, to Him whom the nation abhors, to a

> Servant of rulers, kings shall see and arise, princes also shall worship, because of YHVH that is faithful, and the Holy One of Israel, and He shall choose you …And I will feed them that oppress you (Israel) with their own flesh; and they shall be drunk with their own blood, as with sweet wine; and all flesh shall know that I YHVH am your Savior and your Redeemer, the Mighty One of Jacob.

Isaiah 59:20-21 says,

> And the REDEEMER shall come to Zion, and unto them that turn from transgression IN JACOB, says YHVH. As for me, this is My covenant with them, says YHVH, My Spirit that is upon you, and My words which I have put in your mouth, shall not depart out of your mouth, nor out of the mouth of your seed, nor out of the mouth of your seed's seed, says YHVH, from henceforth and forever.

There is only one way. Through the House of Israel, in loving the Jewish people, the Jewish disciples and all the heroes and heroines of the Bible and the Jewish people returning to their homeland in fulfillment of prophecy today. We will each take hold of the hem of their garment (Zechariah 8:23), or we will not know the true God of all the universe at all. There is only one Messiah, through Yeshua Ha'Mashiach, our Jewish Messiah. There is only one people called to take the message into all the world. They were never replaced, yet there was a time of hardening for many until the end of the time of the Gentiles. A Mystery. Yet, a remnant of faithful Jewish believers has always been in the earth, hidden, until the time of the Gentiles was complete. They are coming back now in fulfillment of Scripture, the blinders coming off to more and more Jewish people, full circle. They are again the light of the world, and we must understand, we are as well when we are grafted into them, as One New Man.

Sailed on the Sea of Galilee June 9, 2018 on the King David Boat.

The view under the fishing pier at Topsail Island, August 2020.

Picture of Temple Mount taken from the Mount of Olives.
The Eastern Gates are to the far right.

From the Garden of Gethsemane, a picture of the
Eastern Gates through the trunks of an Olive Tree.

… Even the rocks cry out.

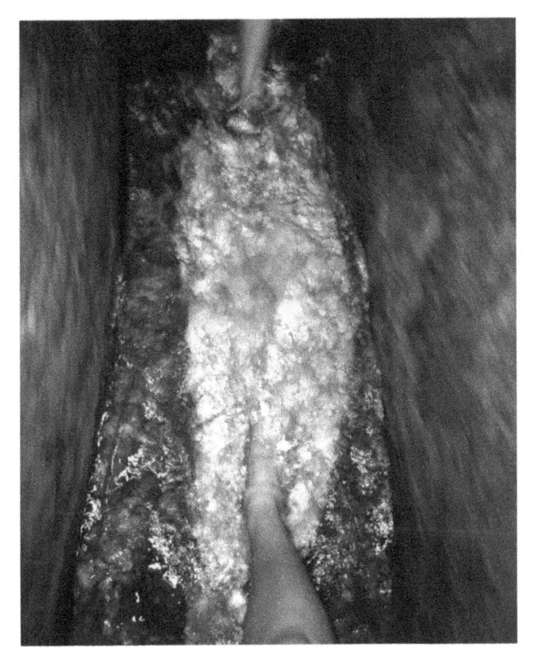

Walking through the Hezekiah Tunnel, pitch dark but flashlights. Fun!

My daughter and I at the Western Wall.

My favorite gate, the Dung Gate, but this is a long story. It has a lot to do with the story of Nehemiah and his walk through the rubble... Nehemiah 2

Open food market in Jerusalem. So many colorful and delicious foods…

Garden Tomb where it is believed Jesus (Yeshua) was buried.

Some of the stones thrown down by the Romans in 70 A.D. in the destruction of the Second Temple. Tears welled up as I touched these stones....

June 15, 2018. Southern Steps to the Temple Mount. As I cross the threshold, I hear in my spirit, "You are Home."

Huldah Gates at the Southern Steps. These gates once led directly onto the Temple Mount. Isaiah 22:22

The Menorah on Mount Zion. A beautiful symbol of keeping the Light of the Holy Spirit burning forever in the House of YHVH God.

The Zion Gate – bullet holes are still visible around this gate to remind everyone of the 1967 Six Day War

An olive tree growing near our hotel in Jerusalem; we are grafted into the olive tree.

Chapter Seven

God's Heart, One New Man, the Acts Disciples

We have covered a lot in the Book of Ruth. It is a beautiful Love Story that points to the unity that YHVH God wants for His children, both Jewish and Gentile people, grafted into the House of Israel. In Ephesians 2, we see once again this union that started in earnest with Cornelius, a gentile, and his family, receiving the Holy Spirit, as Peter ministers and prays for them as commanded by YHVH. I say in earnest because, throughout the Old Testament, there were always "strangers" in the midst of Israel that YHVH said to welcome if they wanted to be a part of their people. But this happened here and there, still with significant outcomes. Yet, now YHVH God, through Jesus on the cross, wanted the Gentiles to be grafted in on a worldwide scale, and it began with Cornelius' house. As stated earlier in chapter two, the prophetic Word, all the people who received the Holy Spirit in Acts 2 were Jewish. So, when Peter has his vision not to think of anything unclean that YHVH says is clean, he is really being told to go to the Gentile peoples and proclaim the gospel to them as well.

Acts 10:9-15 says,

> The next day, as they went on their journey, Peter went up on the housetop to pray about the sixth hour, and became very hungry, and would have eaten, but while they made the meal ready, he fell into a trance. He saw heaven opened and a cer-

> tain vessel descending unto him, as it had been a great sheet knit at the four corners, and it was let down to earth. Within were all manner of four-footed beasts of the earth, and wild beasts, and creeping things, and birds of the air. And there came a voice to him, Rise, Peter, kill and eat. But Peter said, Not so, Lord, for I have never eaten anything that is common and unclean. And the voice spoke unto him again the second time, What Elohim has cleansed, that do not call common. This was done three times; and the vessel was again received up to heaven.

This passage has nothing to do with food! How do we know this? The next verse speaks of Peter trying to figure out what does the dream mean. As he is thinking on this, the Word of God says, "Behold, the men which were sent from Cornelius … stood before the gate." They called and asked if Simon, called Peter, lodged there. While Peter is still thinking on the vision, the Holy Spirit says to him, "Three men are seeking you." The Holy Spirit tells Peter to go and talk with them so that you can know what the dream means. Peter goes, and the three tell him that Cornelius, the centurion, a Roman, a just man, and one that fears the true God, and has a good report from all Jewish people because he treats them with love and kindness, was told by God to send for you and to hear the words you will speak to him.

Wow! Just as Peter has had a vision and is pondering the meaning, the Holy Spirit sends three men to say a man named Cornelius has been told in a vision to call for a man named Simon, whose surname is Peter. The Holy Spirit goes on to say, the man he is looking for is in Simon the tanner's house by the seaside, and he shall tell him what to do (Acts 10:1-6). Cornelius then sends the three men to find this man named Simon, surnamed Peter.

All of this to say, Peter goes to Cornelius' house as called by God. When he gets there, he says to Cornelius and all that are in his house, "you know how that is it an unlawful thing for a man that is a Jew to keep company or come into one of another nation; but Elohim has shown me that I should not call any man common or unclean." Peter now knows the meaning of the dream. God is about to do a new thing, never heard of before. The Jewish believers in Yeshua are to go to the Gentile people who have been searching for truth and tell them about Jesus!

Peter goes on to say, "Therefore I came unto you without delay, as soon as I was sent for; for I ask for what intent have you sent for me?" (Acts 10:29).

Cornelius says to Peter, "Four days ago, I was fasting…and at the ninth hour, I prayed in my house, and behold, a man stood before me in bright clothing, and said, 'Cornelius, your prayer is heard, and your alms (giving to the true God of Israel) are had in remembrance in the sight of God.'" Cornelius goes on to say, "I was told to send for you Peter" (Acts 10:30-33).

Peter, in amazement, says, "Of a truth, I perceive that God is no respecter of persons. But in EVERY NATION, the one that fears Him and works righteousness, is accepted of Him" (Acts 10:34-35). Peter then presents the Gospel (*besorah*) to Cornelius and all that are in his house. "When Peter yet spoke these words, the Holy Spirit fell on ALL of them that heard the Word" (Acts 10:44).

Peter is astonished!

> And they of the circumcision (Jewish people) which believed were astonished, as many as came with Peter, because that on the GENTILES also was poured out the gift of the HOLY SPIRIT.

For they heard them speak with tongues and magnify God.

Acts 10:45-46

Peter goes on to say the Gentiles also should be baptized with water. "Can any man forbid the water baptism, that these should be baptized, which have received the Holy Spirit as well as we (the Jewish believers) have? Then he commanded that they be baptized in the Name of the Lord Adonai" (Acts 10:47-48).

So, the Gentile believers were not grafted in until Acts Chapter 10, about ten years after the baptism that took place in Acts 2 at Shavuot (or Pentecost). With the grafting of Gentile people in mass starting at this point, we see what the God of Israel had in mind all along, that all families of nations would be blessed through the people of Israel, the Jewish people (Genesis 12:3)! This is the very beginning of the One New Man spoken about in Ephesians Chapter 2 and the mystery in Ephesians Chapter 3.

Let's take a look at Ephesians. Paul, like Peter, is commissioned to take the Gospel to the Gentile nations, although his heart longs to also preach to the Jewish people that do not know Jesus yet. In the first verses of Chapter 2, Paul tells the Gentiles that something new has happened in all of history. He says, "In times past you walked according to the prince of the power of the air, the spirit that now works in the children of disobedience. Among whom also we all (both Jewish and Gentile people) have had our conversation in times past" (Ephesians 2:2-3). Paul acknowledges we all have listened to the enemy; it is a fight for every person to hear God's voice and listen only to Him.

> But God, rich in mercy, for His great Love wherewith He loved US, even when we were dead in sins, has quickened us TOGETHER with Christ (Messiah), by grace you are saved; and has raised us up TOGETHER and made us sit TOGETHER in heavenly places in Christ Jesus (Yeshua Ha' MashiacH).
>
> Ephesians 2:4-5

The verses afterward are very well known by most Christians.

For by grace, you are saved through faith, and that not of yourselves; it is the GIFT of God. Not of works, lest any man should boast. For we are His workmanship, created in Christ Jesus unto good works, which God has before ordained that we should walk in them.

Ephesians 2:8-10

But many times, the preaching stops here. Let's look closely at the next half of this chapter.

> Wherefore REMEMBER that you being in times past GENTILES in the flesh, who are called Uncircumcision by that which is called Circumcision (cut away, set apart from the world) in the flesh made by hands, that at that time, you were without Christ (Messiah), being aliens from the Commonwealth of Israel, and strangers from the covenants of promise, having NO HOPE, and without God in the world; but now in Christ Jesus (Messiah Yeshua) you who were sometimes far off are made near by the blood of Messiah. For He is OUR peace, who has made BOTH ONE, and has broken down the middle wall of division between us.
>
> Ephesians 2:11-12

Paul is telling the Gentile people, God has brought you into the Kingdom of God as well. He has brought you into the family of God, the Commonwealth of Israel! The Gentiles did not know the true God at all before the Jewish disciples took the Word of God to them in obedience to YHVH God's commandments. God is doing a new thing! He is putting us both *together*.

The next verse has burned in my heart with a passion ever since returning from Israel, even though it was there all along. It says,

> Having abolished in His flesh the enmity (the hatred and hostility), even the law of commandments contained in ordinance (even the ordinances that have kept Jewish people from even associating with the Gentile nations); for to make in Himself OF THE TWO, ONE NEW MAN, so making peace.
>
> Ephesians 2:15

Again, something new!

Let's see what God had in mind and still has in His heart and mind, especially for the days we live in now. Ephesians 2:16-19 says,

> And that He might RECONCILE BOTH by the cross, having slain the enmity thereby; and came and preached peace to them which were afar off (the Gentiles) and to those who were near (the Jewish people). For through Him (Jesus, Yeshua) we BOTH have access by one Spirit unto the Father. Now therefore, you are no more strangers, and foreigners, but fellow citizens with the saints (ha'kedoshim) and of the household of God.

YHVH, the God of Israel, has a special purpose in putting us *together*, He is building His Tabernacle, the one without human hands. Ephesians 2:20-22 says,

> And are built upon the foundation of the apostles and prophets, Jesus Christ (Yeshua Messiah) Himself being the chief cornerstone; in Whom all the building fitly framed together grows unto a Holy Temple in YHVH. In Whom you are also built TOGETHER for a habitation of God (Elohim) through the Spirit (RuacH).

Only a decade after Jesus ascended to the Father, the beginning of this House of God, this Bride, began in earnest. The Acts believers at first were all Jewish (thousands of them), then ten years later, the Gentiles were grafted in, and together, YHVH God was building His temple, through the work of Jesus the Messiah, the One pointed to by the Jewish prophets and apostles throughout history, that He would surely come and bring peace. This House, this Tabernacle, is the joining of Jewish believers with those from the nations, the Gentiles, that would be grafted into the House of Israel, the Tabernacle of David.

In the last days, it is prophesied that this House will be built and finished. Amos 9:11, Acts 15:14-16, and Haggai 2:9. These are the last days, yet much destruction and separation have again occurred over the last 1700-1800 years, and the tide of antisemitism is rising again in all the earth. The enemy, Satan, hates the Jewish people with a vengeance because they have written the Word of God, preserved it, given it to the world, and through them came the Savior of the world, Yeshua. Because of this, the Acts House of God, in his evil eyes, needed to be separated and destroyed again. We know that this house was soon separated again by a terrible breach, a wound that would fester for at least the next 1700 years.

Chapter Eight

Grafted In, The Remnant, Repentance, Replacement Theology

> And Saul, yet breathing out threatenings and slaughter against the disciples of the Lord, went unto the high priest, and asked him for letters to Damascus to the synagogues, that if he found any of this Way, whether they were men or women, he might bring them bound unto Jerusalem. And as he journeyed, he came near Damascus, and suddenly there shined about him a light from heaven; and he fell to the earth, and heard a voice saying unto him, Saul, Saul, why do you persecute Me? And he said, Who are you Lord? And the Lord said, I am Yeshua whom you persecute… And he trembling and astonished said, Lord, what will You have me to do? And the Lord said unto him, Arise, and go into the city, and it shall be told to you what you must do.
>
> Acts 9:1-6

As Saul turned into Paul needed a bolt of lightning to stop his persecution of God's people, so the church may need this same wake-up call for those who believe the replacement of the Jewish people is in the Bible. This teaching is as dangerous as Paul's persecution of the true believers in Yeshua. Saul, a very religious Jewish man, was persecuting his own Jewish brothers and sisters that believed in Jesus. He was going to the synagogues (because there were no places called churches yet) and taking Jewish believers in Yeshua captive and murdering many of them. He thought with all his heart that he was doing God a favor, as many religious non-believing Jews do today who persecute the Jewish people who believe in Yeshua or are searching to know their Messiah. He thought he was cleansing out people that were dishonoring the true God. He was wrong, yet sincerely so. He sincerely believed he was righteous in his actions and thinking, yet needed Yeshua Himself to turn him completely around.

The church, in many places, has done the same thing. Many in the church have persecuted the Jewish people, if not directly through the Crusades, the Holocaust, and other violent events, covertly, holding them in disdain, rejected, accountable for killing the Lord Jesus. Yet, we forget or were never taught that the Jewish people, by the thousands, were the first to believe. We also forget our own gospel. We all killed Him. We all rejected Him, and only by His grace, the Holy Spirit, can we receive Him as Lord and Savior. The reason the very first Gentiles received Jesus as Lord and Savior and the baptism of the Holy Spirit was because of the obedience of the first-century Jewish disciples that went out to preach the Gospel to the Gentiles as well. The church has done much damage to God's holy temple made without human hands, in the preaching of Replacement Theology, Dualism, and outright hatred for the very people who brought us the Word of God, protected it through the ages, and brought us our Jewish Messiah, Yeshua (Jesus), the King of the Jews, and the King of all creation. So what can we do? We need a wake-up call just as Saul did, no matter how sincerely wrong many have been in our beliefs and in our thinking.

Jeremiah 16:19 says of the Gentiles, in the last days,

> O Lord, my strength and my fortress, and my refuge in the Day of Affliction, the Gentiles shall come unto you (the Jewish believers) from the ends of the earth, and shall say, Surely, our fathers have inherited lies, vanity and things wherein there is no profit.

YHVH God speaks of these last days where the Gentiles will finally see many of us have been wrong, like Saul, and that the God of Israel is the only true God, and we must be re-united with our Jewish brothers and sisters for the building of His tabernacle, the Tabernacle of David. This will take a miracle for some to see this truth. The lies have been entrenched in the Church for at least 1700 years.

Let's Take a Look at History

So what happened? Soon after, exactly fifty days after Yeshua rose from the dead, on the day of Shavuot, or Pentecost, the Jewish disciples were filled with the Holy Spirit. Something new had happened! They were filled with joy, gladness, and deep conviction and courage to carry the message of Yeshua and eternal life to all the people in Jerusalem, then to Judaea, then to Samaria, and then (as started in Cornelius's house) to the four corners of the earth, as Jesus commanded them.

For the first ten years or so, Jewish believers in Yeshua only ministered and preached the gospel to other Jewish people. Thousands of Jewish people came to know the Lord because of their testimony. Then, as we spoke of before, Peter is called to bring the gospel message to Cornelius and his family and then to all Gentile nations. Other Jewish disciples, such as Paul and Barnabas, are also called to preach to the Gentiles, as well as their Jewish brothers and sisters. This time period was full of joy and power as Jews and Gentiles came together as ONE in the Holy Spirit, but also full of persecution and terror. The enemy of us all, satan, made sure that the unbelievers at the time persecuted, tortured, and murdered the believers in Yeshua, the followers of the Way.

First, many Jewish people, as a whole, were targeted. As Yeshua told them, their temple would be burnt down, "not one stone left upon the other." In 70 AD, this happened when the Roman soldiers tore down the temple and killed over a million Jewish people, as attested by Josephus, the historian. By 135 AD, the last of the Jewish community was killed or dispersed from Israel; Israel itself was renamed Palestina by Emperor Hadrian, making it clear that the Jewish people were not allowed to return to Israel.

So, the story continues. The Jewish people were dispersed to the four corners of the earth. Yet, this was all part of God's plan. Their dispersion would lead to the gospel being preached around the world. The Jewish disciples that were still alive would be sent out to be a light in the midst of a dark world. This time period, starting with Alexander the Great (333 BC), but now escalating to full take over is called the Time of the Gentiles by Jesus in Luke 21:24, alluded to in Daniel 8:13, and Matthew 24:14-15. It would be a time of trampling by the Gentiles on Jerusalem. The Jewish people would not be in control of Jerusalem for almost 2000 years. It would be a bitter but necessary trial to endure to bring the gospel to all the world. Why?

Dispersion was necessary, like seeds blowing far away from a parent plant to bring life everywhere… The people of God must go into all the nations. God knew that many would not choose to leave Jerusalem, to leave Israel to go into far countries to preach the gospel. So, He sent them. Some of them were believers in Yeshua, and some were not.

For the next 300 years after the first outpouring of the Holy Spirit, the followers of the Way were true to the Word of God, yet persecution continued and increased. The believers, both Jewish and Gentile, were thrown to lions, burned at the stake, tortured, murdered, used as entertainment; they were killed in the Colosseum by wild animals, made to fight each other to the death in gladiator fights and any other forms of torture the Roman pagan world could think of. The pain and sorrow were never-ending. Yet, many would not renounce their faith in Jesus.

Then, on October 27, 312 AD, Constantine, the current ruler of the Roman empire, on the eve of the Battle of Milvian, had a vision of a cross and was assured that he would win the victory if he would go in the name of Jesus. Many of us know the story. He put crosses on all his soldiers' shields, and he indeed won a great victory. Constantine's heart was changed toward the followers of the Way, also now called Christians (Acts 11:26), and he decided to stop all the persecution and murder. Yet, Constantine's heart was still very much in the world. He would stop the persecution, but the followers of the Way would have to make some changes in their beliefs. It would come with a cost. Even so, there was a sigh of relief for those being persecuted, at least for the moment.

Constantine and another man Licinius Augustus (who also co-ruled the Roman Empire at the same time as Constantine) proclaimed a new law called the Edict of Milan, which in part said, "It has pleased us to remove all conditions whatsoever… concerning the Christians, and now any one of these who wishes to observe the Christian religion may do so freely and openly without any disturbance or molestation." [14]

This law hereby stopped the fierce persecution and murder of the people who followed Jesus, both Jewish and Gentile believers. But the enemy had a plan. In this peace, there would be no peace. Soon thereafter, the division started by some of the fathers of the Christian Church in the people of the Way, the Truth, and the Life, became a huge gaping breach. The people of God were at first called the people of "The Way." They were distinctly Jewish as Gentile believers were grafted into the original Jewish disciples. Yet, slowly, at first, as more Greek, Roman, and Gentile people came to know of the Gospel, while many were true followers, others were wolves in sheep's clothing. One of the first of these voices to widen the breach between the Jewish believers and the Gentile believers was a man named Ignatius of Antioch. In 99 AD, after John, "the disciple that Jesus loved" and who wrote the Book of Revelation, died, Ignatius made this absurd statement to those who followed him, "It is absurd to profess Jesus Christ (Yeshua Messiah, remember He is Jewish) and to Judaize, (practice Jewish laws and customs)." He was essentially saying the very customs and practices that our Lord and Savior Jesus kept and held dear, it is absurd to do the same thing and follow His example.

In the time between 100-165 AD, Justin Martyr, considered another church father, accused the Jews of being solely responsible for killing Jesus. He wrote, "The tribulations were justly imposed on you (Jewish people, believers included), for you have murdered the Just One." [15]

How quickly he forgot that he himself, Justin Martyr, also needed his sins forgiven and was just as much responsible for the death of Jesus as everyone else. Jesus died for all. We all put Him on that cross because He willingly went for all because of His love for us.

In Matthew 27:25, the Scripture says, "May His blood be upon us, and on our children." The Jewish people proclaimed this as they chose Barabbas instead of Jesus to be set free. In so saying, they unknowingly were proclaiming what we all need–Jesus' blood upon us, His blood covering, to wash us clean from our sins. Yes, may His blood covering be on all that proclaim His name. Without the shedding of blood, there is no remission of sins. Jesus came to die on the cross. No one put Him there but He Himself. The people who actually did that work 2000 years ago, however evil their intent may have been, were only doing the will of the Father so that all who called on Yeshua's (Jesus') name could be saved from our sins. If He had wanted to, He could have called the angels in heaven, or even with one word of His own, as fully God, wiped out everyone around Him. He went to the cross because that is what He came to do for us *all*. To hate a particular people for putting Jesus on the cross is absurd theology. Oh God, forgive us, for we are all sinners in need of the blood of Jesus to wash us clean.

In Matthew 16:20-23, Jesus tells His Jewish disciples not to tell anyone that He is Yeshua, the Messiah (Again, Yeshua literally means salvation in Hebrew, and that is what He was called as He walked the earth, so I used the names interchangeably). It goes on to say,

> From that time forth began Jesus to show unto His disciples, how He must go to Jerusalem, and suffer many things of the elders and chief priests and scribes, and be killed, and be raised again the third day. Then Peter (a Jewish disciple that loved Him) took Jesus aside, and began to rebuke Him

> saying, Be it far from You; this shall not happen to You. But Jesus turned and said unto Peter, "Get behind Me Satan; you are an offence to Me; for you savor (or desire) not the things of God, but those that be of men."
>
> Matthew 16:21-23

Here, one of Jesus' closest disciples, a Jewish man, is saying, "No, Yeshua, we will not let this happen to You. We will defend You. They will not kill You on my watch." We know Peter meant well, but Jesus' answer is harsh. He says to Peter; essentially, your words are like Satan's who would try and tempt Me away from the very thing I came to do. I came to lay down my life so that My people would be redeemed. We forget all the Jewish people who loved Him dearly, who cried at the cross for Him, who would have fought for Him. They were told by Jesus, "I came to the earth to do this for you, the Jewish people first, and then for the Samaritans, and then to all the earth." The self-righteous blaming of the Jewish people is an offense to the very God we love. Just like Saul, we need to have a deeper understanding of the Scriptures; even if our intentions are good, we can be sincerely wrong.

This false conversation about the Jewish people continued to be perpetuated by those who should have known better. Another church father named Chrysostom (347-407 AD), a Greek, taught against keeping the Lord's biblical holy days spoken of in Leviticus 23. There were many others who spoke the same thing, and research into this time of history where the breach began is filled with antisemitic sentiments. Why? Because Satan knew the House of God, together with Jewish and Gentile believers, was *unstoppable*, so He needed to cause division. How else do you make a house fall? "And if a house be divided against itself, that house cannot stand" (Mark 3:25).

So, Constantine stopped the persecution and physical warfare. Yet, something more insidious was about to begin–the tearing away from the true gospel to something mixed with the false religions of the day. In 315 AD, Constantine issued a law to stop the dangerous sect of Judaism from persecuting those Jewish people that believed in Yeshua as their Messiah. This, in itself, may have been good, yet the law became not only a protection for those who believed in Jesus but soon became an instrument to use against anything Jewish, including the Jewish believers.

The Way, the first believers, the Acts House of God, was Jewish to its core. Again, we were grafted into the Jewish disciples of Jesus, of Yeshua, not the other way around. The new sect of Jewish belief was given a new name; instead of followers of the Way, the people of Yeshua Messiah were given the Greek name, the followers of Jesus Christ and therefore called Christians. This happened soon after Cornelius and his family were filled with the Holy Spirit and were joined to the Jewish community of believers. In Acts 11:26, it says,

> And when he (Barnabas, a Jewish disciple) found him (Saul, a Jewish disciple) he brought him unto Antioch. And it came to pass, that a whole year they assembled themselves with the assembly, and taught much people. And the disciples were called Christians first in Antioch.

With the new name, slowly yet persistently, came the separation of anything Jewish from increasingly Greek, Gentile-influenced assembly of believers. The original Jewish community was severely persecuted in the early years as they were completely driven from their homeland by 135 AD. The Gentile believers continued to increase in number, but the Jewish community decreased significantly by the Roman Empire clearing out Israel of the Jews. By the time Constantine came in 312 AD, although the House of God was still very much Jewish and Gentile believers together, it was decidedly more Gentile believers than Jewish only because many of the Jewish community had been murdered or dispersed. So, the separation of anything Jewish would be much easier now, as Constantine would stop the persecution of the Christians based on his changing a few things first.

This leads us to the Council of Nicaea called to order by Constantine in 325 AD. The council had 300 bishops to determine what would be true Christianity and what would not. Sadly, there were no Jewish believers in this Council. Although the Council itself brought forth a strong belief in Jesus Christ (Yeshua Messiah) as the Son of God and as the same substance as the Father and Holy Spirit, it also began the process of distinguishing Judaism from Christianity, which in later councils was officially codified. One of the first things determined was to set a new day to celebrate the resurrection of Jesus; it would be called Easter. Passover and First Fruits would no longer be observed. This was in distinct opposition to the way the followers of Jesus had celebrated His resurrection the first 300 years from the outpouring of the Holy Spirit. Passover, the Feast of Unleavened Bread, and First Fruits, this week of celebration and remembrance was replaced with Easter (a mix of the celebration of Jesus with the pagan practices of the day). Constantine was trying to find a way to appease non-believers in the Roman Empire with the now official religion of the land, Christianity.

But Christianity began to look more and more like a completely different belief system than what Yeshua had set into motion at

Shavout (Pentecost) fifty days after His resurrection. First, at the Council of Nicaea, Constantine sent out a letter to all churches everywhere saying,

> When the question arose concerning the most holy day of Easter, it was decreed by common consent to be expedient, that this festival should be celebrated on the same day by all in every place; And truly, in the first place, it seemed to everyone a most unworthy thing that we should follow the custom of the Jews in the celebration of this most holy solemnity, who polluted wretches, having stained their hands with a nefarious crime, are justly blinded in their minds. It is therefore, that rejecting the practice of this people we should perpetuate to all future ages the celebration of this rite, in a more legitimate order… Let us then have nothing in common with the most hostile rabble of the Jews.[16]

The breach was almost complete. The following councils of Antioch and Laodicea solidified the break, the tear, the gaping hole in God's true House. In 345 AD, Christians were no longer allowed to celebrate the Passover seder with the Jewish believers, their Jewish friends, and neighbors. At the Council of Laodicea, in 364 AD, the Biblical Sabbath day called Shabbat (which was celebrated from Friday at sundown to Saturday at sundown for thousands of years) was outlawed, and Christians were told that they *must work* on that day and if they can rather rest on the new Sabbath which would be Sunday. Man had decided to change God's Laws and the times. He would be the one to say what would be the Law. The Law of God, the Word of God, handed down by the Jewish people, their feasts commanded by YHVH, their sabbath commanded by YHVH, would now be changed to man's ways. The Jewish faith, the Way, was completely separated from this new belief system, Christianity. And a new thought became prevalent among Gentile believers–we have taken over. The promises made to Abraham, Isaac, and Jacob now belong solely to us. We are the new Israel.

Replacement Theology has long reared its ugly head in the church. It has kept us from caring about the Jewish people and has kept many of them from knowing their Jewish Messiah, our Jewish Messiah because they have been cast out from their very house. These words may be very difficult for some to accept. We have been taught wrong. In many cases, YHVH God extends mercy in our wrong understanding, and has done so through the centuries, yet now with Israel back on the map in fulfillment of prophecy and Bibles in every home in the United States and in other places around the world, or very easily accessible, we, as God's people, have no excuse to allow this heinous lie to continue. We are in a new dispensation of time. The blinders are coming off the Jewish people, and they *must* come off the Gentile believers as well. The breach *must* be healed. We are the generation that is being held to account to heal this breach.

Replacement theology, or Supersessionism, is the doctrine held by many in the Christian Church that the Church has replaced Israel in God's plans. This is the height of false doctrine that we are warned about. It has led to much sorrow and persecution and hatred of our Jewish brothers and sisters. It is the reason for the antisemitism that caused the Holocaust and so many other atrocities in the last 2000 years against the Jewish people. It has been a war from the beginning, even before Jesus came to the earth. Satan has used people of the world to attack His holy people in the days of Esther through Haman (483-473 BC), in the days of Syrian king

Antiochus (168 BC), and he will persist in trying to annihilate God's chosen people until the day Yeshua returns again and puts an end to all this apostasy. We should not be offended at the truth but do everything in our power to proclaim it and heal the gaping hole in the House of God.

There is a Mystery

We need to repent and love them for what they did, willingly and unwillingly, to bring us the good news. Their hearts were hardened for our benefit, again a Mystery (Romans 11:25). Their hearts are being softened again. Our doors and our arms should be wide open.

Even in all this pain, there is a mystery. Yeshua knew this would happen. It was even part of His plan. Much of the antisemitism that later occurred came partly because the Jewish people had hardened their hearts to the gospel message. Martin Luther (1483-1546 AD), although venerated rightly so for his courageous fight to bring the Bible to people in their own language and to fight against man-made religion, also sadly perpetuated the hatred with comments like "The Jews are a base, whoring people, that is no people of God, and their boast in lineage, circumcision, and law must be accounted as filth."[17] He should have known better because of the Scriptures, but his own frustration at their blindness and Luther's humanness (and maybe part insanity in his old age) caused him to blaspheme God's people and miss the Mystery prophesied in the Bible. Luther's "little" book titled, *The Jews and their Lies* led to so much horror and pain as later generations used his words to justify their hateful actions and words towards the Jewish people. Hence, the Holocaust.

But the antisemitism started way before Martin Luther and was prophesied many times in the Bible. In Acts 11, after the people of the Way started to be called Christians in Antioch (sometime after 30 AD or 40 AD), prophets came from Jerusalem. Acts 11:27-28 says, "And in these days came prophets from Jerusalem unto Antioch. And there stood Agabus and signified by the Spirit that there should be great dearth (famine) throughout all the world; which came to pass in the days of Claudius Ceasar." Then the disciples, determined to send relief unto their brothers which dwelt at Judaea, (and) sent it to the leaders by the hands of Barnabas and Saul.

What I find fascinating in this passage is the prophets proclaim a famine, a dearth in Antioch. It was a famine of food but also a future prophetic famine of the Word of God. The famine of the Word of God would start in Antioch, the very place this Word was proclaimed, even in the Council of Antioch when Christians were banned from celebrating the Passover, the very Passover that recalls our deliverance from Egypt by the blood of the lamb and points to the Passover Lamb that takes away the sins of the world. Again, Amos says there will be a time when it is not just a famine of food but a famine of the Word of God (Amos 8:11). In the next 1000 years, until Martin Luther (1483-1546) brought the Word of God to the common man, there was a great dearth, a great famine of the Word of God. The people lived in darkness and could only do as the church of Rome fathers told them. Whether these men in power told the truth or not was not something most could discern. They could not read. They did not have Bibles, even if they could read. Many were hopelessly at the mercy of those who purported the truth. The church grew rich in the common people's ignorance in the sale of indulgences. Power and wealth were the ambition of most in this false church, not lifting up and glorifying Yeshua and teaching the full Word of God.

As man began to redefine words, replacing the people of the Way with the word Christians (which in itself is not a bad thing but replaces the name Messiah with the Greek word Christ), replacing the Sabbath rest with Sunday (which alludes to the worship of the sun god), replacing the Passover with Easter, replacing all the Jewish feasts and holy days with new names and new ways to celebrate on totally different times, the erasing of our Jewish roots, our Jewish history began. If you can erase history, you can erase identity, purpose, and truth. The enemy's tactics do not change much, calling evil good, and good evil.

Yeshua spoke of the time of the Gentiles, but yet also spoke of a time when this would end, and the Jewish people would come back to a full knowledge of the Word of God, the Old and the New; a time when true Gentile believers would turn their hearts back to their Jewish brothers and sisters. Romans 11 is quite a chapter to tackle. Many times, it is completely ignored. Yet, we need to look much closer at this chapter and see what God has said would happen in the latter days before His second return.

Romans 11–Rightly Dividing the Word of Truth

Romans 11 starts off with a question. "I say then, Has God cast away His people? God forbid. For I am an Israelite, of the seed of Abraham, of the tribe of Benjamin" (Romans 11:1). Paul says even though many, maybe half of the Jews or more, have turned away from the Messiah Yeshua, God has not forsaken His people. Paul goes on to say, "I, even I am one of the Israelites, sent to the Gentiles to preach the Word of God, yet I long for my people (the

Jewish people) as well."

In Romans 11:2, Paul answers his own question.

> God has NOT cast away His people which He foreknew. Do you not know what the scriptures say of Elijah? How he makes intercession to God against Israel saying Lord, they have killed Your prophets, and dug down Your altars; and I am left alone and they seek my life. But what does God answer him? I have reserved to Myself seven thousand people, who have not bowed the knee to the image of Ba'al. Even so then at this present time also there is a REMNANT according to the election of grace.

The Word of God proclaims there is a *remnant* of thousands of Jewish people that will remain faithful to the full Word of God. They will be kept by the Holy Spirit, by grace and not of works. The next question asked, "What then? Israel has not obtained that which it seeks, but the election (the Remnant of Jewish people) has obtained it, and the rest were blinded" (Romans 11:7). God speaks that a remnant of Jewish people will always know the truth and be the first fruit disciples that bless the rest of the world with the gospel message. The rest of the Jewish people will be blinded for a time.

Romans 11:8, "According as it is written, God has given them the spirit of slumber, eyes that they should not see, and ears that should not hear, unto this day."

With this spirit of slumber, is all lost? No, it is part of a Mystery, a plan. Romans 11:11 imparts, "I say then, Have they stumbled that they should fall? God forbid. But rather through their fall, Salvation has come unto the Gentiles, for to provoke them to jealousy." What does that mean? As the Jewish people carried the Word exclusively for 2000 years and became prideful in many ways and fell away, so too, the Gentiles would carry it for the next 2000 years and become prideful and fall away. Yet God has a plan.

Romans 11:12 explains, "Now if the trespass of them (the Jewish people) be the riches of the world, and the diminishing of them the riches of the Gentiles, how much more (blessings will come) from their fullness (from their restoration)." In other words, when the spirit of blindness is cast off the Jewish people, how much more will the blessings come to all the world? It will be a time of great revival!

Romans 11:13-14 makes a point that now Paul is speaking directly to the Gentiles that are beginning to grow in number and becoming predominant in the house of God. Paul gives an exhortation to remember. "For I speak to you Gentiles, inasmuch as I am the apostle to the Gentiles…" but Paul reminds them he is a Jewish disciple and loves his people (the Jewish people) too. "If by any means I may provoke to emulation (inspire to copy) them which are my flesh, and might save some of them." Paul wants the Jewish people that do not yet believe to also see the glory of Yeshua in him and in the rising house of God and become jealous so that they want also what they see in others, the power of the Holy Spirit.

"For if the casting away of them (Jewish people) be the reconciling of the world, what shall the receiving of them (the Jewish people back into the house of God) be but life from the dead?" (Romans 11:15). The receiving of the Jewish people, our brothers and sisters, will initiate the greatest revival we have ever seen! It is time for the Gentile believers to see we *need* our Jewish brothers and sisters and always have.

"For if the first fruit (Yeshua) be holy, the lump (the place of origin) is also holy; and if the root be holy (our Jewish roots), so are the branches (Jewish and Gentiles together)" (Romans 11:16).

> And if some of the branches be broken off (Jewish people), and you, being a wild olive tree (Gentiles), were grafted in among them, and with them (Jewish people) partake of the root and the abundance of the olive tree; BOAST NOT against the branches (original). But if you boast, you do not bear the root (Jewish history and people), but the root bears you.
>
> Romans 11:17-18

"You will say then, The (original) branches (the Jewish people) were broken off, that I may be grafted in" (Romans 11:19). Yes, we say this and stop here. This is replacement theology. But God has an answer through his apostle Paul. Romans 11:20 says,

> Well, because of the unbelief they were broken off, and you stand by faith. BE NOT HIGH MINDED, BUT FEAR. For if God did not spare the natural branches (Jewish people that did not believe), take heed that He also not spare you. Behold, therefore, the goodness and severity of God; on them (Jewish unbelievers) which fell, severity, but on you, goodness, IF you continue in His goodness. Otherwise, you also shall be cut off.

Here is a warning. Do not think you have taken over. Beware of this Replacement Theology which is coming to the House of God. Be careful, I hear Paul emphatically warning and prophesying for the days to come.

Romans 11:23-24 speaks of a turning of events. "And they also if they abide not still in unbelief (all the Jewish people who would come to know Jesus, (Yeshua) in the future) shall be grafted in; for God is able to graft them in again." Again, Paul speaks a warning. "For if you were cut out of the olive tree which is wild by nature, and were grafted in contrary to nature into a good olive tree, how much MORE shall these (the Jewish people), which be the natural branches, be grafted into their own olive tree?"

Romans 11:25 says, "For I do not want you, brethren (and sisters), to be ignorant of this MYSTERY; lest you should be wise in your own conceits, that blindness IN PART is happened to Israel until the FULNESS OF THE GENTILES be come in" and prophesies into the future that this blindness on many Jewish people is part of a mystery, and the blindness is only in part. It will end when the time of the Gentiles is complete. Paul does not know this spirit of slumber will last about 2000 years, but we see it. The Gospel has gone around the world and is back in Jerusalem, where it started. The blinders are coming off the Jewish people. Revival is near!

"And so ALL Israel shall be saved" (Romans 11:26).

This is the New Testament, folks! And we are not Israel unless we are grafted into the Jewish people, our Jewish roots. Jewish and Gentile believers in Yeshua, or as the rest of the world calls Him, Jesus, together. This is the House of God, the God of Israel.

"As it is written, 'There shall come out of Zion the Deliverer, and shall turn away ungodliness from Jacob (renamed Israel). For this is My covenant unto them (Jewish people) when I take away their sins" (Romans 11:26-27). A new covenant written on their hearts and on ours (remember Jeremiah 31).

"As concerning the gospel, they are enemies for your sakes." This speaks of the time when the Jewish people, not all but many, will not listen to the Gospel because of the spirit of slumber put on them for a time. It is also because of the "Church's" historic evil mistreatment of the Jewish people as a whole. "But as touching the election, they are beloved for the fathers' sakes." A remnant of Jewish people will be released from this spirit of slumber and have been and will be some of the greatest evangelists, prophets, pastors, teachers, and apostles ever known. They are with us now, and many more will believe in the years ahead!

For the gift and the calling of God are without repentance. For in times past you have not believed (remember Acts 10, Ephesians 2), yet now you have obtained mercy through their unbelief. Even so, these also have not believed that through *your mercy*, they may also obtain mercy." God speaks again through Paul, that in these last days, when the spirit of slumber is taken off, and the hearts of the Jewish people as a whole are once again able to receive the message of their Messiah in great numbers, *we*, the Gentile believers, are commissioned to love them back into the Kingdom of God, through our mercy, our love, our humility, our understanding of this great mystery and the times we are living in right now. Like Peter went to the Gentiles almost 2000 years ago, we are commanded to purposefully, and with passion and humility, go back to our Jewish brothers and sisters and bring them back into the House of God by knowing their Messiah and our Messiah Yeshua (Jesus). Without them, we are not what God intended. We will either obey this or be in danger of falling into the delusion of the last days and be left behind (Esther 4:14, 2 Thessalonians 2:1-12).

"For God has concluded them all in unbelief (both Gentiles for the first 2000 years, and then many of the Jewish people for the next 2000 years) that He might have mercy on all" (Romans

11:32). No one can boast. It is all God's mercy and His plan from the beginning.

> O the depths of the riches both of the wisdom and knowledge of God! How unsearchable are His judgments, and His Ways past finding out! For who has known the mind, the Spirit of YHVH? Or who has been His counselor? Or who has first given to Him and it shall be repaid to him again? For of Him and through Him and to Him, are all things; to Whom be glory forever. Amen.
>
> Romans 11:33-36

God will receive *all* the glory. As we have received the Word of God and our Messiah from the first Jewish disciples, so we must, in turn, give back to them the Word of God in its entirety and their Messiah, our Messiah in these last days. No one can boast. It is a great Mystery. God has made us dependent on Him alone, and 2000 years ago, He commanded the Jewish disciples to preach Yeshua to the Gentiles. Today, when more and more Jewish people can now see again clearly, we are commanded to give the gospel message (*besorah*), the whole Word of God, back to them.

Many Jewish believers today, Messianic Jewish people, have been positioned, like Paul who desperately wanted to reach his own people as well as the Gentiles, to proclaim the good news to their Jewish brothers and sisters through ministries like One for Israel, shelanu TV, Jewish Voice, and Jews for Jesus, MAOZ Israel, Christians United for Israel, Fellowship of Israel Related Ministries (FIRM) and many others. A list of more of the ministries is given at the end of this book. Many Jewish people are receiving Yeshua (Jesus) as their Savior. It truly is a time of new beginnings (Isaiah 43:19). Supporting these ministries is a wonderful way to bless Israel and the Jewish people. It is a way we can help fulfill this end-time prophetic Word of bringing the Gospel back to those who originally gave it to the world. We will be blessed as we bless Israel (Genesis 12:3).

YHVH God, the God of Israel, is moving in all the earth. His eyes are focused on Israel and the return of the Jewish people to Him in these prophetic days; our eyes should be too. He calls us to be the healers of the breach.

Isaiah 58:12 "And they that shall be of you shall BUILD the old waste places; you shall raise up the foundations of many generations, and you shall be called REPAIRER OF THE BREACH, the Restorer of paths to dwell in."

Isaiah 60:1-3 says,

> Arise shine; for your Light has come, and the glory of the Lord YHVH is risen upon you. For, behold, the darkness shall cover the earth, and gross darkness the people; but the Lord YHVH shall arise upon you, and His glory shall be seen upon you. And the Gentiles shall come to your Light, and the kings to the brightness of your rising.

Israel is rising again.

As the physical temples were destroyed, so the spiritual House has been persecuted and divided. The enemy works on building the third temple (false) where the abomination of desolation will take place; the *true* third temple (Tabernacle of David–Amos 9:11, Acts 15:14-16, and Haggai 2:9) is the spiritual House of God, the living stones, the Jewish and Gentile believers standing together forever.

Amos 9:11 says, "In that day I will raise up the *Tabernacle of*

David that is fallen, and close up the breaches thereof; and I will raise up his ruins and I will build it as the days of old."

Acts 15:14-16,

> Simeon has declared how God at the first did visit the Gentiles (the last 2000 years) to take out of them a people for His name, and to this agree the words of the prophets; as it is written, After this I will RETURN, and will build again the *Tabernacle of David*, which is fallen down; and I will build again the ruins thereof, and I will set it up.

Haggai 2:9 declares, "The glory of this latter House shall be greater than the former, says the Lord of hosts (YHVH tsavaot); and in this place I will give peace (shalom), declares YHVH tsavaot."

This is the true house of God; this is where we build like Nehemiah with our swords by our side (the Word of God) and the instructions of YHVH God through the Holy Spirit in our hearts, to do the work needed for such a time as this…

Romans 12:2 says, "And be not conformed to this world, but be transformed by the renewing of your mind, that you may prove what is that good, and acceptable, and perfect will of God."

Romans 12:21 states, "Be not overcome of evil, but overcome evil with good."

Romans 13:11-12 says, "And that knowing the time, that now it is high time to awake out of sleep; for now, is our Salvation nearer than we believed. The night is far spent, the day is at hand; let us therefore cast off the works of darkness and let us put on the armor of Light."

There is no room for antisemitism in the House of God, overtly or covertly. The damage has been done; the repairers need to come in and heal the House of YHVH.

This has been a tough chapter for some, yet God disciplines those He loves. He corrects us because He loves us. The mistakes of the past, in our misunderstanding, have been held in mercy. God does not condemn us for not seeing, yet He convicts us and is calling out for us to see. If you have this book in your hands, it is because God is calling you deeper into His Word. I hope you will pray about this if the information in this chapter has been new to you, and ask YHVH God for eyes that see, ears that hear, and a heart that understands. Healing often requires a breaking of our own hearts, a repentance deep in the recesses of our spirit so that we can cut off false belief and be renewed in our minds. It is not always easy, but there is great reward in understanding what YHVH God is doing in all the earth for such a time as this.

> For if you altogether hold your peace at this time, then shall their relief and deliverance arise to the Jews from another place; but you and your father's house shall be destroyed; and who knows whether you have come to the kingdom for such a time as this?
>
> Esther 4:14

We are the generation to see all these things and to understand them. We have been born for such a time as this.

Chapter Nine

My Daughters Shall Prophesy

We are called to be Healers of the Breach. The breach between Jewish and Gentile believers in Yeshua is extensive, and sadly, in the last days, antisemitism will continue to grow in all the earth as the enemy sees that his time is drawing near, his final defeat before the millennial reign. Yet, there is another gaping hole in the House of God, the breach that has caused many daughters of God to feel less than their male counterparts. Again, we dive into another deep wound. Only those filled with the Holy Spirit will be able to see the truth when lies of "church fathers" have been perpetrated against women as well as Jewish people in the last 2000 years. Where do we begin?

Defenders, Inheritance, and Builders

Although a whole book could be written on the subject of this chapter, and many have, the purpose of this chapter is to briefly focus on the breach and work to bring healing. Men and women must work together side by side in what the God of Abraham, Isaac, and Jacob has called them to do for the building of His Kingdom.

In the Book of Exodus, the Word of God calls attention to the defenders of God's daughters; although these daughters are of Midian, Zipporah (Tsiporah in the Hebrew, means little bird) will be grafted into the house of Israel later through marriage to Moses. Exodus 2:16 says, "Now the priest of Midian had seven daughters;

and they came and drew water and filled the troughs to water their father's flock. And the shepherds came and drove them away; but Moses stood up and helped them, and watered the flock" (Exodus 2:16-17). Seven is a number of perfection or completion. The daughters are trying to draw water to water their father's flock. In the spiritual realm, we may see they are the daughters of God trying to do what they are called to do by the Father, to water His flock through the calling of the Holy Spirit, but there are those who would stop them. Moses is the man who comes and defends them and allows them to do what the Father, their father, has called them to do. The depth of God's Word is amazing! In the world, there are those men who are like Moses. They will stand and defend the daughters of God and make it easier for them to do their work. They will work alongside the daughters of God without patronizing, without subjugating, and without pride. Then, there are those who would harass, patronize, and try to stop the work of the daughters of God, the false shepherds. The underlying feeling for many women in the church is they are "less than" somehow, for the teaching has been "less than" in the house of God.

When it comes to the inheritance of the daughters of God, we see YHVH God Himself stand for His daughters. Numbers 27:1-8 speaks of the daughters of "Zelophehad, the son of Hepher, the son of Gilead…and these are the names of his daughters: Mahlah, NoacH, Hoglah, Milcah, and Tirzah. Because their father had no sons, the daughters ask Moses, as they stand before Eleazar, and the princes of all the congregation by the door of the tabernacle of the congregation, saying, "Our father died in the wilderness, and he was not in the company of them that gathered themselves together against YHVH in the company of Korah, … and had no sons. Why should the name of our father be done away from among his family because he has no son? Give to us therefore a possession among the brethren of our father." And Moses brought their cause before YHVH. And YHVH spoke unto Moses, "The daughters of Zelophehad speak right. You shall surely give them a possession of an inheritance among their father's brothers and you shall cause the inheritance of the father to pass unto them. And you shall speak unto the children of Israel, saying, "If a man die, and have no son, then you shall cause his inheritance to pass to his daughter." YHVH Himself speaks to this situation. "The daughters speak right. They too have an inheritance of the father."

And there fell ten portions to Manasseh beside the land of Gilead and Bashan, which were on the other side Jordan; because the daughters of Manasseh (Zelophehad) had an inheritance among his sons (Joshua 17:5).

In the days of Nehemiah, when they are rebuilding the temple that was destroyed in 586 BC by the Babylonians, Shallum, the son of Halohesh, the ruler of the half part of Jerusalem, had only daughters. As Nehemiah Chapter 3 names all the people that are helping to repair the walls around Jerusalem, Nehemiah 3:12 says, "and next to him (Milchijah), repaired Shallum, the son of Halohesh, the ruler of the half part of Jerusalem, he and his daughters." Although their names are not listed specifically, the Bible makes it clear that the daughters were building and repairing the walls as well. Shallum also is the ruler of the half part of Jerusalem, he with his daughters. Without sons, half of Jerusalem is inherited by the daughters. Yes, in all the stories of the Bible, God brings out that His daughters are as important as His sons, even when the culture does not always support this view.

On the note of half Jerusalem, half the kingdom to the daughters, the story of Esther intrigues me as to the inheritance of the daughters. Queen Esther goes before King Ahaseurus, to alert him to the plot against her people (the Jewish people); the King extends the golden scepter and says to her, "What will you, Queen Esther? And what is your request? It shall be even given to you the half of the kingdom." The King says to her half the kingdom is hers. Many know the story of how Esther exposes the wicked Haman, and he gets hanged on the gallows he meant for Mordecai. The Jewish people are saved because of her bravery. Although a real person with real history, the symbol of Esther is the daughters of Jerusalem, the daughters of God, that stand for the people of God, the Jewish people, and all those grafted in. Queen Esther, in her defense of God's people, is given the inheritance of half the kingdom, as are the daughters of God given equal inheritance with the sons in the Kingdom of YHVH.

The daughters of YHVH that are lifted up in the Bible as strong women who love God with all their hearts, souls, mind, and strength are many. Strong men stand by these women, and they work together to build God's Kingdom. The daughters are equal in the promises of inheritance. The daughters are building alongside the men.

In the story of Ruth, as the people gather together to bless Ruth after Boaz announces that he is her Kinsman Redeemer, the people in the gate and the elders say,

> We are witnesses, YHVH make the woman that is come into your house like Rachel, and like Leah, WHICH TWO DID BUILD THE HOUSE OF ISRAEL; and do worthily in Ephratah, and be famous in Bethlehem. And let your house be like the house

> of Pharez, whom Tamar bare unto Judah, of the seed which YHVH shall give to you of this young woman.
>
> Ruth 4:11-12

Truly, the women are called to be builders with an equal inheritance in the House of God. We need more men, in humility, to see the truth of God's Word and not to repeat the lies that have been promulgated over the past 1700 years or so.

So what are these lies? And where do they come from? For many, certain passages in the Bible, mostly in the New Testament, not in the Old, have caused much damage to the army of God. Half the army, the women, have been delegated to the back row because of Scriptures that have been translated to fit the purposes of those who would silence women. Second Timothy 2:15 says, "Study to show yourself approved unto God, a workman that needs not to be ashamed, rightly dividing the Word of Truth."

Here are four Scriptures used over and over again to tell women they can not teach or preach the Word of God in the "church." Let's take a closer look at the original Hebrew and at the context of these Scriptures.

First Corinthians 11, 1 Corinthians 14, Ephesians 5:22, 1 Timothy 2:9-15

With all the Scriptures that lift up women, quote women in the scriptures, and display the strength and courage of women to defend the Word of God and YHVH's people, yet there are four main Scriptures that are used again and again as weapons to silence women or to subjugate them: 1 Corinthians 11:10, 1 Corinthians

14:34-35, Ephesians 5:22, 1 Timothy 2:9-15.

In 1 Corinthians 11, Paul needs to address some problems in the Corinthian Church. These are relatively new churches, for the Gentile people have just been introduced to the God of Israel and the Jewish Messiah, Yeshua. Paul needs to help the congregations or assembly of believers to work out their squabbles. In the first nine verses, Paul repeats the problems they are arguing over and their views about these problems, yet in 1 Corinthians 11:10, Paul begins to give his answers. It is the turning point in the conversation or letter. First Corinthians 11:10 says, "For this cause ought the woman to have power on her head because of the angels." The whole argument is whether women should wear something on their heads or not and that somehow men are above women for they were created first, and that man was not created for the woman but the woman for man. Paul steps in and corrects them. First Corinthians 11:12, "Nevertheless (even with all your bickering), neither is the man independent of the woman, neither the woman without the man, in YHVH." Paul speaks that we need each other. "For as the woman is of the man, SO IS THE MAN ALSO BY THE WOMAN; but all things of God." Then Paul says as to the matter of a woman wearing a head covering, "Judge for yourselves," whether it is proper for a woman to pray uncovered. Paul goes on to say that the woman's hair is covering enough. "But if a woman has longer hair, it is a glory to her; for her hair is given to her for a covering." In conclusion, Paul essentially says, if you want to keep fighting over this, go ahead, but the rest of the congregations do not have this problem. Your bickering is for no profit. "Now in this that I declare unto you, I praise you not, that you come together not for the better, but for the worse" (1 Corinthians 11:17). In other words, your words are just divisive.

Second Timothy 2:14, "Of these things put them in remembrance, charging them before YHVH, that they strive not about words to no profit, but to the subverting of the hearers" (2 Timothy 2:14). In other words, Paul, when these verses are taken in context, is telling the Corinthian church that their arguing is useless and only causing division in the House of God.

Yet there are other verses that are referred to again and again to silence women or put them in a place of subjugation.

First Corinthians 14

In 1 Corinthians 14, Paul once again needs to intervene in the newly formed Corinthian church or assembly of believers. Apparently, there is a huge problem with order which is what the whole chapter is about; interruptions and chaos are abounding in the services. This is evident in the first 33 verses where Paul instructs believers how to speak in tongues in public so that it does not end up looking like everyone has gone crazy. Verses 27-33 say,

> If any man *speak* in an unknown tongue, let it be by two, at the most by three, and that by course (one at a time) and let one interpret. But if there be not an interpreter, LET HIM KEEP SILENCE IN THE CHURCH; and let him speak to himself, and to God. Let the prophets speak two or three and let the other judge. If anything be revealed to another that sits by, let the first hold his peace. For you may all (men and women) prophesy one by one, that all may learn, and all may be comforted. And the spirits of the prophets are subject to the prophets. For God is not the author of disorder, but of peace, as in all churches (congregations, assemblies) of the saints.

"And it shall come to pass in the last days, says God, I will pour out My Spirit upon all flesh; and your sons and your DAUGHTERS shall prophesy" (Acts 2:17).

Here starts the problem in misinterpreting the Bible and using it as a weapon against women. In the King James Version, 1 Corinthians 14:34-35 says, "Let your women keep silence in the churches; for it is not permitted to them to speak; but they are commanded to be under obedience, as also says the Law. And if they will learn anything, let them ask their husbands at home; for it is a shame for women to speak in the church."

Now learning some Hebrew over the years, I was interested in what it says originally, so I looked each word up to see. For if the Word of God says to do something, we can only obey in the fear of the Lord. Yet, if the church fathers (some wolves in sheep's clothing) messed with the interpretations, we need to rightly divide the Word of God for ourselves now that we have our own Bibles to read and study. So, what does it say in Hebrew?

Here is a transliteration of the Hebrew: 1 Corinthians 14:34 NesheycHem (Your wives) baK'nesiyot (in the synagogues, temples) tishtoqnah (will be silent) ki lo-nitnah lahen (for it is not given to them) reshut (permission) ledabber (to speak) ki im-le-hikane'a (but if to surrender) ka'asher (when) gam-amrah (also saying) ha'Torah (the Torah, the Law).

And here is the interpretation, word for word, in the English (although my commentary is in parentheses):

Your wives, women in the synagogues (churches), temples, will be quiet, silent, (stop talking for the moment), for it is not given to them permission to speak, but if (in this situation) to surrender (the floor), (you are interrupting) when also saying the Torah.

First Corinthians 14:35 transliterated says, "Ve'im (And if) cHeftzan (they desire) lilmod (to learn) davar (a thing) tishalnah (she will ask) et-ba'alehen (their husbands) ba'bayit (at home) ki-cHerpah (for it is a disgrace) hi la'nashim (the women) ledabber (to speak) ba'qahal (in the audience)."

The interpretation in English:

"And if they desire to learn a thing, she will ask their (her) husband at home. Because it is a disgrace that the women to speak in the audience (a disgrace to interrupt, a matter of order)."

What a difference! This, like the rest of the chapter, is about order, not about silencing women in the church! These two verses speak to the women who were interrupting from the audience. They were not the ones invited to speak and were interrupting. It was a correction that Paul was making to the women as he had also spoken to the men earlier in verses 27-31, specifically where it says, "but if there be no interpreter let *him* keep silence in the church." This is not silencing men. The verses above are not about silencing women. It is about order and should not be taken out of context to weaponize it as a silencer of God's daughters who are filled with the Holy Spirit. We need to rightly divide the Word of God!

In biblical passages, three words are all translated as church, but they are not the same word: Knesiyot, this is the physical temple; eder, witness or witnesses (spiritual temple); and ba'qahal (in the audience or congregation). These very different meanings give a whole new context to what is being said. These three words are differentiated for a reason and should be translated as so. The women were not to speak out loud and interrupt from the audience those that were invited to teach, prophesy, or pray aloud, whether men or women. No one was to interrupt, especially when the Torah was being read, spoken. The men also were not to interrupt so that all things could be done in order.

Ephesians 5

Ephesians 5:22 says, "Wives submit yourselves unto our own husbands." There is no problem with this unless you use it as a weapon of subjugation. We are to submit one to another equally. We are to honor each other and strengthen one another. Let us look closer at this verse as well.

Ephesians 5:22 Hebrew transliteration, "Ha'nashim, hika-na'anah le'baaleken c'mo la'adonenu."

It translates, The women submit yourselves to your husbands as to our Lord. The previous verse says to all, "Submitting yourselves one to another in the fear of God" (Ephesians 5:21).

Galatians 5:23-33 goes on to describe how a man and wife ought to love each other and reverence each other. For the husband is head of the wife, even as Messiah is the head of the congregation of the House of God; and He is the Saviour of the body. Therefore, as the House of God, the witnesses (ha'edah) are subject to Messiah, so let the wives be to their own husbands in everything.

Again, an order is established here. The husbands are to be under the headship and leadership of Yeshua, the Messiah. Even as the husbands are following Yeshua and His example, so the women can follow their husband's example. There is a qualification here, though. It is not all wives submit to all husbands. How are the husbands treating their wives? As the Messiah treats His followers?

Husbands are then commanded to *love* their wives, even as Messiah also loved the witness (ha'edah), and gave Himself for it. Why?

> That He might sanctify and cleanse it with the washing of water by the Word, that He might present it to Himself a glorious witness (le'edah), not having spot or wrinkle, or any such thing; but that it should be holy and without blemish. So ought men to LOVE their wives as their own bodies. He that loves his wife, loves himself.
>
> Ephesians 5:25-28

A deeper mystery is that husband and wife represent the Messiah Yeshua and His Bride. "This is a great MYSTERY; but I speak concerning Messiah and His witness (edato). Nevertheless, let every one of you in particular so love his wife even as himself; and the wife see that she reverence her husband" (Ephesians 5:33).

For sure, there is order. Yet, Jesus, our Messiah, would never silence His Bride. He does not condemn us for past sins but redeems us and gives us power to do His work. A cruel master tries to silence those under him. A true leader brings out the very best in those that are under His care. Blame is the weapon of the enemy used to silence God's people. Redemption and the washing of the Water of the Word is the weapon of our King, who calls us to *speak* His Word, with humility, with order, and with reverence. Yet Speak! He constantly nourishes us with His Word. He calls us to be His witnesses in all the world. He wants us, male and female, made in the image of Elohim, to proclaim the Word of God, to teach it, to preach it, to prophesy, and to pray. This is how we build the House of God, with His building blocks, with His Word, and with Truth. We are to work together just as Yeshua works with His Bride to accomplish the Father's will through the Holy Spirit.

First Timothy 2

One last Scripture that we must grapple with is 1 Timothy 2:9-15. Again, we must look at and understand context. We have all seen what the newscasters in our day can do with words taken out of context. They can make someone say anything they want to according to their intentions by taking out words and adding in new words or even putting together words in different places that were never meant to be together.

Revelation 20:19 warns, "And if any man shall take away from the words of the book of this prophecy, God shall take away his part out of the book of life, and out of the holy city, and from the things which are written in this book." This verse applies to the Book of Revelation but is a warning to not tamper with the Word of God, especially to twist it to say things it does not say.

So let us take a look at this Scripture 1 Timothy 2:7-15 in the original Hebrew. Paul says, "Whereunto I am ordained a preacher, and an apostle, (I speak the truth in Messiah and do not lie), a teacher of the Gentiles in faith and truth. I will therefore that men pray everywhere, lifting up holy hands without wrath and doubting."

> In like manner also, that women adorn themselves in modest apparel, (with shamefacedness and sobriety), not with braided hair, or gold or pearls, or costly array; but (which becomes

> women professing godliness) with good works. Let the woman learn in silence with all subjection. But I suffer not a woman to teach, nor to usurp authority over the man, but to be in silence. For Adam was first formed than Eve. And Adam was not deceived but the woman deceived was in the transgression. Notwithstanding she shall be saved in childbearing, if they continue in faith and charity and holiness with sobriety.
>
> 1 Timothy 2:9-15

Well, it looks like that's it; women are not to teach and remain in silence. I have cried many tears over this passage and the others that we have already examined, for, with all my heart, all I want to do is YHVH's will to be about my Father's business. I am sure many other women feel the same way and have been silenced with a few verses that were never intended for this purpose. Instead of just ignore them and move on, or focus on them and be stopped and silenced, I felt YHVH God encourage me to look closer to rightly divide and understand the Word of God. If we look at the original text in Hebrew, what does it say? It is a lot to transliterate and understand, but it is worth it.

First Timothy 2:9 in the English text, "In like manner also, that women adorn themselves in modest apparel, with shamefacedness, and sobriety, not with braided hair, or gold, or pearls, or costly array."

First Timothy 2:9 in the Hebrew says,

> Ve'ken gam ha'nashim tityapeynah betilboshet na'ah im-boshet panim utzni'ut lo bemacHlefot harosh lo ve'zahav lo vefninim ve lo bemalbushim yeqarim, which interpreted means, And therefore also the women, they shall dress nicely with inward dress, and modesty not in interchanges of the head (braided hair) not with gold, not with pearls, not in ex-

pensive clothes.

The interpretation is similar, but the words "with shamefacedness and sobriety" are not in this passage; they are added.

First Timothy 2:10 says, "But (which is proper for women professing godliness) with good works."

First Timothy 2:10 transliterated in the Hebrew, "ella c'mo she'hu hagun (but like that he is decent), la'nashim asher (to the women that) becHaru (choose) la'hen (unto them) yirat (to fear) Elohim (God) bema'asim tovim (in good works)."

The interpretation is as follows: "But to be like he is, decent, to the women who choose the fear of God in good works." This passage inserts words that are not there and deletes others that are. First, the passage says the women should be like the men in that they dress modestly and in decency, knowing that they are in the assembly to worship Elohim. Remember, this is a Gentile group of people just learning how to behave in the House of God (knesiyot). Paul goes on to say that for the women who choose the fear of God, it will be evidenced by their good works, just like it is evidenced in the men. It does not say women who profess godliness or who are saying they are godly to behave themselves. It says those women who choose the fear of Elohim, will do good works. By their fruit, you will know them.

First Timothy 2:11 in Hebrew transliteration:

"Ha ishah tilmad dumam be'cal hakno'ah." The interpretation is, "The woman will be taught silently in all submission." Paul pivots his attention from "the women" plural, and now speaks of "the woman," singular. The article "the" tells us that he is speaking of a particular woman who is causing trouble in the House of God. The word for women is nashim in Hebrew. The word for "a woman" is isha; the word for "the woman" is ha'isha.

First Timothy 2:12, "Ve'eineni noten reshut la'ishah lelamed af lo-lehitnasea al-ha'ish ella tidom." The interpretation, "And I do not give reshut (permission) "to the woman" (la'ishah) to teach and not to rise over the man, but to be in silence." We see that Paul, in speaking to this situation, is saying to this particular woman, who has talked down to a man, maybe even patronizingly so, is not to teach anymore; she needs to learn in silence. She needs humility.

First Timothy 2:13, Ki Adam notzar ba'rishonah ve'acHerav cHavah. For Adam was created first, and afterward, Eve. No extra comment here. This is true.

First Timothy 2:14, "Ve'Adam lo niftah, ki ha'ishah shama'ah le'qol ha'Mashia va'tavo liydei averah." The Hebrew interpretation, "And Adam was not deceived, for the woman heard the voice of the 'officiating teacher,' the Messiah (ha'Mashia), and came to understand, to know sin."

Comparing this to the English, "And Adam was not deceived, but the woman being deceived was in the transgression." Wow! What a difference! In Hebrew, it says the man was not deceived. He knew what he was doing. He knew he was disobeying God. Yet, the woman did not understand sin until she heard the voice of Messiah. She did it all in innocence, for she was tricked, deceived. When she understood, she repented. This passage, when rightly divided, puts the blame on Adam more than on Eve! It does not say what is interpreted in English. The English translation leaves out all the words that speak of Eve, clearly hearing the voice of her

Messiah and then knowing the sin. It does not say she was the one solely in the transgression as if Adam is above this. Pure nonsense.

First Timothy 2:15, the last verse to grapple with, says in Hebrew, "Aval tivasha'a be'lidtah banim im ta'amodnah ba'emunah, uva'ahavah, uva'qdushah, im-hatzniyut." But she will be rescued in her birth of children if she stands in faith and love and holiness with humility.

Paul is addressing again the way the services of the house of God should be orchestrated. His letter is addressing a letter(s) sent to him from Ephesus concerning questions for the newly formed congregation, so we see the answers in the letter but not the original questions. In summary, women and men need to dress appropriately. Women, of course, have many more options, so this would be a more necessary topic to address with them, especially in a newly formed Gentile congregation. The woman spoken of here is one who was usurping power over all in this particular church or congregation. She was caught teaching with an air of superiority and patronizing a particular man. This could not be tolerated. Of course, men patronizing and talking down to women is the same offense. The spirit of the feminist movement in our day causes the same animosity between men and women. Man is not over woman in the sense that he is better. Woman is not over man in the sense that she is better. As fully filled with the Holy Spirit, working together as equals in the Kingdom of God was, and is and will always be God's plan for us all.

To put it all together, 1 Timothy 2:9-15 says in the Hebrew:

And therefore, also the women shall dress nicely with the

> inward dress and modesty not in braided hair, not with gold, not with pearls, and expensive clothing, but like he is, in decency. To the women who choose to fear Elohim (God), they will do good works.

Turning to the *particular woman* that is causing problems in this congregation, Paul says,

The woman will be taught silently in all submission. And I do not give permission to the woman to teach and to rise up over the man, but she will be still, silent. For Adam was created at first, and after him Eve. And Adam was not deceived, for the woman (Eve), she heard the voice of the officiating teacher (the Messiah) and came to understand, to know sin. But she will be saved, rescued, in her birth of children if she stands in faith and love and holiness, with humility (1 Timothy 2:11-15).

We will get back to the birth of children in this passage later in the book, for this is not a put-down, but a prophetic Word showing that women are the bearers of life, and bring forth, through birth pangs, a new thing in all the earth, prophetically, as well as the children of the living God. We are the builders, through bringing forth living stones, for the constructing of God's holy temple as we birth the children and teach them the Word of God.

Yet, the passage ends with the word humility. This particular woman needed to be reminded of humility. Don't we all? Yet YHVH's plan is that every Holy Spirit-filled believer be treated as One in Him. As Galatians 3:28 reminds us, "There is neither Jew nor Greek, there is neither bond nor free, there is neither male nor female; for you all are ONE in Messiah Yeshua (Christ Jesus)."

We are distinct as Jew and Gentile, male and female, employer to employee, yet we all have the same value and are all One in Yeshua. No one is under another as a "lesser than" in the Kingdom of God. No one that is filled with the Holy Spirit is silenced from teaching the Word of God. This is the difference. Those without the Holy Spirit should remain quiet until they are taught and understand and are filled with His presence. Otherwise, pride and apostasy abound in both men and women, Jew or Gentile, bond or free, and we try to take pre-eminence over others which causes much pain and division in the House of YHVH God. For the one that is greatest in the Kingdom of God is the servant of all (Luke 22:24-27).

Ezer and Prophetess

So how is a wife to relate to her husband? As it says in Genesis, woman came out from man, the same essence, to be His ezer k'negdo (Genesis 2:20), for it was not good that man should be alone. The word *ezer* has been interpreted in this passage as helpmeet, helper, fitting helper, and denotes a picture of a child to an adult, maybe the child that goes and gets the tools that the builder needs but is not the one building. But what does *ezer* really mean, and where else is this word found in the Bible?

The word *ezer* is found twenty-one times in the Bible: two in describing the woman to the man in Genesis 2:18 and 2:20; three times in a military sense, Isaiah 30:5, Ezekiel 12:14 and Daniel 11:34, and sixteen more times when describing YHVH as defender and protector of the nation of Israel. The word *ezer* is a powerful word meaning strength, warrior. *Kenegdo* means opposite of him, like two wings on a bird. One cannot fly without the other.

Briefly, the word helpmeet is a very poor choice for the interpretation of ezer and is only used when referring to the woman in Genesis. In all other verses, it is interpreted to mean strength and help in times of distress. YHVH God comes to be our ezer.

Deuteronomy 33:7 says, "And this is the blessing of Judah; and he said, Hear, YHVH, the voice of Judah, and bring him unto his people; let his hands be sufficient for him; and be to him a help (ezer) from his enemies."

Psalm 33:22 declares, "Our soul waits for YHVH; He is our help (ezer) and our shield."

Psalm 121:1-2 says, "I will lift up mine eyes unto the mountains, from where comes my help (ezer). My help (ezer) comes from YHVH, which made heaven and earth."

Hosea 13:9 states, "O Israel, you have destroyed yourself; but in Me is your help (ezer)."

Woman was made to walk alongside man as his ezer k'negdo to build alongside him the Kingdom of God. She is not just his help meet as an underling; she is his equal and very courageous counterpart. She is the other half of the army rising up.

We have covered a lot of Scriptures that have been used as weapons against women when that was not their original intent. Rightly dividing the Word of God was necessary to release women to see that we are equally made in the image of God, and we are also the teachers, apostles, preachers, evangelists, and prophets needed in the House of God (Ephesians 4:11); yet we are never to be high-minded, conceited, overbearing, usurping authority over anyone, just as the men are also commanded to be in humility as they serve the people of God by doing the will of the Father

YHVH.

So now we finally come to the heart of this chapter… My daughters shall prophesy…

Joel 2:27-29 says,

> And you shall know that I am in the midst of Israel, and that I am the Lord YHVH your God, and none else; and My people shall never be ashamed. And it shall come to pass afterward, that I will pour out My spirit upon all flesh and your sons and your daughters will prophesy, your old men shall dream dreams, your young men shall see visions; and also upon the servants and upon the handmaidens in those days, I will pour out My Spirit.

Acts Chapter 2:16-18 says,

> But this is what was spoken by the prophet Joel; and it shall come to pass IN THE LAST DAYS declares Elohim, I will pour out My Spirit upon all flesh; and your sons and your daughters shall prophesy, and your young men shall see visions, and your old men shall dream dreams: and on My servants and on My handmaidens, I will pour out IN THOSE DAYS of My Spirit; and they shall prophesy.

Throughout the Bible, women have been anointed by the Holy Spirit as prophetesses, speaking the Word of God to the nation of Israel to direct them in the ways of YHVH God. There are many, but for the sake of space and time, we will focus on a few. Miriam, the sister of Aaron (Exodus 15:20), Deborah (Judges 4 and 5), Huldah (2 Kings 22:14, 2 Chronicles 34:22), unnamed prophetess that Isaiah marries (Isaiah 8:1-4), Anna, the prophetess, who prophesies over Yeshua (Luke 2), the daughters that prophesied in the Old Testament and the New, such as the daughters of Philip, four prophetesses in Acts 21:9. Each of these women spoke God's Words and taught the people through the words God gave to them to speak. So, the prophetic Word is arising in the hearts of the daughters and sons of the God of Israel as we approach these latter days or are already in them. We shall prophesy the words of God from the Word of God. They will be proclaimed "whether they will hear, or whether they will forbear" (Ezekiel 3:11).

Here, I am reminded of the day I stood at the Gates of Huldah in June of 2018 near the Temple Mount in Jerusalem. I did not know at the time these gates were called the Huldah Gates but found out over a year later as the Holy Spirit showed me. Yet, as I stood there, I proclaimed Isaiah 22:22. "And the key of the House of David will I lay upon His shoulder; so He shall open and none shall shut, and He shall shut and none shall open." Amazing! I was standing at the gates named for a woman prophetess, proclaiming prophetic words. Only the Holy Spirit can lead us this way! Many other times, as I joyfully walked the paths that Yeshua walked in Israel and Jerusalem, the Holy Spirit would bring Scriptures to mind that I would proclaim aloud, many times not even knowing the significance of the Scripture to the place I was standing until later. It was glorious! A sweet presence of Yeshua through the Holy Spirit seemed to fill almost every place we placed the sole of our feet in Israel, in Jerusalem.

So today, we are called to build the House of God His way, not ours, not the way it has been done for the past 1700-1800 years or so. We are to turn, return (teshuvah) totally to YHVH, the God of Israel and build His spiritual House. So, what does this look like? The closest example that comes to me is the re-building of the second temple by Ezra and Nehemiah.

In the book of Ezra 4:24, it says, "Then ceased the work of the House of God which is at Jerusalem. So, it ceased until the second year of the reign of Darius, king of Persia." Because of persecution, lies, opposition, and deceitfulness, the building of the House of God was called to a halt. Yet Ezra 5:1-2 says,

> Then the prophets, Haggai the prophet, and Zechariah, the son of Iddo, prophesied unto the Jews that were in Judah and Jerusalem in the name of the God of Israel, even unto them. Then rose Zerubbabel, the son of Shealtiel, and Jeshua, the son of Jozadak and began to build the House of God which is at Jerusalem; and with them were the prophets of God helping them.

The prophetic Word was the encouragement they needed to keep going even in the midst of all the spiritual warfare. The prophetic voice was the cheering voice saying to keep going despite what you see all around you. It encouraged the people to keep working. Nehemiah 4:6 reports, "But it came to pass that when Sanballat, and Tobiah, and the Arabians, and the Ammonites, and the Ashdodites, heard that the walls of Jerusalem were made up, and that the BREACHES BEGAN TO BE STOPPED, then they were very angry."

And Judah said, "The strength of the bearers of burdens is decayed, and there is much rubbish; so that we are not able to build the wall" (Nehemiah 4:10). There is much rubbish in the House of God, much false teaching, shallow teaching, and breaches that must be cleansed and healed. What to do?

Nehemiah calls out to the nobles, the rulers, and to all the people, "Be not afraid of them; remember YHVH, which is great and awesome, and fight for your brethren, your sons, and your daughters, your wives, and your houses," (Nehemiah 4:14). Nehemiah sends forth words to encourage, exhort, and strengthen the people. "And it came to pass, when our enemies heard that it was known unto us, and YHVH had brought their counsel to nothing, that we returned (teshuvah!) all of us to the wall, everyone to his work" (Nehemiah 4:15).

We have work to do together: Jewish and Gentile believers together, Holy Spirit-filled men and women together. The prophet Haggai was one of the prophets that encouraged Ezra and Nehemiah. He was a contemporary, working alongside the builders. Haggai 2:7 declares, "And I will shake all nations, and the desire of all nations shall come (to Jerusalem); and I will fill this House with glory, says YHVH tsava'ot." Haggai 2:9 prophesies, "And the glory of this LATTER HOUSE shall be greater than the former, says the Lord of hosts, and in this place, I will give Peace, says YHVH tsava'ot."

This is what we are building with our Lord and King Yeshua, the House of God without human hands, the living stones together.

In John 17, Yeshua prays for the people that God the Father has given unto Him before He ascends back to heaven after He had finished the work the Father had given Him to do. He prays,

> I have manifested Your Name unto the children of Adam, le'bnei ha'Adam (does not say men in the Hebrew) which You gave Me out of the world; Yours they were, and You gave them to Me; and they have kept Your Word. Now they have known that all things whatsoever You have given to Me are from You. For I have given them the words which You gave Me; and they have received them and have known surely that I am come out from You (just as woman came out from man, my comment), and they have believed that You did send Me.
>
> John 17:6-8

Jesus goes on to pray,

> I pray for them; I do not pray for the world, but for them which You have given Me; for they are Yours. And all Mine are Yours, and Yours are Mine, and I am glorified in them. And now I am no more in the world, but these are in the world, and I come to You. Holy Father, keep them through Your own Name those whom You have given to Me, that they may be as One, as we are.
>
> John 17:9-11

Yeshua's final prayer is that He knows those that are truly the Father's and those that are truly His. He says that His children know that He has come out of the Father, for the Father, and the Son and the Holy Spirit are One. He prays for the people of God, Jewish and Gentile believers, male and female Holy Spirit believers to be One in Him, One in the Father through the Holy Spirit. The whole chapter is a beautiful prayer that, like the Our Father prayer, should be lifted up much more, even memorized. Yeshua prays for us to be One. Again, Galatians 3:28 tells us what that means; "There is neither Jew nor Greek, there is neither bond nor free, there is neither male nor female; for you are all ONE in Messiah Jesus."

The lie that women are more at fault for the fall of man and must be silenced in the churches because they were deceived and not Adam is straight from the pit of hell. This lie must be countered with truth. The men who stand with the women as God's end-time army will be blessed. Those who perpetuate this lie, this breach, will be corrected if they are filled with the Holy Spirit. If not, in their pride and self-righteousness, they will continue to try to weaken God's end-time army but will not prevail.

So daughters *PROPHESY* as the Word of God proclaims; speak in the House of God the words that Abba Father Himself, through the Holy Spirit, has given to you. Discern true prophesy from false by a deep understanding and Berean study of God's Word every day. You daughters, just as the sons, are equal partners in the building of God's House, the Tabernacle of David. The daughters of God will not be silenced by the incorrect interpretations of God's Word by church "fathers" of long ago with ill intent. It is time to heal the breaches in God's house (Isaiah 58:12).

Psalm 68:11

The Lord (Adonai) gives a command (Adonai yiten-omer)

The women who bring the news are a great host (ha'mvasrot tzava rav)

The Israel Bible,תנך

Edited by Rabbi Tuly Weisz

Chapter Ten

The Lord Our God Is One, EcHad One! (Zeroah)

In previous chapters, we have spoken of the importance of unity in the House of God. Ephesians 2:13-15,18 speaks of unity between the Jewish and Gentile believers in Yeshua.

> But now through the blood of Messiah Jesus (Yeshua) you who were sometimes far off are made near by the blood of Messiah. For He is our peace, who has made both ONE and has broken down the middle wall of division between us, having abolished in His flesh the enmity (hatred), even the law of commandments contained in ordinances; for to make in Himself of the two, ONE New Man, so making peace.

"For through Him we both have access by ONE Spirit unto the Father" (Ephesians 2:18).

Galatians 3:27-29 takes it further:

> For as many of you as have been baptized into Messiah have put on Messiah. there is neither Jew nor Greek, there is neither bond nor free, there is neither male nor female; for you all are ONE in Messiah Yeshua. And if you be Messiah's, then you are Abraham's seed, and heirs according to the promise.

One of my favorite Psalms is Psalm 133. It speaks of unity in the Holy Spirit, for without the indwelling of the Holy Spirit, there is no unity in truth.

> Behold how good and how pleasant it is for brethren (all people of God) to dwell together in unity! It is like the precious ointment (oil) upon the head, that ran down upon the beard, even Aaron's beard; that went down to the edge of his garments; as the dew of Hermon, and as the dew that descended upon the mountains of Zion. For there, the Lord YHVH commanded the blessing, even life forevermore.

The oil represents the Holy Spirit. It is poured upon the head of the anointed and runs down to the edge of the garment, filled to overflowing. It is like the dew (Holy Spirit) flowing from the highest mountain in Israel (Hermon) to the mountain of Zion. There is an outpouring of God's Holy Spirit signified here that leads to unity among God's people.

One of the most popular prayers in Judaism is the Shema; it has three very important parts (Deuteronomy 6:4-9, Deuteronomy 11:13-21, and Numbers 15:37-41), but the main essence of the prayer is–Hear O Israel, YHVH our God, YHVH is One…In Hebrew it is transliterated, "Shema Yisrael, YHVH Eloheinu, YHVH ecHad." Many times, the Jewish people that do not know Messiah yet, are confused as to how we can worship three gods (Father, Son, and Holy Spirit) when there is only One God. They are right! There is only ONE God, and the mystery lies in zeroah!

One of the elements placed on the Passover Seder plate every year in the celebration of Passover is called *zeroa*. Zeroa, the lamb shank bone, represents the part of the story (the Haggadah) where the Jewish people every year tell of the blood of the lamb required on every doorpost of those who wanted to be protected from the tenth plague to come to Egypt, the death of the firstborn male in every household. The blood covering would protect those households whose doorposts had the blood on them. With the blood of the lamb, the angel of death would pass over them, and no one would be harmed under this covering! Zeroa is, therefore, the most significant symbol on the seder plate. It speaks of their deliverance through the blood of the lamb. We, as Holy Spirit-filled believers, can see that the zeroa, the lamb shank bone signifying the blood of the lamb, points to Yeshua! The Passover celebration would be a shadow of what was to come and would, every year, point to the day when Jesus would come upon the earth as the "Lamb of God who takes away the sins of the world" (John 1:19).

One morning the Holy Spirit got my attention with the question, "What does the actual word *zeroa* mean in Hebrew?" I was just beginning to learn about Passover and wanted to celebrate it with my family every year with the Jewish people as it points to our Savior, Yeshua, the Lamb of God. I found that the actual word *zeroa* means "arm" in Hebrew. The Lord YHVH drew me in further: "How many times is the word arm or *zeroa* found in the Bible, and what does it refer to?" This is where the Mystery began to pour out! I got out my Strong's Concordance and looked up how many times the word arm is used in the Bible. Then I looked up these verses in the King James Bible and in the Hebrew language to find the word arm and *zeroa* זרוע, respectively. Hold on to your hats, for here is *some* of what I found! Yes, and this is what I do for fun![18]

> Wherefore say unto the children of Israel, I am YHVH, and I will bring you out from under the burdens of the Egyptians and I will rid you out of their bondage and I will redeem you with a stretched out *arm (בזרוע bi'zeroa)* and with great judgements…And I will take you to Me for a people, and I will be to you Elohim…
>
> Exodus 6:6-7

> Or has God assayed to go and take him a nation from the midst of another nation, by temptations, by signs, and by wonders, and by war, and by a Mighty Hand, and by a stretched out ARM (*ubi'zeroa*), and by great terrors, according to all YHVH your God did for you in Egypt before your eyes? Unto you it was shown, that you might know that YHVH, He is God; there is none else beside Him.
>
> Deuteronomy 4:34-35

Deuteronomy 5:15 says, "And remember that you were a servant in the land of Egypt, and that YHVH thy God brought you out from there through a mighty hand and by a stretched out *arm* (ubi'zeroa); therefore YHVH thy God commanded you to keep the sabbath day."

> The great temptations which your eyes saw, and the signs and the wonders and the mighty hand, and the outstretched *arm* (*veha'zeroa*), whereby YHVH your God brought you out; so shall YHVH your God (Eloheka) do unto all the people of whom you are afraid.
>
> Deuteronomy 7:19

Deuteronomy 9:29 says, "Yet they are Your people, and Your inheritance, which You brought out by Your mighty power and by Your stretched out *arm* (*ubizeroa'kHa*)."

> Therefore, you shall love YHVH Eloheka, and keep His charge, His statues, and His judgements, and His commandments, always. And know this day, for I speak not with your children which have not known, and which have not seen the discipline of YHVH ElohekHa, His greatness, His mighty Hand, and His stretched out ARM (*uzeroa'o*).
>
> Deuteronomy 11:1-2

And YHVH brought us forth out of Egypt with a mighty hand, and with an outstretched ARM (*ubizeroa*), and with great terribleness and with signs, and with wonders. And He has brought us into this place, and has given us this land, even a land that flows with milk and honey.

Deuteronomy 26:8-9

Moreover concerning a stranger, that is not of Your people Israel, but comes out of a far country for Your Name's sake; For they shall hear of Your great Name, and of Your strong Hand and of Your stretched out ARM (*uzeroa'kHa*) when He shall come and pray towards this House. Hear in Heaven Your dwelling place, and do according to all that the stranger calls to You for, that all people of the earth may know Your Name, to fear You, as do Your people Israel; and that they may know that *this House, which I have built*, is called by Your Name.

1 Kings 8:41-43

Second Kings 17:36: "But YHVH, who brought you up out of the land of Egypt with great power and a stretched out *arm (ubizeroa)*, Him shall you fear, and Him shall you worship, and to Him shall you do sacrifice."

Second Chronicles 6:32-33: "Moreover concerning the stranger, which is not of Your people Israel, but is come from a far country for Your great Name's sake and Your mighty hand, and Your stretched out ARM (*uzeroa'kHa*); if they come and pray in this House; Then hear from the heavens..."

Job 40:9 "Do you have an ARM (זרוע zeroa) like God? Or can you thunder with a voice like Him?"

Psalm 44:3 "For they did not get the land in possession by their own sword, neither did their own arm save them, but by Your right Hand, and *Your ARM* (*uzeroa'Kha*), and the light of Your countenance, because You had favor towards them."

Psalm 77:15 "You have, by *Your arm (be'zeroa)* redeemed Your people, the sons of Jacob and Joseph. Selah."

Psalm 89:10, 12-13, and 21

> You have broken Rahab (not RacHab in the story of Joshua) in pieces, as one that is slain; You have scattered Your enemies with *Your strong arm (bi'zeroa).* The north and the south You have created them; Tabor and cHermon shall rejoice in Your Name. You have *a mighty arm (zeroa*); strong is Your hand, and high is Your right Hand. With whom My Hand shall be established; *Mine arm (zeroa'i)* also shall strengthen him.

Psalm 98:1-3 says,

> Sing unto YHVH a new song; for He has done marvelous things; His right Hand (yemino) and *His Holy Arm (uzeroa)* have gotten Him the victory. YHVH has made known His Salvation (Yeshuato); His righteousness He has openly showed in the sight of the nations (goyim). He has remembered His mercy and His truth toward the House of Israel; all the ends of the earth have seen the Salvation (Yeshuat) of our God (Eloheinu). The Yeshua (Jesus) of our God!

And brought out Israel from among them; for His mercy endures forever. With a strong hand and *a stretched-out arm (ubizeroa),* for His mercy endures forever (Psalm 136:11-12).

In the prophetic books of the Bible, still, there are many more Scriptures speaking of the mighty arm of God; it is the word zeroa in the Hebrew text, which is the name given by the Jewish people to the lamb shank bone on the seder plate at Passover. With the power of the Holy Spirit, this *zeroa* has been revealed; it means arm and is the arm of YHVH. Let's look at more scripture to show how many times YHVH has put this mystery in the Word of God for us to all see YHVH God is *ONE*, even in Yeshua through the power of the Holy Spirit.

Isaiah 30:30 "And YHVH shall cause His glorious voice to be heard, and shall show the *lightning down of His arm*, with the indignation of His anger, and with the flame of a devouring fire, with scattering, and tempest, and hailstones."

Isaiah 33:2 "O YHVH, be gracious unto us; we have waited for You. *Be their ARM every morning, our Salvation* also in the time of trouble."

> *Behold YHVH God will come with strong Hand and His ARM shall rule for Him*; behold, His reward is with Him and His work before Him. He shall feed His flock like a shepherd; He shall gather the lambs with *His arm*, and carry them in His bosom, and shall gently lead those that are with young.
>
> Isaiah 40:10-11

> All you, assemble yourselves, and hear; which among them has declared these things? YHVH has loved him; He will do His pleasure on Babylon, *and His arm shall be on the Chaldeans*. Come you near unto ME, hear this; I have not spoken in secret from the beginning; for the time that it was, there am I; and now, YHVH God, and His Spirit has sent ME (Yeshua!).
>
> Isaiah 48:14,16

> My righteousness is near; My Salvation is gone forth, and Mine arms shall judge the people; the isles shall wait upon Me, *and on Mine arm shall they trust. Awake, awake, put on strength O arm of YHVH*; awake, as in the ancient days, in the generations of old. Are you not it that has cut Rahab, and wounded the dragon?... *Are You not the one which has dried the sea, the waters of the great deep; that has made the depths of the sea a way for the ransomed to pass over?*
>
> Isaiah 51:5, 9-10

Isaiah 52:10 "YHVH has made bare *His holy Arm* (*et-zeroah kad'sho*) in the eyes of all the nations; and all the ends of the earth shall see the Salvation (et Yeshuat) of our God (Eloheinu)."

The following is a *key verse* that ties the other scriptures with Passover *zeroa* together very clearly. We can see without a doubt that the Arm of YHVH (*zeroa*) is Yeshua (Jesus). The mystery of *zeroa* revealed. A treasure hid in plain sight quickened by the Holy Spirit for our day.

> "Who has believed our report? *And to whom is the ARM of YHVH (zeroa YHVH) revealed?* For He shall grow up before Him as a tender plant, and as a Root out of a dry ground; He has no form or comeliness, and when we shall see Him, there is no beauty that we should desire Him. He is despised and rejected of men…Surely He has borne our griefs and carried our sorrows"… Yeshua!
>
> Isaiah 53:1-4

Isaiah 59:16 "And He (YHVH God) saw that there was no man, and wondered that there was no intercessor*; therefore His own ARM* (*zeroa'o) brought Salvation unto Him*; and His righteousness, it sustained Him." Wow!

> *YHVH has sworn by His Right Hand, and by the ARM of His strength*, Surely, I will no more give your grain to be food for your enemies; and the sons of the stranger (that are not grafted in) shall not drink your wine, for which you have labored. But they that have gathered it shall eat it, and praise YHVH; and they that have brought it together shall drink it in the courts of MY holiness.
>
> Isaiah 62:8-9

Isaiah 63:5 "And I looked, and there was none to help; and I wondered that there was none to uphold; therefore Mine own ARM (zeroa'i) brought Salvation (Yeshua) unto Me; and My fury, it upheld Me." Again, Wow!

Let's take a look at Jeremiah–

Jeremiah 21:5 "And I Myself will fight against you with an outstretched hand and with a strong arm (*zeroa*), even in anger, and in fury, and in great wrath." This is a sad verse that reminds us of the holiness of YHVH God and that He will discipline His children when they are consistently rebellious and turning away from Him.

Jeremiah 27:5 "I have made the earth, the man and the beast that are upon the ground, by My great power, and by My outstretched Arm (zeroa'i), and have given it unto whom it seemed right unto Me."

> Ah, YHVH God! Behold, *You have made the heaven and the earth by Your great power and by Your stretched out ARM* ־ובז רעך *(uve'zeroakha),* and there is nothing too hard for You. And You have brought forth Your people Israel out of the land of Egypt with signs, and with wonders, *and with a strong hand,*

> *and with a stretched out Arm (zeroa)*, and with great terror…
>
> Jeremiah 32:17, 21

And Ezekiel–

> *As I live says YHVH God, surely with a mighty Hand, and with a stretched out Arm (zeroa),* and with fury poured out, I will rule over you. And I will bring you from the people, *and I will gather you out of the countries wherein you are scattered, with a mighty hand and with a stretched out Arm,* and with fury poured out. And I will bring you into the wilderness of the people, and there I will plead with you face to face.
>
> Ezekiel 20:33-35

In the New Testament (*B'rit cHadashah*), *zeroa* is directly associated with Yeshua. The connection is made but only by the revelation of the Holy Spirit's direct teaching, for such a time as this…

Luke 1:51 "*He that has showed strength with His arm*, He has scattered the proud in the imagination of their hearts."

John 12:38 "That the saying of Isaiah the prophet may be fulfilled which he spoke, YHVH, who has believed our report? And to whom has the ARM of YHVH been revealed?" (Refers to Isaiah 53).

As Paul preaches in AntiocH, in part he says,

> "The God of this people of Israel chose our fathers and exalted the people when they dwelt as strangers in the land of Egypt, and *with a high ARM* (*zeroa*), He brought them out of it. And about the time of forty years, He suffered their manners in the wilderness. And when He had destroyed seven nations in the land of Canaan, He divided their land to them by lot."
>
> Acts 13:17

The arm of YHVH God is Yeshua! Every time Passover is celebrated, the lamb shank bone (*zeroa*) points to the Lamb of God that takes away our sins and to the Arm (*zeroa*) of God that delivers us from the power of all evil! It is Yeshua, King of kings, and Lord of lords. The Jewish people celebrate the arm of YHVH God every year, and whether they know it or not, they are celebrating Yeshua, who is ONE with YHVH God. Yeshua is His right *arm* (extending to His right hand, *yeminekHa*). Through the Holy Spirit of God, He is ONE with the Father, Abba, the God of Israel. He is the same essence and has come from the side of YHVH, manifested in the flesh to die for our sins as the Lamb of God who takes away the sins of the world! He goes to be at the right hand of the Father because He has come from His right side, His right arm! Here are a few of the Scriptures that say so, even though there are many more!

Exodus 15:6: "*Your right hand* (*yeminekHa*), O YHVH, is become glorious in power; Your right hand, (ימינך) O YHVH has dashed in pieces the enemy."

Psalm 16:11: "You will sow me the path of Life; in Your presence is fulness of joy; at *Your right hand* (*yeminekHa*) there are pleasures forevermore."

Psalm 17:7: "Show Your marvelous lovingkindness, O You that *saves by Your right hand* all those who put their trust in You from those that rise up against them."

Psalm 18:35: "You have also given me the shield of Your salvation, and *Your right hand* has held me up, and Your gentleness has made me great."

Psalm 20:6: "Now I know that YHVH saves His anointed; He

will hear him from His holy heaven with the saving strength of *His Right Hand.*"

Psalm 21:8): "Your hand shall find out all Your enemies; *Your right hand* shall find out those that hate You."

Psalm 44:3: "For they did not get the land in possession by their own sword, neither did their own arm save them; but *Your Right Hand*, and *Your Arm* (*zeroa'kha*), and the light of Your countenance, because, You had favor unto them."

Psalm 78:54: "And He brought them to the border of His sanctuary, even to this mountain, which *His right Hand had purchased.*" Acts 20:28 says, "Take heed therefore unto yourselves, and to all the flock, over which the Holy Spirit has made you overseers, to shepherd the congregation of God, *which He has purchased with His own blood.*"

Psalm 91:7: "A thousand shall fall at Your side, and ten thousand at *Your right hand*, but it shall not come near unto you." Yeshua walks with us and fights for us.

Psalm 110:1,5: "*YHVH declares to my Lord, Sit at My Right Hand* until I make Your enemies Your footstool."

Second Kings 22:19: "And He said, Hear the Word of YHVH, I saw YHVH sitting on His throne, and all the host of heaven standing by Him on His *Right Hand* and on His left."

> Behold, I go forward, but He is not there; and backward, but I cannot perceive Him. On the left hand, where He does work, but I cannot behold Him. He hides Himself on the *Right Hand*, that I cannot see Him. But He knows the way that I take; when He has tried me, I shall come forth as gold.
>
> Job 23:8-10

A mystery being revealed in our day!

Matthew 25:33-34: "And He shall set the sheep on *His Right Hand*, but the goats on the left. Then shall the King say unto them on *His right Hand*, 'Come, You are blessed of My Father, inherit the kingdom prepared for you from the foundation of the world.'"

Matthew 26:64: "Jesus (Yeshua) said, … I say unto you, Hereafter you shall see the Son of man sitting on the *right hand of power*, and coming in the clouds of heaven."

Mark 16:19: "So then after the Lord had spoken unto them, He was received up into heaven, and sat on *the right hand of God.*"

Ephesians 1:20: "Which He wrought in Messiah (Christ), when He raised Him from the dead, and set Him at *His own Right Hand* in the heavenly places."

Colossians 3:1: "If you be then risen with Messiah, seek those things which are above, where *Messiah sits on the right hand of God.*"

Hebrews 1:3: "Whom being the brightness of His glory, and the express image of His person, and upholding all things by the Word of His power, when He had by Himself purged our sins, sat down on the *Right Hand of the Majesty* on high."

Hebrews 1:13: "But to which of the angels said He at any time, Sit on *My Right Hand* until I make Your enemies Your footstool?" (refers to Psalm 110:1, A Psalm of David).

> Now of the things which we have spoken, this is the sum; We have such a high priest, who is set on the *Right Hand of the Throne of the Majesty in the heavens*, a minister of the sanctuary, and of the true tabernacle, which the Lord pitched, and not man.
>
> Hebrews 8:1

Hebrews 10:12: "But this man, after He had offered one sacrifice for sins forever, sat down on the *Right Hand of God*; From henceforth waiting till His enemies be made His footstool."

Hebrews 12:2: "Looking unto Yeshua (Jesus), the author and finisher of our faith, Who for the joy that was set before Him, endured the cross, despising the shame, and is set down at *the Right Hand of the throne of God*."

First Peter 3:22: "Who is gone into heaven, and is *on the Right Hand of God*; angels and authorities and powers being made subject unto Him."

> The Mystery of the seven stars which you saw *in My Right Hand* (in Yeshua) and the seven golden candlesticks. The seven stars are the messengers of the seven congregations (qehilot); and the seven candlesticks which you saw are the seven congregations.
>
> Revelation 1:20

Revelation 2:1: "Unto the angel of the congregation of Ephesus, write, These things says *He that holds the seven stars in His right Hand*, who walks in the midst of the seven golden candlesticks."

The mystery, by YHVH's right hand (Yeshua), He has saved His people; the Harvest is being gathered in, the remnant that are truly His in all the congregations, communities of people who are listening to the Word of God.

> And I saw in the *Right Hand of Him* that sat on the throne a book written within and the backside, sealed with seven seals. And I saw a strong angel proclaiming with a loud

> voice, Who is worthy to open the book, and to loose the seals thereof? And no man in heaven, nor in earth, neither under the earth, was able to open the Book, neither to look thereon. And I wept much, because no man was found worthy to open and to read the book, neither to look thereon. And one of the elders, says unto me, Weep not, behold the Lion of the Tribe of Judah, the Root of David, has prevailed to open the book, and to loose the seven seals thereof. And I beheld, and lo, in the midst of the throne and of the four beasts, and in the midst of the elders, stood a Lamb as it had been slain, having seven horns and seven eyes, which are the seven Spirits of God sent forth into all the earth. *And he came and took the Book from the right hand of Him who sat upon the throne.*
>
> Revelation 5:1-7

YHVH God looked down upon the earth and saw that there was none to help, so He saved His people by His own Arm, His own Right Hand, the manifestation in the flesh, Yeshua! Once again, we review Isaiah 63…

> *And I looked, and there was none to help; and I wondered that there was none to uphold; therefore Mine own ARM (zeroa'i) brought Salvation unto Me; and My fury, it upheld Me.* Then He remembered the days of old, Moses and his people, saying, Where is HE that brought them up out of the seas with the shepherd of his flock? Where is He that put His Holy Spirit within him? That led them by the right hand of Moses *with His glorious ARM* (*zeroa tifarto*), dividing the water before them, to make Himself an everlasting Name.
>
> Isaiah 63:5, 12

Yeshua was the One who parted the waters. He was the glorious Arm of YHVH standing next to Moses when Moses lifted His right hand with the staff to part the waters. Yeshua manifests Himself many other times in the Old Testament as well, such as in the stories of the promise of a son to Abraham and Sarah (Genesis 17), the changing of Jacob's name to Israel (Genesis 32), the crossing of the Jordan by Joshua and YHVH's people (Joshua 5:13-15).

Yeshua came from the right side of YHVH. He is God Himself manifested in the physical, fully God, yet not all of God, for YHVH God was always on the throne even as Yeshua walked the earth. They always spoke together, even as they were ONE. What a mystery! For YHVH, God does not have a physical body as we do but has revealed Himself to us through what we can understand, the arm (*zeroa*) of YHVH, Yeshua! Hallelu*yah*! Meditate on this for a moment. It is overwhelmingly beautiful! Healing a breach in understanding for both sides.

ONE, ONE, ONE! The Lord, our God, is *ONE!* We are ONE together in YESHUA, through the Holy Spirit. Let's look again at Yeshua's prayer before He left from the Mount of Olives. John 17 –Yeshua prays, starting in verse 21,

> That they all may be One as You, Father, are in Me, and I in You, that they also may be ONE in us; that the world may believe that You have sent Me. And the glory which You gave to Me I have given to them; that they may be *One*, even as we are One; I in them, and You in Me, that they may be made perfect in One and that the world may know that You have sent ME, and have loved them, as You have loved Me.

Yeshua speaks of unity, *oneness*, but He speaks of Truth first!

In John 17:17, Jesus prays, “Sanctify them through Truth; Your Word is Truth.” Unity in truth, truth *must* come first, otherwise, it is unity in rebellion against YHVH. Again, unity without truth is rebellion. Peace, peace, but there is no peace. “They have healed also the hurt of the daughter of My people slightly, saying Peace, peace, but there is no peace” (Jeremiah 6:14).

The one-world religion will speak of unity, but there will be no truth. They will persecute those who say I follow Jesus (Yeshua) and Him alone, for He is the Way, *THE TRUTH* (not a truth), and the Life. This will be considered hate speech. They will say, “All must agree that every belief has equal value and must get along in unity. There can be no exclusiveness. All must be included.” So, to say there is only *ONE WAY* will not be tolerated. YHVH God gives us warning of the spirit of delusion that will come upon the earth in the last days, and it will disguise itself in unity. Yet, Unity without Truth may make people “get along” for a while, but it will only lead to the path of destruction. In Matthew 7:13, Yeshua says, “Enter in at the narrow gate; for wide is the gate, and broad is the way, that leads to destruction, and many there be which go in there; because narrow is the gate, and narrow is the Way, which leads to Life, and few there be that find it.”

Only Unity in Truth is Love and leads to eternal life. Jesus says, “I am the Way, the Truth, and the Life and no one comes to the Father except through Me” (John 14:6). We may have to rock the boat, folks! Cry out the whole Word of God, so we may be unified in Truth!

Ground breaking! Earth-shattering revelation! The earth will shake with revelation in these last days–before the Great and Terrible Day of the Lord comes upon the earth!

> The voice of Your thunder was in the heaven; the lightnings lightened the world; the earth trembled and shook. Your way is in the sea, and Your path in the great waters, and Your footsteps are not known. You led the people like a flock by the hand of Moses and Aaron.
>
> Psalm 77:18

> Whose voice then shook the earth; but now He has promised saying, Yet once more I shake not only the earth, but also heaven. And this Word, Yet once more, signifies the removing of those things that are shaken, as of things that are made, that those things which cannot be shaken may remain.
>
> Hebrews 12:26-27

We should celebrate Passover with the Jewish people as One. We should be a Light unto them that zeroa is the Arm of YHVH and the Arm of YHVH is Yeshua!

The Lord our God is *ONE!* Hear O Israel, YHVH, Eloheinu, YHVH ecHad.

שמע ישראל יהוה אלוהינו יהוה אחד

"And the Word was made flesh, and dwelt among us, and we beheld His glory, the glory as of the only begotten of the Father, full of grace and Truth" (John 1:14).

> Who (Yeshua) being the brightness of His glory, and the express image of His person (YHVH), and upholding all things by the Word of His power, when He had by Himself purged our sins, sat down on the right hand of the Majesty on High; being made so much better than the angels, as He has by inheritance obtained a more excellent Name than they.
>
> Hebrews 1:3-4

The angels were spoken into being, yet Yeshua came from the Father God YHVH Himself. He was always there, eternal as the Father, for He came from the inside of God, from the Right arm of YHVH God, from His Right Side, *zeroa*!

Chapter Eleven

Ha'SHEMEN, Holy Spirit Oil vs. Worldly Oil

Have you ever come before YHVH Father, before Yeshua (Jesus), in your morning prayer time with certain expectations of how the morning may go, but find as the Holy Spirit leads, you are so far down another path of new information and knowledge that God truly wants you to see. I hope it happens to you all the time. This happens to me more and more, and when I come from where God has led me, I am always amazed and overwhelmed that He would reveal such things to me. Who am I anyway? Who are you? In Jesus, we are far more than we can think or imagine. He has glorious plans for those who love Him. He has amazing treasures for those who will dig deep in His Word.

All this to say, recently, while in the middle of writing this book, I delved into my Bible and prayer and found my heart was focused on the oil industry. No, not the olive oil but the crude petroleum oil that comes from the depths of the earth. What was this all about? And did God want me to see something that He wanted me to share, even in this book? At first, I thought because this has just been revealed, maybe it belongs somewhere else, but then an idea came of how this is very relevant to the days we are living in. So, with that thought, I will attempt to explain.

I opened the Bible that morning to Isaiah 54. The very first verse has had me confused for some time; for years, it just didn't seem to fit the rest of the verses in context, so instead of reading it quickly and moving on as I usually do, I felt God speak I was to look up the original meaning in Hebrew.

Mystery of Isaiah 54:1

Isaiah 54:1 says, "Sing O barren, you that did not bear; break forth into singing and cry aloud, you that did not travail with child; for more are the children of the desolate than the children of the married wife, saith the Lord."

When I looked it up word for word, here is the transliteration:

Rani aqarah lo yaladah pitzcHi (solve a puzzle). Rinnah ve'tsa-hali lo-cHalah ki-rabim benei-shomemah mibnei ve'ulah, amar YHVH.

Sing uprooted, displaced woman that did not bear the solving of a riddle (maybe even puzzle or mystery). Sing aloud and rejoice that did not apply or occur. Because many more are the children of the desolate from the children of her burden, says YHVH.

When interpreted and understood this way, all of a sudden, the verse made sense with the rest of the chapter. The word *Beulah* which means married woman is actually ve'ulah in this passage. The Bet has been changed to a vet. Hebrew words do not start with vet, so why is the dagesh left out here that makes this letter change from bet to vet? I explain all this to those who may know a little Hebrew too and not understand the translation I have presented. I believe this change in one dot or tittle is for a reason, and it speaks of a mystery. The word ve'ulah could be interpreted as her burden, and the whole phrase "mibnei ve'ulah" as "from the children of her burden. Interpreted as such, Israel will not understand it until the end of days. Yet, she will be made desolate in order to bear the burden of the nations. She will be the mechanism or the vessel YHVH God uses to graft in the children of the nations into Israel, and many more will be the children of Israel when this puzzle, this mystery, is finally understood and resolved.

Yes! YHVH God, this makes sense to me. A barren woman can not have more children than anyone else, for she does not bear. This verse says she does not bear the understanding. But we are seeing more now and can understand as the day of Yeshua draws near and Israel will stretch forth her tent and break forth on the left and the right as YHVH brings them back together from the nations, and the strangers grafted in as well, to the re-born land of Israel.

So, as I continue to read, there is more good news. In Isaiah 54:5, 9-10, it says,

> For your Maker is your Husband; YHVH of hosts is His name; and your Redeemer the Holy One of Israel; The God of the whole earth shall He be called. For this is as the waters of Noah unto Me; for as I have sworn that the waters of Noah should no more go over the earth so I have sworn that I would not be angry with you, nor rebuke you. For the mountains shall depart, and the hills be removed, but My kindness shall not depart from you, neither shall the COVENANT of My Peace be removed says the Lord that has mercy on you.

I feel YHVH's Spirit then remind me of Hosea, where again God says He is our Husband.

> And I will give her vineyards from there and the Valley of AcHor for a Door of Hope; and she shall sing there, as in the days of her youth, and as in the day when she came up out of

> the land of Egypt. And it shall be at that day, says YHVH, that you shall call Me Ishi (My Husband) and shall no more call Me Baali. For I will take away the names of Baalim out of her mouth, and they shall no more be remembered by their name. And in that day, I will make a COVENANT for them with the beasts of the field, and with the birds of heaven, and with the creeping things of the ground; and I will break the bow and the sword and the battle out of the earth and will make them to lie down safely. And I will BETROTH you to Me forever; Yea, I will BETROTH you unto Me in righteousness and in judgement and in lovingkindness and in mercies. I will even BETROTH you unto Me in faithfulness; and you shall know YHVH. And it shall come to pass in that day, I will hear, says YHVH, I will hear the heavens, and they shall hear the earth. And the earth shall hear the grain, and the wine, and the OIL; and they shall hear Jezreel (Yizrael, יזרעאל). And I will sow her unto Me in the earth; and I will have mercy upon her that had not obtained mercy; and I will say to them which were not My people, you are My people; and they shall say You are my God.
>
> Hosea 2:15-23

This is the end of the matter. God will fulfill His covenant with us, His Marriage covenant. Yet, the people of the earth will make covenants that are not of Him. He will need to break our covenants with death.

Hosea 8:1,13b says, "Set the trumpet to your mouth. He shall come as an eagle against the House of YHVH because they have transgressed MY COVENANT and trespassed against My Law… they shall return to Egypt."

As I continue to read the Book of Hosea, YHVH makes it clear to me that this is about Covenant, the true and the false. Hosea 9:7 says the days of visitation are come. Hosea 10:4 goes on to say, "They have spoken words swearing falsely in making a COVENANT; therefore judgment springs up as hemlock in the furrows of the field." Hosea 10:10 declares, "It is My desire that I should chastise them, and the people shall be gathered against them, when they shall bind themselves (in covenant) in their two furrows."

The covenant that Israel will make in the latter days that will lead to the building of the third temple as part of the agreement will cause the judgment of YHVH God. He will see that their heart is divided (Hosea 10:2) because they do not KNOW the God of Israel in their hearts; they do not know as a nation their own Messiah, Yeshua. Therefore, they will place themselves back *under* the Law, which will grieve YHVH.

These covenants that are made between nations will ultimately lead to the final "peace" agreement spoken of in Daniel 9:27,

> And he shall confirm the COVENANT with many for one week (seven years); and in the midst of the week (three and a half years) he shall cause the sacrifice and the oblation to cease, and for the overspreading of abomination he shall make it desolate, even until the consummation and that determined shall be poured upon the desolate.

So, are these Scriptures in Hosea really pointing to the last days, the days we are living in? Hosea 10:8 speaks of the judgment of YHVH on this last temple that will re-instate the animal sacrifices without understanding that Yeshua came as the Lamb of God and His sacrifice was payment for the sins of all those who would and will call upon His Name and believe in what He did on the cross for them. Hosea 10:8 says, "The high places also of Aven, the sin of Israel, shall be destroyed; the thorn and the thistle shall come up on their altars and they shall say to the mountains, Cover us; and to the hills, Fall on us."

When Yeshua is telling of the last days to His disciples, He speaks of this exact event. Luke 23:30 says, "Then shall they begin to say to the mountains, Fall on us; and to the hills, Cover us." Revelation 6:16-17 says of these last days before Yeshua returns, "And they said to the mountains and to the rocks, Fall on us, and hide us from the face of Him that sits on the throne, and from the wrath of the Lamb; For the great day of His wrath is come; and who shall be able to stand?" Surely, Hosea speaks of the last days.

In the midst of judgment, YHVH also pours out mercy. In Hosea 11:7-9, we see the heart of our Father. "And My people are bent on backsliding from Me, though they (believe points to the two witnesses that will stand in the last days spoken of in Revelation 11:1-13) called them to the Most High, none at all would exalt Him." We hear YHVH God's sadness as He asks,

> How shall I give you up Ephraim? How shall I deliver you, Israel? How shall I make you as Admah? How shall I set you as Zeboim? My heart is turned within Me, My repentings are kindled together. I will not execute the fierceness of Mine anger; I will not return to destroy Ephraim; for I am God, and not man; The Holy One in the midst of you; and I will not enter into the city (Jerusalem).
>
> Hosea 11:8-9

Because of His great mercy, Hosea 11:10-11 says,

> They shall walk after YHVH; He shall roar like a lion (Lion of Judah!). When He shall roar, then the children shall tremble from the west (that includes the United States!) They shall tremble as a bird out of Egypt, and as a dove out of the land of Assyria; and I will place them in their houses, says YHVH.

O Praise YHVH! Praise Yeshua! His righteousness and His mercy will prevail!

At the beginning of 2020, the Lord YHVH placed on my heart the Burden of Dumah spoken of in Isaiah 21:11-12, "The burden of Dumah. He calls to me out of Seir, Watchman, what of the night? Watchman, what of the night? The watchman said, The morning comes, and also the night; if you will inquire, inquire; Return, come."

I hear the Holy Spirit speak from the Word of God that the days are coming when the dark will get darker, but the Light of YHVH God shining in His people will grow ever brighter as He pours out His Holy Spirit upon us to strengthen us for the days ahead. As His sons and daughters, we will have what we need for these days to proclaim His Word.

So as I continue to read the Book of Hosea that morning, I am stopped at Hosea 12:1.

"Ephraim feeds on wind and follows after the east wind; he daily increases lies and desolation, and they do make a COVENANT with the Assyrians (modern day Turkey, Iran, Iraq, and Syria), and OIL is carried into Egypt."

Again, the Holy Spirit focuses my attention on the word *COVENANT* but this is a covenant of oil. I wonder what oil this is since people in those days could not see the importance of crude oil on the earth as it is today. For this reason, many commentators believe Hosea is speaking of olive oil; but YHVH says no to my spirit. Hosea is a prophetic book and therefore, Hosea sees what cannot be seen yet with the physical eye. I go to do more research on when the crude oil industry began in earnest on the earth because now, we understand the power of this deep, dark liquid from the ground.

Oil Industry

Here is a brief history found from the very informative website (ekinteractive.com).[19] The first black oil discovered was by the Chinese in 600 BC. I was surprised at this early discovery, but nothing really came of it. Not until the nineteenth century did people begin to understand the power of this underground treasure. In 1859, the discovery of oil in Pennsylvania and the Spindletop discovery in Texas set the stage for the new oil economy.[20] With the dawn of the twentieth century, the energy source for much of the world went from coal to oil. In the early 1900s, in World War I, the ships, trucks, tanks were all oil-powered. A great industrial shift had taken place in all the earth.

Some of the supermajors in the field of the oil industry are well-known names such as Rockefeller, who founded Standard Oil Company in 1865, which was succeeded by the name Exxon Mobil. Nobel and Rothschild discovered oil fields in Russia and made great names for themselves. Samuel founded Shell Transport in 1897, which was called back then Royal Dutch Petroleum, backed by oil from the Dutch East Indies. Also, in 1907, oil was discovered in Iran, at first called Anglo-Persian Oil Company. In 1954, the British purchased this oil company and called it British Petroleum, better known as BP.

Exxon Mobil, Shell Transport, and BP were the original three supermajors. Others included Texaco from oil found in the Gulf of Mexico. By the 1930s, Chevron was also included. Major discoveries of oil were also found in Kuwait, Saudi Arabia, and Libya. This resulted in what was called the "Seven Sisters:" Exxon, Royal Dutch/Shell, BP, Mobil, Texaco, Gulf, and Chevron.

By the 1950s, more shifts occurred in the oil industry. The control of the oil fields was taken back by most of the original countries from where the oil was found. The Middle East, in particular, wanted to control their own oil fields and take back control from Britain. South America also struck oil. By 1960, OPEC, the Organization of the Petroleum Exporting Countries, was formed. OPEC, as many know, is now a considerable political and economic force. Eighty-one percent of oil reserves in the world belong to the members of OPEC. Today, Saudi Arabia has the majority of ownership, followed closely by Iran and Venezuela. The United Kingdom, Denmark, Germany, and the Netherlands are other major players. Canada and Brazil are also members. OPEC headquarters is based out of Vienna, Austria.

How does the United States fit into all of this? With new oil reserves found in the US, the United States, especially with the new technology of fracking, has been able to keep OPEC oil prices lower. When our nation is allowed to harvest this oil, we become another superpower in the midst of those controlling the wealth and power of the oil industry. Those that hold the key to the major energy sources, of course, hold the most power and wealth in the world and, therefore, the most control over the economic system of the world. Why is it certain administrations will allow our production of oil in the United States and others who would like to see a world government come into power, hold back, as much as they can, or sell overseas, the rights to our oil? It's just a question.

Recently, the US oil and gas production has been higher than at any other time in the last twenty years. The global community has been watching. But again, this can change quickly with new administrations in the US government who would like to see our influence on the world stage diminished. Either way, the world is watching.

Overall, there is lots of attention on this industry around the world. It is where much wealth and power are concentrated–in those who own the oil fields and control the earth's main source of energy and power.

So let's get back to the Hosea 12:1 covenant. Has it been established? By the leading of the Holy Spirit, I go to look. The answer maybe, a probable yes. In just this past year, 2020, an agreement was made between Israel and Egypt concerning oil. A little history will help explain.

In 2003, the Arab Gas Pipeline was established. In 2004, Egypt, Jordan, Syria, and Lebanon agreed to connect the existing pipeline with Iraq for the flow of gas to Europe. Egypt, at first, through this underground gas line was pumping oil to certain Middle East countries, but because of an attack on Egyptian oil fields starting in 2010, Egypt needed the oil; the other countries in the agreement now had the oil, so the pipelines were reversed for a time between 2010 and 2018. In 2020, just last year, the nation of Israel began exporting gas to Jordan through the Israel-Jordan pipeline. Also, the real big news concerning the prophetic Word, in 2020, the gas flow was reversed in the underwater branch of the

Arab Gas Pipeline to flow from Israel into the nation of Egypt.[21] It is a lot to take in, and you may ask, why does this even matter?

Again, Hosea 12:1 says, "Ephraim feeds on wind, and follows after the east wind; he daily increases lies and DESOLATION; and they do make a COVENANT with the Assyrians, and OIL is carried into EGYPT." From my understanding by the power of the Holy Spirit, this one small verse that I would normally never pay any attention to has been prophetically fulfilled in just the last year, 2020, by the agreement of Israel to allow oil to come through their nation from other Middle East countries, into Egypt. It matters because YHVH God, the God of Israel, is in the smallest details. Not one word of Scripture is overlooked. Every single word will be fulfilled to the tiniest detail. It shows He is and will always be in full control.

The next war will have a lot to do with gaining control over the oil fields. This is obvious to many watching world events and what is going on in the Mediterranean Sea with Turkey and other nations vying for power. Yet, the Word of God gives a clear indication that this was also prophesied. God saw the oil wars (building up to World War III) coming and the false covenants being made, even the recent China-Iran deal just signed on March 26, 2021.[22] On a side note, by the Holy Spirit's leading, I found March 26 is the same day as Nisan 13, the day Haman (the Agagite, the Jews' enemy, Esther 3:10) made an agreement with Persian King Ahasuerus to annihilate the Jewish people in the Book of Esther; he drew lots to see the actual day the extermination of this people group would happen, the 13th day of the 12th month of the Hebrew calendar, Adar 13, which translates next year to February 14, 2022. Iran is modern-day Persia. Maybe all this covenant-making between China and Iran (the enemy of the Jews) happened on the same day by coincidence, and then maybe not. China wants oil and computer technology, essentially world power. But what does Iran want more than anything? The destruction of the Jewish people and their nation. It is the spirit of Haman, alive and well on the earth today, and maybe the covenant of black oil includes the siding with China with Iran against Israel (one of the most technologically advanced nations in the world) in the days ahead, for the details of this covenant, have been kept secret, but not secret to YHVH God's eyes.

Black Oil vs. Golden Oil

Yet in all this, YHVH God has the perfect covenant sealed with a perfect oil, with more power, and more treasures than anything the world's oil can give–the Holy Spirit sealing and anointing!

So, I get out the Strong's Concordance and look up the word oil which shows oil is spoken of in the Bible over 200 times. Yet, there are certain passages that are key to seeing how God's holy oil was always used throughout the Bible, from the first book of Genesis to the last Book of Revelation. It was His way to establish a covenant with a people separate from the world and to keep the light of His Salvation burning throughout all generations.

From the very beginning of calling out a nation unto Himself, a covenant of oil was poured forth. In Genesis 28, Jacob, the son of Isaac, the son of Abraham, has a dream in a certain place. Genesis 28:11-17 says,

> He took stones of that place and put them for his pillows (at his head) and lay down… to sleep. And he dreamed, and behold a ladder set up on the earth, and the top of it reached to heaven…and angels of God were ascending and descend-

> ing on it. And behold, YHVH stood above it and said, I am YHVH God of Abraham, thy father, and God of Isaac; the land whereon you lay, to you will I give it, and to your seed. And your seed shall be as the dust of the earth, and you shall spread abroad to the west and to the east and to the north, and to the south; and in you and in your seed shall ALL the families of the earth be blessed. And behold, I am with you and will keep you in all the places where you go, and will bring you again into this land; for I will NOT leave you, until I have done that which I have spoken to you of. And Jacob awakened out of his sleep, and he said, Surely YHVH is in this place; and I knew it not. And he was afraid, and said, How dreadful is this place! This is none other but the House of God, and this is the gate of heaven.

YHVH knows how to get our attention, and He called on Jacob to acknowledge Him as the God of all the earth. This is a fearful dream for Jacob, for he knows he has been in the presence of the Holy God of all the earth. He wakes and decides he must place a memorial here.

Genesis 28:18-19 says,

> And Jacob rose up early in the morning and took the stone that he had put for his pillows, and set it up for a pillar, *and poured OIL upon the top of it.* And he called the name of that place Bethel (which means beyt El, House of God, in the Hebrew) but the name of that city was called Luz at the first.

Jacob then makes a vow that if YHVH God takes care of him, he will dedicate his life to serving God. Genesis 28:20-22 says,

> And Jacob vowed a vow saying, If God be with me, and will

> keep me in this way that I go and will give me bread to eat and clothing to put on, so that I come again to my father's house in peace; then shall YHVH be my God. And this stone which I have set for a pillar, shall be God's House; and of all that You shall give me I will surely give to you back the tenth.

Jacob set up the stone he had used for a pillow as a pillar, signifying the beginning of the building of God's House. He anointed the stone with olive oil, signifying this covenant was sealed.

Jacob then goes on to meet Laban, his mother's brother, and there begins to build his family; by the trickery of Laban, he marries Leah first, and then Rachel. Over twenty years later, Jacob leaves Laban with eleven sons (Benjamin is born later), two wives, two concubines, many servants, cattle, and goats. He comes away as a very rich man but now must face his brother Esau that he tricked out of his birthright. Jacob is terrified that his brother is still angry. In Genesis 32, again, Jacob meets with God's angels. Genesis 32:1-2 says, "And Jacob went on his way, and the angels of God met him. And when Jacob saw them, he said, this is God's host; and he called the name of that place *MacHanaim*" (which means Double Camp in Hebrew).

Jacob is walking towards his brother's land, and with every step, he becomes more afraid. Maybe because he has just seen the double camp of God's army, he divides his family in two and hopes that if one gets attacked, maybe the other side will escape. He is desperate. He begins to pray desperately to God. Jacob sends both camps before him over the Jabbok River (front cover picture of this book, bibleplaces.com/jabbok), and he is left alone behind them. That night, he meets with a man and wrestles with him until the break of day. Genesis 32:25-30 recounts this magnificent event where Jacob is renamed Israel (means fighter of God in Hebrew), and the very beginning of a great nation is established.

> And when He saw that He prevailed not against him (would not give up), He touched the hollow of his hip and the hollow of his hip was out of joint, as He wrestled with him. And He said, Let Me go, for the day breaks. And Jacob said, I will not let You go, except You bless me. And He said unto him, "What is your name?" and he said, Jacob. And He said, your name shall be called no more Jacob, but Israel, for as a Prince you have power with God and with men and have prevailed. And Jacob asked him, tell me your name, and He said, "Why do you ask for My Name?" And He blessed him there. And Jacob called the name of the place Peniel for he said, "I have seen God face to face and my life is preserved."

Jacob knew he had been in the presence of God again. From this encounter, he was given a new identity, from Jacob (means deceiver in Hebrew) to Israel (fighter of God). He had wrestled with God and came away blessed with a new name and a new purpose. He was to fight for the true God of all the earth. We know that Jacob wrestled with YHVH, manifesting as a man, Yeshua, even all the way back in Genesis. Genesis 35:10 says, "And God appeared unto Jacob again, when he came out of Padanaram and blessed him. And God said unto him, your name is Jacob; your name shall not be called any more Jacob, but Israel shall be your name; and He called his name Israel." God promises Israel that he will become a great nation and a company of nations (Gentile remnant grafted in) and that kings will come forth from him. And God promises to give him the land that he is now on, what we know as Israel today, and much more than the boundaries of today.

Again, Jacob (Israel) sets up a pillar of stone in the place that

He (God) spoke with him, "And he poured a drink offering thereon, and he poured out OIL thereon" (Genesis 35:14). This occurred again in the same place as the first, the place Jacob had renamed Bethel (Beyt El, בית-אל the House of God).

This is the beginning of the nation of Israel and the building of the House of God "built without human hands." The anointing oil is the substance that seals the covenant just as the Holy Spirit (living water and oil) washes us clean and seals us with the promise of Salvation.

But this is only the beginning. The oil pours like a living stream throughout the Bible, although only certain passages will be highlighted here. In Exodus, as the tabernacle ordained by YHVH is established, God commands in Exodus 27:20 that "Moses shall command the children of Israel, that they bring you pure olive oil beaten for the light, to cause the lamp to burn (literally the word means to ascend) always." The oil was to give Light in the House of God continually and not to go out.

The children of Israel are told to make a specific oil to anoint the tabernacle. They were to take pure myrrh, cinnamon, sweet calamus, cassia, and olive oil and mix them to "make an oil of holy ointment," and it was to be "a holy anointing oil" which they would "anoint the tabernacle of the congregation with it, and the ark of the testimony and the table and all the vessels and the candlestick and his vessels and the altar of incense, and the altar of burnt offering with all his vessels, and the laver and its base. And you shall sanctify them, that they may be most holy; and whatsoever shall touch them shall be holy (Exodus 30:23-29).

The priests were also to be anointed with this oil. "And you shall anoint Aaron and his sons, and consecrate them that they may minister unto me in the priest's office" (Exodus 30:30).

This oil was used to seal the tabernacle and the priests in holiness unto YHVH.

We see places in the TanakH or Old Testament where people are anointed with oil and then filled with the Holy Spirit. In the TanakH, the Holy Spirit was poured out on individuals chosen by YHVH God to lead His people. One of the first mentions of this anointing was on many Israelites in the building of YHVH's tabernacle and in the workmanship needed to make everything exactly as God spoke. Exodus 35:10 says,

> And every wise hearted among you shall come and make all that YHVH has commanded. The tabernacle, his tent, and his covering, the taches, and boards, bars, pillars, and sockets. The ark, and the staves, the mercy seat, and the vail covering. The table, and staves and vessels and shewbread, the candlestick (menorah) also for the Light, and furniture, and lamps with the oil for the light. And incense altar, and staves, and the anointing oil, and the sweet incense, and the hanging for the door at the entrance of the tabernacle. The altar of burnt offering, with the brazen grate, staves and vessels, the laver and foot. The hanging of the court, his pillars, and their sockets, and the hanging for the door of the court. The pins of the tabernacle, and the pins of the court, and their cords. The cloths of service to do work in the holy place, the holy garments for Aaron the priest and for his sons, to minister in the priest's office.

The whole congregation, men and women, heard the work to be done. Then they departed and listened for the voice of God. What was their part? What were they anointed to do? No one just started working without having their hearts stirred by the Holy Spirit to do the work assigned to them. They all had their part, and if they were listening, they knew exactly how and where they were to build the House of God.

Moses singles out Bezaleel and specifically says God has "filled him with the Spirit of God, in wisdom, in understanding, and in knowledge, and in all manner of workmanship" (Exodus 35:31). Bezaleel was to teach others what the Holy Spirit had given to him. He was filled with the Holy Spirit, and now he was to teach so that others could also be filled and help him with the work that needed to be done.

As commanded, Moses did all that YHVH God asked of him. Leviticus 8:12 says of Moses, "And he poured of the anointing oil upon Aaron's head, and anointed him, to sanctify him." In Psalm 133, David sings of this anointing.

> Behold how good and how pleasant it is for brethren to dwell together in unity! It is like the precious ointment upon the head, that ran down upon the beard, even to Aaron's beard, that went down to the edge of his garments… It sounds like a lot of oil was poured that day upon Aaron's head. He was anointed to do the work of God through the Holy Spirit and the Holy Spirit would bring unity in the house of God, unity in Truth, unity in Salvation, "for there the Lord commanded the blessing, even life forevermore."

The tabernacle was built in the wilderness, where the Israelites had to stay for forty years because of their unbelief. But YHVH God planned to take them to the Promised Land, "A land of wheat and barley (the harvest), and vines, and fig trees, and pomegranates; *a land of olive oil*, and honey" (Deuteronomy 8:8). The land would be fruitful and sweet; the land would be anointed with oil.

Joshua leads them into the land after forty years. At first, YHVH brings Holy Spirit-filled judges and prophets such as Othniel (Judges 3:9-10), Deborah (Judges 4 and 5), and Gideon (Judges 6-8). There are many more, but in each of these leaders, the Holy Spirit comes upon them to help them to fight, to lead, and to teach the children of Israel about the true God of Israel. "But the Spirit of YHVH came upon Gideon and he blew a trumpet" (Judges 6:34). An anointing of the Holy Spirit, a pouring out of oil…

After the judges, Israel wants a king like the nations around her. Saul, the first king, is anointed by Samuel the prophet. In 1 Samuel 10:1, it says, "Then Samuel took a vial of oil, and poured it upon his (Saul's) head and kissed him, and said, Is it not because the Lord YHVH has anointed you to be captain over his inheritance?" Yet Saul did not do as YHVH commanded and feared the opinion of people more than that of YHVH. In 2 Samuel 1:21, we see that Saul's anointing has been taken away. "Ye mountains of Gilboa, let there be no dew, neither let there be rain, upon you, nor fields of offerings, for there the shield of the mighty is vilely cast away, the shield of Saul, as though he had not been anointed with oil."

Samuel is sent to look for another king. He is sent to Jesse's house. Samuel looks at all Jesse's sons, but YHVH's Spirit does not indicate that it is any of them. Samuel asks Jesse if he has any other sons. Jesse calls for David, who is out in the fields tending the sheep. "And he sent and brought him in. Now he was ruddy and had a beautiful countenance… And YHVH said, Arise, anoint him; for this is he" (1 Samuel 16:12).

What a surprise this must have been to David, a young lad

pulled from the fields. How did I go from singing songs to YHVH as I care for the sheep to being anointed as king of all Israel? "Then Samuel took the horn of oil, and anointed him in the midst of his brethren; and the Spirit of YHVH came upon David from that day forward" (1 Samuel 16:13).

In 1 Kings 1:38-39–King Solomon is anointed as king. He was the son of David and Bathsheba. YHVH God does work in mysterious ways!

> So Zadok the priest, and Nathan the prophet, and Benaiah the son of Jehoiada … went down and caused Solomon to ride on King David's mule and brought him to Gihon. And Zadok the priest took a horn of oil out of the tabernacle, and anointed Solomon. And they blew the trumpet; and all the people said, God save king Solomon.

The holy oil was used to anoint kings and priests.

> But you are a chosen generation, a royal priesthood, a holy nation, a peculiar people; that you should show forth the praises of Him who has called you out of darkness into His marvelous Light. Which in times past were not a people, but now are the people of God.
>
> 1 Peter 2:9-10

Both Elijah and his successor Elisha performed miracles concerning oil in two women's homes. In 1 Kings 17:14 and in 2 Kings 4:2, Elijah and Elisha keep the oil flowing for two households that had blessed them. The Holy Spirit released the miracle of the flow of oil in their homes even as they blessed the prophets of YHVH God.

"Quench not the Spirit. Despise not prophesyings" (2 Thessalonians 5:19-20).

Elisha is also called to anoint Jehu, the one that will destroy the wickedness of the house of Ahab and Jezebel. In 2 Kings 9:1-3), Elisha the prophet calls one of the children of the prophets and says to him,

> Take this box of oil … and go to Ramoth-gilead, and when you come there, look for Jehu, the son of Jehoshaphat (YHVH judges), the son of Nimshi, and go in, make him rise up from among his brethren, and carry him to an inner chamber; then take the box of oil and pour it on his head, and say, thus says YHVH, I have anointed you king over Israel…

The oil flowed during the anointing and dedication of the first Temple of God that Solomon built. Second Chronicles 4:20 says, "Also the lampstands (were made), that they should burn after the manner before the oracle, of pure gold." The oil lamps were full and burning bright. After all the people praise God with thanksgiving and the sounds of the shofars and other instruments, and dedicate the House of God on Mount Moriah, "the glory of YHVH filled the House of God," so much so, "that the priests could not stand to minister by reason of the cloud."

Shekinah Glory! Holy Spirit power! The oil flows.

It flows during the anointing and dedication of the second Temple. The House of God is filled with good things, including the oil.

> For the children of Israel and the children of Levi shall bring the offering of the grain, of the new wine, *and the oil*, unto the chambers, where are the vessels of the sanctuary, and the priests that minister, and the porters, and the singers; and we will not forsake the House of our God.
>
> Nehemiah 10:39

Without the oil, there is no Holy Spirit power. David sings of this in some of his psalms. One of the most well-known psalms, Psalm 23, speaks of this anointing. The Lord is my Shepherd; I shall not want, He makes me lie down in green pastures, He leads me beside the still waters, He anoints my head with oil (Psalm 23:1-2). I wonder if David wrote this psalm after he meets Samuel the prophet for the first time or if he was prophesying a future event.

In Psalm 89:20-21, it says, "I have found David, My servant; with My Holy Oil I have anointed him, with whom My Hand shall be established, My ARM (zeroa, Yeshua) also shall strengthen him."

Isaiah prophesies of Yeshua the Messiah in Isaiah 61,

> The Spirit of YHVH is upon Me, because YHVH has anointed Me to preach good tidings to the meek; He has sent Me to bind up the brokenhearted, to proclaim liberty to the captives, and the opening of the prison to them that are bound; to proclaim the acceptable year of YHVH and the day of vengeance of our God; to comfort all that mourn, to appoint unto them that mourn in Zion, to give them beauty for ashes, the OIL of Joy for mourning and the garment of praise for the spirit of heaviness.
>
> Isaiah 61:1-3

Yeshua the Messiah, the Anointed One, who sets us free and fills us with the Oil of Joy. He is our Kinsman Redeemer, that washes us clean and anoints us with Holy Spirit oil (Ezekiel 16:8-9).

And in the last days, the days upon us now, we have a promise from the Almighty.

> And it shall come to pass in that day, I will hear, says YHVH, I will hear the heavens, and they shall hear the earth. And the earth shall hear the grain, and the wine, and the OIL; and they shall hear Jezreel (Yizrael, God will sow). And I will sow her unto Me in the earth; and I will have mercy upon her that had not mercy; and I will say unto them which were not My people, you are My people; and they shall say You are my God.
>
> Hosea 2:21-23

Joel prophesies,

> Yes, YHVH will answer and say unto His people, Behold, I will send you grain and wine and OIL, and you shall be satisfied therewith; and I will no more make you a reproach among the heathen (unbelieving people). Be glad then, ye children of Zion, and rejoice in YHVH your God, for He has given you the former rain moderately, and He will cause to come down for you the rain, the former rain, and the latter rain in the first month. And the floors shall be full of wheat, and the vats shall overflow with new wine and OIL.
>
> Joel 2:19, 23-24

HalleluYAH! These days are upon us. All the oil poured in the Old Testament was given to chosen people to lead Israel. Sadly, it could be taken away, as we saw with Saul. The oil poured out in Acts was the former rain. It poured out on all the Jewish people in the house in Jerusalem that were gathered together waiting upon the promise of Yeshua, "that you shall be baptized with the Holy Spirit, not many days from now" (Acts 1:5). Yet Joel prophesies two outpourings, the former and the latter. The greatest outpouring is yet to come. It is before us, and many of us are feeling the sprinkles of a coming outpour as we begin to get our feet wet!

In Acts 2:16-18, Luke quotes the prophet, Joel,

> But this is that which was spoken by the prophet Joel; and it shall come to pass in the last days, says God, I will pour out My Spirit upon all flesh, and your sons and your daughters shall prophesy, and your young men shall see visions and your old men shall dream dreams. And on My servants and on My handmaidens I will pour out in those days of My Spirit, and they shall prophesy.

The Spirit of God, the holy oil, causes the prophetic Word to go forth…and to accomplish that which it is sent out to do and not return void (Isaiah 55:11).

In Acts 10, the Holy Spirit outpour goes from the Jewish nation also to the Gentiles. And so, for the next 2000 years, the Holy Spirit oil has been poured out where hearts are humble and will receive the truth of God's Word. The remnant is being gathered in. The people of God from around the world are grafted into the Tabernacle of David, the House of God. The story has come full circle.

We await this final outpour to come against the growing evil. When the enemy comes in like a flood, YHVH raises a standard against Him (Isaiah 59:19).

Even in growing darkness, God's people can be filled with joy just as Yeshua was as He faced the evil head-on. "You have loved righteousness, and hated iniquity; therefore God, Your God, has anointed You with the Oil of Gladness above your fellows" (Hebrews 1:9). "Looking unto Yeshua, the author and finisher of our faith, Who for the joy set before Him endured the cross, despising the shame, and is set down at the Right Hand of the throne of God," (Hebrews 12:2).

So what will happen in these last days? The book of Zechariah gives us more understanding. Zechariah sees a vision of a golden lampstand, "with a bowl upon the top of it and seven lamps thereon and seven pipes to the seven lamps" "and two olive trees by it" one on the right side and one on the left. Zechariah wants to know "what does this mean"? The angel answers, "This is the Word of YHVH unto Zerubbabel saying, *'Not by might, nor by power, but by MY SPIRIT, says YHVH tsavaot'*" (Zechariah 4:6). The angel continues to speak,

> The hands of Zerubbabel have laid the foundation of this HOUSE; his hands shall also finish it; and you shall know that YHVH tsavaot (The Lord of hosts) has sent me to you. For who has despised the day of small things? For they shall rejoice and shall see the plummet in the hand of Zerubabbel with those seven; they are the eyes of YHVH which run to and fro through the whole earth.
>
> Zechariah 4:9-10

God is looking for all those who will come to Him. He will gather all those that are His. He is building His House made without human hands, even as the enemy, Satan himself, is trying to build his kingdom on the earth.

Zechariah 4:11-14 says,

> Then answered I (Zechariah) and said unto him (an angel), What are these two olive branches which through the two golden pipes empty the GOLDEN OIL out of themselves? And He answered me and said, Do you not know what these be? And I said, No, my lord. Then said he, These are the two anointed ones, that stand by YHVH of the whole earth.

In the very last days, two anointed ones will proclaim God's Word to anyone who will hear. These two will stand in Jerusalem crying out for the people to not come under the delusion of the antichrist. They will cry, "Come out of her!" Come out of the apostate church and be grafted into the House of God (Revelation 18:4).

In Revelation 11:3-4, God says,

> And I will give power unto My two witnesses, and they shall prophesy a thousand two hundred and sixty days (three and a half years), clothed in sackcloth. These are the two olive trees, and the two candlesticks standing before the God of the earth.

In these days of tribulation, 144,000 Jewish people will be anointed to speak forth the true Word of God and proclaim Yeshua in these last days, calling all those who will listen to the Jewish people first and then to the whole earth. By the power of the Holy Spirit, they will cry, "Come out of her!" Revelation 7:3-8 and Revelation 14:1-4.

A small note of clarification. Revelation 14:4 says, "These (the 144,000) are those that were not kinsman redeemers (lo-ngoel'u) to women; for they were virgins." They were set for a special purpose to focus solely on proclaiming Yeshua in the last days. The word *goel* means kinsman redeemer, not defiled. Just another example of interpreting scripture the wrong way and putting women in a bad light. God's daughters do not defile. We bring forth life!

In the end, we will be separated by the oil we carry. We can either carry the golden oil of God or the black oil of the world. One brings forth truth and eternal life. The other brings forth greed for power and wealth on the earth. Only the pure oil of YHVH God will be the entrance to heaven, and we can only be filled with this oil after accepting Yeshua as our Lord and Savior, laying down our lives, our wants, and our desires in exchange for the desire that the Father's will be done in all the earth, and that we are His servants, His family, His Bride.

Many are familiar with the parable of the ten virgins in Matthew 25:1-13. The difference between those that entered into the Marriage Supper of the Lamb and those who did not was the *oil.* Who was ready? Who was already His when He came?

> Then the kingdom of heaven is like ten virgins, which took their lamps, and went forth to meet the bridegroom. And five of them were wise and five were foolish. They that were foolish took their lamps, and took NO OIL with them. But the wise TOOK OIL in their vessels with their lamps. While the bridegroom tarried, they all slumbered and slept. And at midnight, there was a cry made, Behold, the Bridegroom comes; go out to meet Him! Then those virgins arose and trimmed their lamps. And the foolish said unto the wise, Give us of your OIL; for our lamps are gone out. But the wise answered, saying, Not so, because there might not be enough for us and you together; but go to them that sell and buy for yourselves. And while they went to buy, the Bridegroom came; and they that were ready went in with Him to the marriage; and the door was shut. Afterward, the other virgins came saying, Lord, Lord, open to us. But He answered and said, Truly I say unto you, I do not know you. "Watch therefore, for you do not know the day nor the hour (yet we do know the time and season) that the Son of man comes."

Many in the House of God are not filled with the Holy Spirit. They may look very similar to those who are, when in the church building, but their hearts are not with Yeshua. They go to church on Sunday, but the rest of the week, not much or not any time is given to the Word of God. They have not been filled with the Holy Spirit that causes us to crave knowing God more, the Holy Spirit that makes us more and more like Yeshua every day as we study His Word and pray and spend time with Him. What is really on the inside is what matters. Appearances mean nothing. If you are not sure that you are filled with the Holy Spirit, cry out to YHVH God, the God of Israel, the God of all the earth. Pray that He will fill you with Him. Religion is an offense to Him. Truly knowing Him means everything.

In Luke 7, Yeshua is invited to a Pharisee's house, so Jesus goes to his house. Soon after He enters, a woman (Mary Magdalene) abruptly enters the house as well. She is on a mission. She does not care if she was invited or not. She does not care what others think of her. She must anoint the feet of Yeshua. By the Holy Spirit of God, Mary must know that the anointing of Jesus must occur before His crucifixion. YHVH God has given her an assignment, and she will fulfill it. She brings to the house an alabaster box of ointment (oil). "And she stood at His feet weeping, and began to wash His feet with tears, and did wipe them with the hairs of her head and kissed His feet, and anointed them with the ointment" (Luke 7:38).

The Pharisees were not happy about this at all. They start to speak among themselves, saying if Jesus really were a prophet, He would know this woman was a sinner, defiled, not worthy of their attention. Jesus has a message for this house of men. He speaks of the parable of a certain creditor who had two debtors. "The one owed 500 pence and the other 50." They both could not pay, so the creditor forgives them both. Jesus asks them, "Tell me, which will love him most?"

Simon answers the one who was forgiven most. Jesus says, "You have judged right." Then Jesus turns to the beautiful woman at His feet. "See this woman?" He says to all the self-righteous men in the group.

> I entered your house, and you gave Me no water for My feet; but she has washed my feet with her tears and wiped them with the hairs of her head. You gave me no kiss, but this woman since the time I came in has not ceased to kiss My feet. My head with oil you did not anoint; but this woman has anointed My feet with ointment. Wherefore I say unto you, her sins, which are many, are forgiven. For she loved much, but to whom little is forgiven (those who do not think they have much to forgive), the same loves little.
>
> Luke 7:44-45

They still do not get what Jesus is saying in their self-righteousness, as many do not. "And they that sat at the meal with Him began to say within themselves, Who is this that forgives sins also?" or in other words, "Who does He think He is?" And Jesus said unto the woman, "Your faith has saved you; go in peace."

The oil makes the difference here. Mary, filled with the Holy Spirit, brings the oil into the house. She fills the house with a beautiful fragrance when all there was before her entrance was judgment and self-righteousness. Mary, filled with Holy Spirit oil on the inside, could pour the oil at Yeshua's feet and anoint Him, as the Holy Spirit led her to, to prepare Jesus for the cross.

Cry out before the Lord YHVH! Know Him! And you will love Him more and more.

Heaven and earth will touch, a great love story!

> Surely His Salvation is near to them that fear him; that glory may dwell in our land. Mercy and Truth are met together; righteousness and peace have kissed each other. Truth shall spring out of the earth; and righteousness shall look down from heaven.
>
> Psalm 85: 9-11

For everything YHVH God does, the enemy Satan has a temptation to lure people away. Smoke and mirrors. We must have discernment and to see far beyond what this earth and the world have to offer–Colossians 3:23 says, "And whatsoever you do, do it heartily, as to YHVH, and not unto men." Yeshua is coming soon! Will you be ready? What is drawing you away from the real treasure to be found? What is your black oil?

In Isaiah 28:14, the Word of the Lord comes to the self-righteous,

> Wherefore hear the Word of YHVH, ye scornful men (rulers in the earth), that rule this people which is in Jerusalem (that have power over My people for a time). Because you have said, WE have made a covenant with death, and with hell are we at agreement; when the overflowing scourge shall pass through, it shall not come unto us; for we have made lies our refuge, and under falsehood have we hid ourselves, Therefore thus says the YHVH God, I lay in Zion for a foundation as stone, a tried stone, a precious corner stone, a sure foundation; He that believes shall not make haste. Judgement

> also will I lay to the line, and righteousness to the plummet (remember Zerubbabel); and the hail shall sweep away the refuge of lies, and the waters shall overflow the hiding place.

For all of God's people who are being persecuted by the rulers of this earth who have made a covenant with death, YHVH has an answer–Yeshua! The tried stone, the precious cornerstone, a sure foundation. And for those who will come to Him, the "covenant with death shall be disannulled, and your agreement with hell shall not stand" (Isaiah 28:18).

Yet, in the last days, there will be an overflowing scourge to wipe out all that will not come to Him.

> When the overflowing scourge shall pass through, then you shall be trodden down by it. From the time that it goes forth, it shall take you; for morning by morning it shall pass over, by day and by night; and it shall be a vexation only to understand the report. For the bed is shorter than that a man can stretch himself on and the covering narrower than he can wrap himself.
>
> Isaiah 28:18-20

The scourge shall come, and it will leave the people with not enough to take care of their needs.

> For YHVH shall rise up as in Mount Peratzim (in the breaks, in the breaches), he shall be angry as in the valley of Gibeon, that He may do His work, His strange work; and bring to pass His act, His strange act. Now therefore do not be as mockers, lest your bands (of slavery to sin) be made strong; for I have heard from YHVH God of hosts, a consumption, even determined upon the whole earth. Give ear, and hear MY Voice; hearken, and hear MY speech.
>
> Isaiah 28:21-23

In the middle of this vexation, scourge, consumption determined upon the whole earth, YHVH God will be separating those that are His from those that are not. Could the consumption determined upon the whole earth be this Covid-19 or something like it coming soon? Biological warfare is now a stark reality and is being used to gain control over all the earth. It is for the wicked who hide in lies to conquer the population and gather power and riches of the earth for themselves.

Yet in the midst of this, in the next few verses of Isaiah 28, God speaks of reaping His greatest harvest and that there are different harvests as there will be different ways and times to bring in His people. It is a great mystery, but YHVH God will separate out His people and bring them Home at the appointed time, and He will do His strange work, His strange act, "which is wonderful in counsel, and excellent in working."

What if you gain the whole world but lose your own soul? (Matthew 16:26). The people who follow after the wealth and power of this world will have their reward here, and then there will be nothing more to look forward to, for they have made their choice. The dark black oil, in itself, is not evil, but many have made what it represents their god and have made the riches of this world and the power obtained through riches to be their true heart's desire. They have become evil in turning away from the true source of treasure and power, and *love*.

YHVH God, Yeshua Messiah, One in the Spirit of God!

The tsunami of evil will bow at His feet. For even the wind and the waves obey Him. And the earth thunders at His presence, and the rocks cry out even as a recent discovery of biblical text (The

Times of Israel, Bible Scroll Fragments among Dazzling Artifacts found in Dead Sea Cave..., by Amanda Borschel-Dan, March 16, 2021)–reveals scriptures from Nahum and Zechariah. Part of the text of Nahum is Nahum 1:5-6,

> The mountains quake at Him, and the hills melt, and the earth is burned at His presence, yea, the world, and all that dwell therein. Who can stand before His indignation? And who can abide in the fierceness of His anger? His fury is poured out like fire, and the rocks are thrown down by Him.

These words have just come out of the earth, hidden in caves only accessed through rappelling steep cliffs to get to them; they have been hidden for almost 2000 years. Yes, the rocks cry out! The earth will shake at His soon return, and YHVH is giving us warning to be prepared. Be filled with the Holy Spirit! It is the mark of those who are YHVH God's children.

The greatest outpouring of Holy Spirit power is coming–the former and latter rains combined! Water the harvest! Blow the trumpet! Repent and come out of her! Get ready for the Marriage Supper of the Lamb. The final touches are being put upon the head of the Bride. The final touches are being added to the pillars of the House of God. Then, it is finished!

"And I heard a voice in the midst of the four beasts say, A measure of wheat for a penny (denarius) and three measures of barley for a penny; and see that you do not hurt the OIL and the WINE" (Revelation 6:6).

Chapter Twelve

Out of His Side, The Bride!

One morning as my feet hit the floor, I heard in my spirit, "Out of His Side, the Bride." I immediately went to write it down in one of my journals. It was something to think about. I knew YHVH God was speaking, but I could not see it clearly at that moment. Since then, there has been more revelation. Man and woman have been made in the image of God. Adam was formed first and then Eve, from the side of Adam. Therefore, shall a man leave his father and his mother, and shall cleave unto his wife; and they shall be *one* flesh (Genesis 2:21-24).

As we have studied, YHVH God, through the revelation of *ze-roa*, shows us that Yeshua came from the side of YHVH. He is the arm of God the Father. He comes from the side of the Father! The same essence, now made flesh, the arm of God! Yeshua and the Father are *ONE!* He is fully God, yet made visible to people. Yeshua came many times on the earth as a Messenger of YHVH, not as an angel, but as the image of God, made flesh, so that He could interact with people face to face. Even in the Garden of Eden, we see Yeshua walking and talking with Adam and Eve before the fall and after (Genesis 2 and 3).

In Genesis 18, Abraham meets the Lord Yeshua, who gives him the message that Sarah will have a child, even at age ninety!

> And the Lord appeared unto him in the plains of Mamre; and he sat in in the tent door in the heat of the day and he lifted

> up his eyes and looked, and lo, three men stood by him. And when he saw them, he ran to meet them from the tent door, and bowed himself toward the ground.
>
> Genesis 18:2

Before Joshua passes over the Jordan into the Promised Land to take Jericho, he sees Yeshua.

> And it came to pass, when Joshua was by Jericho, that he lifted up his eyes and looked, and behold there stood a man opposite him with his sword drawn in His hand; and Joshua went unto Him, and said unto Him, Are you for us, or for our adversaries? And He said, No, but as captain of the host of YHVH am I now come. And *Joshua fell on his face to the earth, and did worship*, and said unto Him, What do You say unto your servant? And the captain of YHVH's host said unto Joshua, Loose your shoe from off your foot; for the place where you stand is holy. And Joshua did so.
>
> Joshua 5:13-15

Yeshua shows up many times in the Old Testament, and of course, He is revealed to all in the New. Through the virgin birth of Mary, He not only comes into the world to appear for a short time but reveals Himself as the Son of God. He stays with us for about thirty-three years as fully man and fully God!

Yes, Yeshua came from the side of YHVH. For He always spoke with the Father even as He was on the earth. So, we have Yeshua coming from the side of YHVH together as One in the Holy Spirit. In the image of God, we have Eve coming from the side of Adam, made together in spirit as One flesh. And then YHVH reveals to me Yeshua, the second "Adam" on the cross.

He dies only to birth His Bride. When Yeshua gave up His Spirit, He is pierced by a spear on His side; out pours blood and water. It signifies a birth. A birth that came from His giving up His own life. It signifies the cleansing of His Bride by His own blood and the Holy Spirit living water which would be poured out on those who are His to fill them with Holy Spirit power. As YHVH and Yeshua are One in the Spirit, so is the Bride of Yeshua, One with Him in the Spirit. That is why the people of God were told to wait in Jerusalem so they could be filled with the Holy Spirit, to be sealed and made One with Him! It was the birth of His Bride, the true House of God!

Adam and Eve were a shadow of what YHVH God would do. The image of God was shattered when the accuser of the brethren stepped into the garden and deceived Eve. She and Adam disobeyed YHVH God. Adam sided with the enemy in accusing Eve and blaming God for sending her. Eve sided with God in accusing the accuser, yet the damage was already done. A deep wound was now the chasm in the relationship between man and woman. This accusing has not stopped. It was never meant to be. They were made in the image of YHVH God.

The true Bride of Yeshua would be born in Yeshua's death; He would love her so much that He would lay down His life for her. The Bride and Yeshua would be made together as One in His Resurrection! We are ONE with Him, for we came out of His side, all those who receive the Holy Spirit! He is in us, and we are in Him! This may be hard to hold on to, but pray and ask YHVH God to reveal this to your heart and mind. Think about it. Meditate on it. Yeshua died to birth His Bride, just as Adam was put into a deep sleep to bring forth Eve. Yeshua gave His life so that He could be a Husband unto us! Even more so, each of us a living stone, which together, is made not only the Bride but also the holy Temple of YHVH made not with human hands, in which He will reside forever. It is more than beautiful! Out of His Side, the Bride…

The Bride, all of us together that are His or will come to be His, is being built together ever since the resurrection of Yeshua. The outpour of the Holy Spirit in Jerusalem to the first born-again believers seals us and makes us One with Him. This harvest of His Bride started in the Old Testament by faith in the coming Messiah (Abraham and others who knew YHVH God by the individual giving of the Holy Spirit) and continued in earnest with the death, burial, and resurrection of Yeshua! For almost 2000 years now, the Holy Spirit has been poured out on everyone that calls upon His Name (Yeshua, Jesus!). The final touches are being put upon His Bride; even a golden crown like He wears will be set upon her head! They will rule and reign together for 1000 years! It is almost too much to comprehend, but yet it is there in God's Word.

Revelation 14:14, "And I looked, and behold, a white cloud, and upon the cloud sat One like the Son of man having on His head a *golden crown*, and in His hand a sharp sickle."

Like Yeshua, the Bride will also wear a crown.

In the Old Testament (or TanakH as the book was originally called), the crown symbolizes those that were anointed by the Holy Spirit to do the Father's will from the beginning. In Leviticus 8:9, Moses is commanded by YHVH to place a crown on Aaron's head, "And he put the mitre upon his head; also upon the mitre, even upon his forefront, he did put the golden plate, the holy *crown*; as YHVH commanded Moses." The priests were to be crowned. *The born again Israel, first delivered out of slavery, begins to show us what it means to be a royal priesthood in the Tabernacle of YHVH.*

Zechariah 6:11-13 says,

> "Then take silver and gold and make crowns, and set them upon the head of Joshua, the son of Josedech, the high priest; and speak unto him, saying, Thus speaks YHVH tsavaot saying, Behold the man whose name is The BRANCH; and He shall grow up out of His place and He shall build the temple of YHVH." (Joshua symbolizes Yeshua, who will be born from the people of Israel. He will be a priest after the order of Melchisedek, Hebrews 5). "He shall be crowned with everlasting glory. Even He shall build the temple of YHVH; and He shall bear the glory, and shall sit and rule upon His throne; and He shall be a priest upon His throne; and the counsel of peace shall be between them Both, (Jewish and Gentile believers together!)."

"And they that are far off shall come and build in the temple of YHVH" (Zechariah 6:15).

Isaiah 28:5 says, "In that day shall the Lord of hosts be for a *crown of glory*, and for a diadem of beauty unto the residue (the remnant) of His people."

Zechariah 9:16, "And YHVH their God (Eloheyhem) shall save them in that day as the flock of His people, for they shall be as the (jewels) *stones of a crown*, lifted up as an ensign upon His land."

> Come here, I will show you the Bride, the Lamb's wife. And he carried me away in the Holy Spirit to a great and high mountain, and showed me the great city, the holy Jerusalem, descending out of heaven from God. Having the glory of YHVH and her light was like unto a stone most precious, even

like a jasper stone, clear as crystal…

Revelation 12:9-11

Revelation 20:6 says. "Blessed and holy is he that has part in the first resurrection; on such the second death has no power, but they shall be priests of YHVH and of Messiah and shall reign with Him a thousand years."

God speaks in the end days He will crown His Bride. Psalm 65:11 was the Word of the Lord YHVH given to me for 2021, which says, "You crown the year with Your goodness; and Your paths drop abundance." I believe YHVH God is putting on the final touches to His Bride, the crowning glory before Yeshua returns again soon. He is getting us ready!

Again, YHVH by His Spirit confirms the Word given to me clearly that this is so. On January 30, 2021, I wrote this in a journal:

> "An hour ago, I went walking in the woods on the path surrounding my home. I was about one-third of the way around when a little bird came very close, about five or six feet away within eye level, and just flew from branch to branch, not seeming to care how close I was. I stopped to watch her. She was such a small bird about the size of a wren and had a beautiful, yellow cap on her head. She stayed for about three minutes or so and then flew away. I wondered what kind of bird she was, so I asked Elijah, my seven-year-old son, when I got back around the loop to go get the Audubon Bird Book so I could look it up after I went around the loop again. The second time around, I was thinking of corona and crown, and all of a sudden, there was the little bird again. This time in a different location about two-thirds the way around the loop,

> literally on the other side of our woods. This time she draws even closer and then flies directly towards me as if she would land on my shoulders but decides at the last second to instead fly to a little one-foot tall pine seedling tree and hang from there. The tree is about two or three feet from me. She just stays there and gives me a good look at her. I see distinctly her golden crown, and tears start to come. I feel God speak, the golden crown, on my Bride. The little bird flies away, and I know my KING has spoken to me. I finally finish my hike in the woods and open the Audubon Book to find the name of the bird. I think it could be a white-eyed vireo or something like that. I look at the vireos and other perching birds, but none of them look like this bird. Then I see it, a little 3 1/2 inch-4 inch bird with a golden crown–her name/his name, the Golden Crowned Kinglet! Of all the birds to come so close to me, of all the years crowned with sorrow (2020), Yeshua (Jesus) says I have a better crown coming, and I know, because a little bird told me."

Tsiporah qatanah amrah li means in Hebrew, "A little bird told me."

His bride has a much better crown coming than anything this world can give, and He is preparing us now for this final coronation.

Psalm 68:13 says, "Though you have lain among the pots, yet shall you be as the wings of a dove covered with silver, and her feathers with yellow gold."

YHVH God longs for His Bride. His sweetness to those who love Him is so much more than we can imagine. He is calling out to us all the time if we would just be still and listen.

Psalm 45:13 says, “The King’s daughter is all glorious within; her clothing is of wrought gold.” YHVH God is adorning us with His jewels, with a crown, with clothing wrought with gold.

Hanukkah (חנוכה) Revelation

The Bride of Yeshua is being prepared for the day He returns. In the book of Esther, when Esther prepares to go before the king, there was quite a process for her to undergo. Hegai, keeper of the women, was pleased with Esther as he got to know her, so he “quickly gave her the things for purification with such things that belonged to her and seven maidens to help her” (Esther 2:9). This process of purification took twelve months! Six months with oil of myrrh, and six months with sweet perfumes and with other things for purification… (Esther 2:12). Similar to Esther, the Bride of Messiah must be washed clean by the washing of the Water of the Word (Ephesians 5:26). We must be cleansed from apostasy, shallowness, lies of the world by delving deep into the Word of God and knowing it so well that we are washed clean of anything that is not truth.

This past year, we celebrated *Hanukkah* again. The Holy Spirit led me to study the word’s meaning in Hebrew. I found that *Hanukkah* means dedication. So this year, we prayed to rededicate our lives to Yeshua and to the truth of God’s Word. We lit candles and the hanukkiah (*menorah*) as we learned about Hanukkah and how it was and is celebrated throughout the Bible and throughout His story. The dedication of the House of God is through sacrifice, for without the shedding of blood, there is no purification, sanctification from sin. Each temple must be purified and dedicated to YHVH before the light of the Holy Spirit can shine.

So as I continued to study the word Hanukkah, the next question was, "Is the word Hanukkah in the Bible?" As revealed, the word Hanukkah means dedication. So I found the verses that had the word dedication in English. Then I went to look up these same verses in my Hebrew Bible. Each time the people of God dedicated the House of God, the word in the Hebrew Bible is cHanukah חנוכה! So, in the Tabernacle of Moses (Numbers 7:10, 84, 88, 1500 BC), the first Temple built by Solomon (2 Chronicles 7:9, 1000 BC), the Second Temple built by Ezra (Ezra 6:16-17, 515 BC), and the walls of Jerusalem by Nehemiah (Nehemiah 12:27), the re-dedication of the Second Temple after the defilement of Antiochus (although this story is not in the Bible, but in books of history, 167-164 BC), we see the celebration of Hanukkah (Dedication). Mattathias and Judah Maccabee, leaders, courageous, willing to fight for truth at any cost, not willing to bow the knee to pagan idols or pagan teaching, are our examples (like Daniel, like Esther, like MordecHai). Because of their courage and those who followed them, the light of God's House was preserved, and the seed of Israel continued to bring forth our Messiah, Yeshua.

His Name, Yeshua, in Hebrew means salvation. Salvation has come to any that believe in Him and follows Him (meaning knowing, loving, and obeying His Word). Yeshua died on the cross, and by His blood, He came to sanctify and dedicate (cHanukah) His Temple, His Body, His Bride, first to the Jewish people and then to those grafted in from among all nations. Yeshua came to re-dedicate His spiritual House, living stones. Yeshua, our Jewish Messiah, the Light of the world, re-dedicated His people back to Him and then called us to be the light of the world. His Holy Spirit shines in us.

Most people would say the word cHanukah (or Hanukkah in English) is not found in the Bible, but we see, it is! It is a celebration of Light (Holy Spirit) found from the dedication of the first tabernacle with Moses even until now. A remnant has always prevailed who have kept the light burning, just as God said to in Exodus 29:20, "And you shall command the children of Israel that they bring to you pure olive oil beaten for the Light, to cause the lamp to burn always." Jesus (Yeshua) celebrated the Feast of Dedication in John 10:22, the Feast of cHanukah. He came to separate the holy from the profane.

Every time God's temple or tabernacle is dedicated to Him, it is a celebration of cHanukah–this word, dedication, is in the Bible eleven times and also about thirty more times in the words dedicated, dedicate, and dedicating. So, all in all, cHanukah (or a derivative thereof) is found in the Bible over forty times!

The celebration of cHanukah is a celebration of dedication to YHVH, the God of Israel, and the God of all the remnant of nations who are grafted in. God calls us, His Holy Temple made from living stones, to re-dedicate our temples; we are the living temple of God if we have His Holy Spirit. We are called to purity and to separate ourselves from the world's religion and dedicate ourselves to Him. We should all stand with our Jewish brothers and sisters in the true celebration cHanukah–it is for all God's people that love Him, will stand for Him, that truly know YHVH, and want to dedicate (cHanukah) their lives to the Way, the Truth, and the Life. In these days of growing darkness, we must shine forth His Light, no matter the cost. The celebration of Hanukkah is a way to re-connect with our Hebrew roots and see how far back this light has always been kept burning. It has never gone out. There has always been a remnant of Jewish believers who knew Yeshua was the Light of the world, and they are the ones who brought this truth to the world. They have been hidden because of persecution and the apostasy that overtook the House of God, but they have always been there, shining the lights of Hanukkah. All those who have been grafted in from the nations have been shining this light as well. All those who have not understood this can be grafted in with understanding, be re-dedicated unto Yeshua, our Jewish Messiah, and joined together with our Jewish family, those who know Yeshua. His Bride is both Jewish and Gentile believers together as One in Him.

Hanukkiah vs. Menorah

Hanukkah, in the physical sense, was the celebration of the victory over those who were trying to destroy the Jewish people during the period between 200 and 100 BC; Antiochus and others of the pagan world had defiled the House of God, and the Maccabees and those strong Jewish people that stayed true to their faith amidst great persecution, needed to cleanse the house and re-dedicate it to the only true God, the God of Israel, YHVH. It was the time between the Book of Malachi and Matthew. It seems the enemy never sleeps; there is always an attack on God's people who were chosen to carry His message of Salvation to the world. The lampstand (hanukkiah) for this celebration has nine candles, four on one side, one taller in the middle (Shamash, Servant King candle), and four on the other side for the eight days the oil continued miraculously burning in the House of God. However, the menorah used normally in the tabernacles of God had seven candles on the lampstand. Three on each side, and the One in the middle. Again the middle candle represents Yeshua! Seven is a very important number as it signifies completion. After seven days, seven millenials, the Bride will be completely consecrated. In Leviticus 8, we get a glimpse of this as YHVH God speaks to Moses to tell Aaron and his sons how to perform the duties of the priesthood. Leviticus 8:33 says, "And you shall not go out of the door of the tabernacle of the congregation in seven days, until the days of your consecration be at an end; for seven days shall He consecrate you." It is a picture of the seven millennials. The last millennial that we are about to enter, the Bride will reign with Yeshua on the earth in a day of Rest. At the end of this millennial reign (Revelation 20:7-15), the eighth day (the Shemini atzeret mystery of the Feast of Tabernacles) will start, and all will be made new, a new heaven and new earth (Revelation 21). It will all be rolled up like a scroll, the end of this story and the beginning of a brand new one!

We see seven in many other places in the Bible, but one more I want to bring forth. Isaiah 11:1-2 says,

> And there shall come forth a rod out of the stem of Jesse, and a Branch shall grow out of his roots (our Jewish roots); and the Spirit of YHVH shall rest upon Him, the spirit of wisdom and understanding, the spirit of counsel and might, the spirit of knowledge and the fear of YHVH.

In this verse, we see the menorah. The middle candle represents Yeshua filled with the Spirit of YHVH, and on each side of this shamash (Servant King) candle are three candles, each representing the attributes of the Holy Spirit found in believers who know Yeshua, the King of kings: wisdom, understanding, counsel and on the other side, might, knowledge and the fear of YHVH God. The light of the House of God is the Spirit of YHVH! The lamp will always be kept burning in the hearts of true believers! Hallelu*Yah*!

The Sabbath rest, which occurs every seven days, and the seven holy convocations to be held each year are also a picture of the menorah, the seven candles put together as one on a lampstand that brought the *Light* into the Tabernacle of God. The lamp was to be kept continually burning. Three candles on one side, one in the middle, and three on the other side. They all point to Jesus! The Light of the World.

Just like the Maccabees did in the celebration of the first Hanukkah, we need a re-dedication in the House of God. We need to clean out that which has been defiled, that which is false, that which is shallow, that which is apostate and heal the breaches in the House of God.

Ezekiel 47 Revelation

To explain this revelation, I will need to tell a story. At the beach last year during my prayer time one morning, I felt the Lord prompt me with a new idea; instead of sitting on the beach chair and then jumping in the ocean to play and refresh like we had been doing each day, I felt excited to walk down the beach, with whoever would go with me, for about three miles until we reached a fishing pier we had visited a few days before. My three daughters decided to go with me while the rest of the family would drive to a nearby smaller pier on the bayside of Topsail Island and do some fishing there. They would meet us at the beach and pick us up at the ocean pier at the end of the journey. All that said, we set out enjoying the sunshine, warm waves, and sand beneath our feet as the Lord ordered our steps. Finally, we made it to the pier, which jutted out into the sea. The tide was coming in, and I was in awe of what God wanted to show me and my daughters and family. The picture below shows what the pier from underneath "hidden" looked like; to me, it reminded me of a Tabernacle, a House of God, a long temple with many pillars set high above the waters; at the end was a post with branches that looked just like a *TREE*. Oh Lord, this beautiful Story You have written ends where it all began, with the Tree of Life; yet this time You reign over all the waters forever, all the nations, and we who are Yours, are again given access to the Tree of Life. All those who humble themselves under the mighty Hand of God and the Kingship of Yeshua HaMashiacH, who is the Tree of Life, will eat from this tree and drink from this fountain of Living Waters freely and forever. I praise You YaHaVaH God Who is over all the nations and all powers, and all kingdoms and over all authority and principalities. You, Yeshua, reign over all forever and ever. YaHaVaH (with the YAH at the beginning and possible ahava in the middle of His Name, meaning Love in Hebrew) is again building His Tabernacle of David, but this time, with living stones. We are that Tabernacle!

Psalm 29:3: "The voice of the Lord is over the waters; the God of glory thunders; The Lord is heard over many waters."

Revelation 17:15: "And He says unto me, The waters which you saw,…are peoples, and multitudes, and nations and tongues."

> In the midst of the street of it, and on either side of the river, was there the tree of life, ... and the leaves of the tree were for the healing of nations. And there shall be no more curse (tree of knowledge of good and evil is gone forever); but the throne of God and of the Lamb shall be in it; and His servants shall serve Him.
>
> Revelation 22:2-3

Blessed are they that do His commandments, that they may have right to the Tree of Life, and may enter in through the gates into the city (Revelation 22:14).

But this was just the beginning of what YHVH God wanted to show me. About four or five months later, I went to a prophetic conference, which I have not done in years. The inside of the conference building had a sanctuary, hotel rooms, and a few shops to peruse. I was drawn to an Israeli shop. It was the only one like it, for the conference was not at all about Israel, although I wish it had been. Here, I felt at home. I began to talk with the shop owner of all kinds of things as we both shared some of our experiences in the nation of Israel. He had visited Israel many more times than I did, but our love for Israel was the same. I then went to look at the things he had for sale in his shop, and my eyes rested on a beautiful picture of a Bride making her way to the Lion of Judah. She was in a great white majestic hall; water was poured out across the hall and had made it to her ankles. She was lifting her wedding dress and walking toward an arch that within stood a great symbol of Yeshua, a beautiful, strong Lion whose eyes were riveted on her. I knew YHVH God was speaking for the picture reminded me strongly of the pier at the beach. It looked just like it except with a lot more details and different symbolism. Yet the water at the ankles was there even as the waters were coming in under the pier and rushed around our feet and then our knees and continued to get higher as the tide came in. Of course, I bought the picture the next day after praying about it. I wanted to make sure it was for me. YHVH God confirmed it was. He was telling me again that He is coming soon for His Bride, and He will rule over all the waters, all the nations, even as He is preparing His Bride. To see the picture visit https://jnesbit.com/products/awaiting-the-king.

A month or so later, I was looking for a Scripture that I can't remember now. All I know is what I was searching for was not where God led me that morning. He led me straight to Ezekiel 47 and said in my spirit, this is the picture I gave you. Ezekiel 47:1-3 says,

> Afterward He brought me again unto the door of the House; and behold, waters issued from under the threshold of the house eastward; for the forefront of the house stood toward the east, and the waters came down from under from the right side of the House, at the south side of the altar. Then He brought me out of the way of the North Gate and led me about the way without to the outer gate by the way that looks eastward; and behold, there ran out waters on the right side. And the man that had the line in his hand went forth eastward, he measured a thousand cubits, and he brought me through the waters; the waters were to the ankles.

The next few verses speak of the man measuring out another 1000 cubits (which is about 1500 feet) and the water rising to the knees, and then another measurement, and the waters rising to the waist, and then once again measuring and the waters overflowing and becoming so deep that "I could not pass over, for the waters were risen, waters to swim in, a river that could not be passed over" (Ezekiel 47:5). As I meditated on this passage of Scripture, I knew YHVH God was speaking of His Holy Spirit outpour upon His Bride. It will be as the days of Noah. The waters will wash His Bride, yet the waters will drown all wickedness at the same time. Only those in the ark, in the safety of Yeshua, will survive this Holy outpour. More than survive, God's people will be empowered to do YHVH's will in times of great darkness.

I was overwhelmed by this message. I felt God speak that the washing will begin with the feet of His Bride. It reminded me of when Yeshua knelt before His disciples and washed all their feet. Peter did not want this to be so. Yet Yeshua said to Peter, "If I do not wash your feet, you can have no part with me." Of course, Peter essentially responds, "Then not only my feet but wash all of me." Jesus says to Peter, only your feet need to be washed. The rest of you will follow your feet, as your feet follow Me (John 13:1-17).

God speaks, "The Bride needs to be cleansed and rededicated to Me." Over and over, I hear this same message. It is time for the Bride to turn and rivet her eyes on Yeshua even as His eyes are upon us. We must turn away from shallowness, unity with the world's ways, fear of man's opinions, apostate teaching that would divide and separate Ruth (Gentile) from Boaz (Jewish), Deborah (prophetess) from Barak (military commander), God from His Name, the God of Abraham, Isaac, and Jacob, the God of Israel, YHVH, Yeshua, the *arm* of the Almighty God, the only true God of all the earth. It is time for the Bride to rise up to do the will of the Father, even as our King is rising up and coming back to us soon to take us Home!

As I was asking YHVH for ideas for the cover of this book, I came across a picture of the Jabbok River, the location where Jacob becomes Israel in Genesis 32. Through a series of events, the front cover was put together and I saw the same vision for the third time. The Bride of Yeshua washing her feet in the living water, getting ready to meet Yeshua, the Lion of Judah. Three is a number of completion. I hear the vision is true. This is where we are in time. Like Jacob, the Bride of Yeshua must also understand her lost identity and gain her true identity in Israel and the God of Israel. This is where Jewish and Gentile believers come together as One, and where heaven and earth meet again.

And in the Twinking of an Eye–The Raptures Revelation

Yet before we are taken out of this world, we have work to do. Isaiah 62:11 says, “Behold YHVH has proclaimed unto the end of the world, Say ye to the daughter of Zion, Behold, your Salvation comes; behold, His reward is with Him and His work before Him.” And Isaiah 40:10 says, “Behold, YHVH God will come with strong hand, and His arm shall rule for Him; behold His reward is with Him and His work before Him.” And once again, Revelation 22:12

says, "And behold I come quickly; and My reward is with Me, to give every person according as his work shall be."

Still, there is coming a day when after our work is done here… the great lifting up, raising up of God's people after the sound of the Trumpet will occur, also known as the rapture. The great controversy is the timing, pre-tribulation, or post-tribulation. I believe that briefly, here is a good place to address what YHVH spoke to me about this, even though I know these are deep waters and each person must go before the Lord YHVH themselves and find peace on this issue, although it is not at all a Salvation issue.

One morning, as I pondered the timing of the "rapture," I felt the Holy Spirit ask me how many "raptures" happened in the TanakH or, as we call it, the Old Testament. Immediately my mind went to two people: Enoch and Elijah. So, there are two. The Holy Spirit reminds me of Isaiah 46:9-10, which says,

> Remember the former things of old; for I am God, and there is none else; I am God (Elohim), and there is none like Me, declaring the end from the beginning, and from ancient times the things that are not yet done, saying, My counsel shall stand, and I will do all My pleasure.

The Holy Spirit reminds me that much of the Old Testament is a shadow of things to come, and it points to and symbolizes future spiritual events. I see that God is telling me there will be two "raptures" or gatherings up to Him. One that is pre-tribulation like Enoch, and one post-tribulation like Elijah. Could it be that both sides of this debate are correct? The Lord YHVH speaks to me through the Holy Spirit, Enoch represents My Bride; as Enoch pleased Me, so does My Bride in these days. She will be taken out before the Tribulation gets severe. I believe we will be taken at or soon after the three and a half years mark when the Tribulation begins. The "rapture" of Elijah happens at the end of the Tribulation; it is for those who are His but have not been committed to God's Word; yet when they see and understand the first rapture and realize they have been "left behind," they will know there is a fight ahead of them (like Elijah against the 850 false prophets). They will have to endure the Tribulation, and many will be executed, but they will not receive the mark of the beast and will also be a light to those still on the earth that will come to Yeshua because of their testimony during this horrific time.

So what are the Scriptures that support this? Some Scriptures seem to point to a pre-tribulation rapture, while others very clearly point to a post-tribulation gathering. Let's look at a few. Maybe both camps on this issue are right but only seeing part of the picture!

Scriptures supporting the Enoch rapture are 1 Corinthians 15:51 (written above).

First Thessalonians 4:16-18 says,

> For the Lord Himself shall descend from heaven with a shout, with the voice of the archangel, and the Trump of God, and the dead in Messiah shall rise (יקומו, yiqumu) first. Then, we which are alive and remain, shall be caught (taken) up (נלקח nilaqacH) together with them in the clouds, to meet the Lord in the air, and so shall we ever be with the Lord. Wherefore comfort one another with these words.

We are comforted because we, as Yeshua's Bride, are not to go through the Tribulation. Yeshua calls us out before the wrath of satan hits the earth, and the vials of God are poured out upon men.

Second Thessalonians 2:1-7, and 17 which says,

> Now we beseech you, brethren, by the coming of our Lord Jesus Christ, and by our GATHERING together (the Hebrew word asiftenu, אסיפתנו meaning a HARVEST gathering, not just gathering, is used in this passage) unto Him, that you be not soon shaken in mind, or be troubled, neither by spirit, nor by word, nor by letter as from us, as that day of Messiah is at hand. Let no man deceive you by any means; for that day shall NOT come, except there come a falling away first (the love of people for God will fall away), and that man of sin (anti-christ) be revealed, the son of perdition; who opposes and exalts himself above all that is called God, or that is worshipped; so that he as God sits in the Temple of God, showing himself (or proclaiming) that he is God. Do you not remember that when I was yet with you, I told you these things? And now you know what restrains that he might be revealed in his time (the appointed time). For the Mystery of iniquity does already work; only He who now restrains will restrain, until He be taken out of the way.

This passage of Scripture speaks of the end times when the Bride of Yeshua shall be harvested, taken out of the way as soon as we see a great falling away and the anti-christ just being revealed. Many will begin to follow him and leave YHVH's House for this new god. Soon thereafter, the Bride of Yeshua will be taken out (asif, harvested) before the Tribulation begins in earnest. The Holy Spirit in us restrains the anti-christ from taking full power until the Bride of Yeshua has completed her work on the earth and then is taken up at the three and a half years mark of the beginning of the Tribulation or very soon, within days, thereafter. With the Bride taken, the earth becomes very dark and evil. Those left will have to fight every day for their lives if they refuse to worship the beast, the antichrist.

Zechariah 14:4-5 gives a picture of Jesus returning to fight the final battle of Armegeddon, to fight for His people still left on the earth that have "fought the good fight" like Elijah. The Scripture says,

> And His feet shall stand that day upon the Mount of Olives (where Jesus returns), which is before Jerusalem on the east, and the Mount of Olives shall cleave in the midst (great earthquake) toward the east and toward the west, and there shall be a great valley; and half of the mountain shall remove toward the north, and half of it toward the south. And you shall flee to the valley of the mountains; for the valley of the mountains shall reach unto Azal; yes, you shall flee (these are the Jewish people that are fleeing from the Palestinians that live in the West Bank, after the seven year peace plan is established). These Jewish people and all other persecuted living in this horrific time of Tribulation are commanded to flee to the valley …Yes, you shall flee, like as you fled from before the earthquake in the days of Uzziah king of Judah; and the Lord YHVH my God shall come, and all the saints with you.

Here it speaks of Yeshua coming back again with His saints (Jewish and Gentile believers together). We have already met Him in the air, and now this time, His feet touch the earth. This lets us know that the Bride has already been taken and has been in heaven with Jesus celebrating but also preparing for the day when we will come back with Yeshua to see the Battle of Armageddon, maybe even to fight with Jesus. Although He can defeat the enemy with a Word, He may choose to make us full participants in His glory.

There are other Scriptures that speak of God hiding His Bride, such as in Joel 2:16.

Joel 2:16 says, "Gather (asifu, אסיפו) the people, sanctify the congregation, assemble the elders, gather the children, and those that suck the breasts, let the Bridegroom go forth of His chamber, and the Bride out of her closet."

Isaiah 26:20-21 is similar to Joel 2:16 and says,

> Come My people, enter into your chambers and shut your doors about you; hide yourself as it were for a little moment, until the indignations be overpast. For behold, the Lord YHVH comes out of His place to punish the inhabitants of the earth for their iniquity; the earth also shall disclose her blood, and shall no more cover her slain.

The Bride is to be hidden for a time. For such a time as this… Esther. Again, the Lord YHVH pours out revelation. Esther's original name was cHadassah which means Myrtle, like a Myrtle tree. Her name was changed to Esther when she became Queen so that she could hide her identity. Many have interpreted her name to mean Star, from the Greek. Yet in Hebrew, the Lord revealed to me, Nistar means hidden, and Estar would be "I will hide." The Esthers of today will be hidden from the wrath to come because of their faithfulness to God's Word and to His people; we serve the God of Abraham, Isaac, and Jacob; we serve the God of Israel; to the Jewish people who gave us the Word of God and our Jewish Messiah, we are to be forever grateful and to love them back into the Kingdom of God, and we are to raise up our voices, like Esther, to stand against antisemitism in all its forms, and to stand with and love our Jewish brothers and sisters. To be an Esther is to be hidden in the time of wrath. The Bride will have Jewish roots. She has gained the King's favor and is to be given authority for such a time as this.

Esther 9:29 says, "Then Esther, the Queen, the daughter of Abi-haEL (which means My Father God) and Mordecai the Jew wrote with all authority… to confirm the second letter of Purim."

Jude 14:15-23 says,

> And Enoch also the seventh from Adam, prophesied of these, saying, Behold the Lord YHVH comes with ten thousands of His saints (kedoshim, holy ones)… We will come back with Yeshua to execute judgement on all who are left on the earth. Many will be mockers and completely evil and will not turn to YHVH even with all the tribulation going on, but others (those to be saved in the second "rapture"), God says, we His Bride, "need to have compassion on them, making a difference. And others save with fear, pulling them out of the fire, hating even the garment spotted by the flesh."

Colossians 3:1-4 says, If you then be risen with Messiah, seek those things which are above, where Messiah sits on the right hand of God. Set your affection on things above, not on things on the earth. For you are dead (to the world), and your life is *hid* with Messiah Jesus in God. When Messiah (Greek word Christ), who is our life, shall appear, then shall you also appear with Him in glory.

Scriptures supporting the Elijah's "rapture" include Matthew 24:29, Revelation 20:4. Matthew 24:29-31 says,

> Immediately AFTER THE TRIBULATION of those days, shall the sun be darkened, and the moon shall not give her light, and the stars shall fall from heaven, and the powers of the heavens shall be shaken, and then shall appear the sign of the Son of man in heaven, and then shall all the tribes of the

> earth mourn, and they shall see the Son of man coming in the clouds of heaven with power and great glory. And He shall send His angels with a great sound of a trumpet and they shall gather (Hebrew word here for they shall gather is ve'qabetzu, root word qabetz, קבץ which means grouping together and differentiated from asif, harvest gathering) His ELECT (those that were always His but did not come to know Him until the days of Tribulation) from the four winds, from one end of heaven to the other.

Clearly, this "gathering" occurs after the days of Tribulation but before the outpour of YHVH Yeshua's wrath on the rebellious nations. God gathers these people out of the way so they will not be destroyed in the outpour of His wrath at the Battle of Armageddon. These are the ones that will go into the millennial age as mortals and live long lives in the presence of Yeshua. Isaiah 65:19-25 says,

> And I will rejoice in Jerusalem, and joy in My people; and the voice of weeping shall be no more heard in her, nor the voice of crying. There shall not more be an infant of days, nor an old man that has not filled his days; for the child shall die one hundred years old; but the sinner being a hundred years old shall be accursed. And they shall build houses, and inhabit them; and they shall plant vineyards, and eat the fruit of them. They shall not build, and another inhabit; they shall not plant, and another eat; for as the days of a tree are the days of My people, and mine ELECT shall long enjoy the work of their hands. They shall not labor in vain, nor bring forth for trouble; they are the seed of the blessed of the Lord YHVH and their offspring with them.

These are those who will be on the earth as mortals for the next

1000 years bearing children. They are the ones like Noah, set aside in the ark, saved from God's judgment on the earth. In the days of Noah, God judged the earth with a flood, and so in these days, just like in the days of Noah, YHVH God will judge the earth, but this time by fire. But before He does this, He will gather (qebatz) and save in the ark of Yeshua His elect that will repopulate the earth for the next 1000 years, and these are those who make it through the Tribulation period alive that refused the mark of the Beast.

Revelation 20:4-5 says,

> And I saw thrones, and they sat upon them, and judgement was given unto them; and I saw the souls of them that were beheaded for the witness of Jesus, and for the Word of God, and which had not worshipped the beast neither his image, neither had received his mark upon their foreheads, or in their hands; and they lived and reigned with Messiah a thousand years. But the rest of the dead lived not again until the thousand years were finished. This is the first resurrection.

The word for resurrection is *hatcHiYah*, התחיה and is also different from the words asif (harvest gathering for bride), and qebatz (grouping and hiding in ark away from God's fire judgment which are those who make it alive through the Tribulation). The word resurrection is used for those who died during the Tribulation and were resurrected at this time to join Yeshua and His Bride to reign as priests over the people separated as elect and left on the earth to again repopulate the earth for the next thousand years, as Noah and his family did. We see the elect will be saved like Noah and remain as mortals on the earth and will birth children, some that will love Yeshua and then some who will not. At the end of the next thousand years, Satan will be released again, and there will be those on the earth, mortals, who will join him once again. A final final battle will occur where satan is permanently defeated and all those who aligned themselves with him. After the seventh millennial begins the eighth (Shemini atzeret), and forevermore, all will be rolled up like a scroll with a completely new heaven and earth. (Read Revelation 20:1-15 and Revelation 21:1-2).

So, in reality, there is a rapture (asif) of His Bride before the Tribulation. There is a separation or grouping of the Elect who do not take the mark of the beast during Tribulation who will continue to live during the seventh millennial on the earth (qebatz), and there is a resurrection of those beheaded (hatcHiYah) during the Tribulation that will join the Bride to rule and reign with Yeshua those left on the earth for the next 1000 years. So maybe not two raptures (especially since this particular word is never really used in the Bible), but there are definitely gatherings and separation of His people (wheat and barley from the tares) at the beginning of the Tribulation and at the end.

Filling the Sea of Galilee
(my experience in Israel, the news in 2020!)

We are getting ready for the greatest outpour! From Mt. cHermon, to the Sea of Galilee, to the Jordan, to Mt. Zion to the Dead Sea… It's coming alive again!

Ezekiel 47 goes on to say,

> And he said unto me, Son of man, have you seen this? Then he brought me, and caused me to return to the brink of the river. Now when I had returned behold, at the bank of the river were very many trees on the one side and on the other. The he

> said unto me, These waters issue out toward the east region, and go down into the desert, and go into the sea; which being brought forth into the sea, the waters shall be healed. And it shall come to pass, that everything that lives, which moves, whithersoever the rivers shall come, shall live; and there shall be a very great multitude of fish, because these waters shall come there; for they shall be healed; and everything shall live where the river comes.
>
> Ezekiel 47:6-9

It is a prophesy coming true in our day. When I was in Israel, we sailed on the King David boat on the Sea of Galilee. The Sea was drying up and in danger of getting to very low levels that could not sustain the amount of water being taken out. I remember being touched by the Holy Spirit, crying almost the whole time on that boat tour. I was so deeply touched that I was on the Sea of Galilee, the place where Yeshua calmed the storm and walked upon the waters, yet something more was going on. I could feel His presence standing right there with me! In the back of my mind, I wanted the waters to rise again. I wanted the Sea of Galilee to be healed. When I got back home to the United States, I watched the Israeli newspapers to see the status of the Sea of Galilee. Miraculously the waters, after decades of decline, were beginning to rise again. My heart rejoiced and still rejoices to see the Sea of Galilee water levels rising so high that the dams may need to be opened to release some of the overflow! Yes, God does in the physical what He is about to do in the spiritual.

Here are some of the words I wrote about this just last year. On April 17, 2020, I wrote, the Sea of Galilee water levels are healthy and strong again! I rejoice! I have been watching this climb in water level for two years since sailing on the Sea in 2018 when waters were very low. Isaiah 43:19 "Behold, I will do a new thing; now it shall spring forth; shall you not know it? I will even make a way in the wilderness, and rivers in the desert." God pours water (living water) on a dry and thirsty land (His people) even as we watch Him heal the Sea of Galilee. Praise You Abba Father, Yeshua, Holy Spirit (EcHad)!

"As the dew of Hermon, and as the dew that descended upon the mountains of Zion–for there the Lord commanded the blessing, even life forevermore" (Psalm 133:3).

The water and snow that fall on the mountains of Bashan, Mt. Hermon in Northern Israel, make their way to the Sea of Galilee, which pours out waters to the Jordan River and eventually into the Dead Sea. As the Dead Sea receives these waters, it is beginning to heal slowly. Miraculously, scientists in Israel are beginning to find small pools around the edges of the Dead Sea with life in them! This has never been seen before! Quietly, in His still small voice, God is working behind the scenes, and only those who are seeking, searching, looking for Him will see He has been with us all along.

This is in fulfillment of the rest of Ezekiel 47, which says,

> And it shall come to pass that the fishers shall stand upon it from Engedi even unto Eneglaim; they shall be a place to spread forth nets; their fish shall be according to their kinds, as the fish of the great sea, exceeding many. But the miry places thereof and the marshes shall not be healed; they shall be given to salt.
>
> Ezekiel 47:10-11

This prophecy speaks of the healing of the Dead Sea. It is happening before our eyes. God is working in our midst. He will bring what is dead back to life, yet there will always be a portion that will refuse life, the miry places that will not be healed.

He is pouring out His Spirit to build. This year, 2021, the waters will come to our ankles but will rise ever higher in the coming years to overflow. YHVH Yeshua is putting on the final touches to His Bride and His Holy Temple. We must notice. We must respond. We must run to Him.

> And he made the pillars, and two rows round about upon the one network, to cover the chapiters that were upon the top with pomegranates; and so, he did for the other chapiter. And the chapiters that were upon the top of the pillars were of *lily work* in the porch four cubits. And the chapiters upon the two pillars had pomegranates also above, over against the belly which was by the network; and the pomegranates were two hundred in rows round about upon the other chapiter. And he set up the pillar in the porch of the temple; and He set up the right pillar and called the name thereof Jachin; and he set up the left pillar, and called the name thereof Boaz. And upon the top of the pillars was *lily work, so was the work of the pillars finished.*
>
> 1 Kings 7:18-22

This is the Tabernacle of David, the final touches. And this is lily work…

Chapter Thirteen

A Song, a Prayer, Warriors of God

Twelve chapters was the original plan, but I hear YHVH God speak once more. Since coming back from Israel, I have learned a little Hebrew and continue to study this beautiful language that Jesus (Yeshua) spoke (Acts 26:14) as much as I can, biblical and conversational, almost every day. It is a language the Lord YHVH promised to restore in the last days as He knew much of it would be lost or destroyed after the Jewish dispersions of 70 AD and 135 AD and the controversies and separations during the Councils of Nicaea and Laodicea that we have studied earlier. Zephaniah 3:9 says, "For then (in the last days) I will restore to the people a pure language, that they may all call upon the name of YHVH to serve him with one accord." In the late 1800s to early 1900s, YHVH God called a man named Eliezer Ben Yehuda and his family to do exactly that–to revive the Hebrew language in the promised reborn Israel![23]

So as I study this revived language, one of the things I learned is that each Hebrew letter has a numerical value. God reminds me of the word *ahava*, the word for love in Hebrew. It is spelled אהבה or Alef (numerical value 1), Hey (5), Vet or Bet (2) and again Hey (5). If you add these up, Ahava has a numerical value of thirteen. Okay, so I see His Story is all about Love, and a thirteenth chapter is a perfect way to speak Love, for surely all of History was for the union of Yeshua with His Bride. We could end with the Song of Solomon yet, I believe the song of Deborah is what is needed. It is the song really of Deborah and Barak together. As we stand together in unity, Jewish and Gentile true believers in Yeshua, man, and woman filled with the Holy Spirit, a great victory is coming, and Yeshua is the Lord of hosts who leads us on! He goes before us, and in Him, we are victorious!

In Judges 4, Deborah prophesies unto Barak,

> Up; for this is the day which YHVH has delivered Sisera (the captain of the host of King Jabin, a Canaanite) into your hand; Is not YHVH gone out before you? So Barak went down from Mount Tabor and ten thousand men after him. And the Lord YHVH discomfited Sisera, and all his chariots, and all his host, with the edge of the sword before Barak; so that Sisera lighted down off his chariot, and fled away on his feet.
>
> Judges 4:14-15

Barak, the military commander, was used by YHVH to take down the whole army of King Jabin, yet Sisera, the captain, the head of the army, escapes. Now God uses a woman to finish this war. Sisera runs to the house of Jael, Heber's wife, looking for refuge. She hides him but not for his good. She knows that King Jabin and the Canaanites have oppressed her people for twenty years. She is brave as a warrior. Sisera, exhausted from the battle, falls asleep.

Judges 4:21 tells what happens next. "Then Jael, Heber's wife took a nail of the tent, and took a hammer in her hand, and went softly unto him (Sisera) and smote the nail into his temples, and fastened it into the ground, for he was fast asleep and weary. So he died."

The victory is complete.

> And behold as Barak pursued Sisera, Jael (meaning to ascend or mountain goat) came out to meet him, and said unto him, Come, and I will show you the man whom you seek. And when he came into her tent, behold, Sisera lay dead, and the nail was in his temples. So God subdued on that day Jabin the king of Canaan before the children of Israel. And the *hand* of the children of Israel prospered and prevailed against Jabin the king of Canaan, until they had destroyed Jabin king of Canaan.
>
> Judges 4:22-24

It is prophetic, these words. YHVH God will use man and woman together to defeat the enemy, with the prophetic word (Deborah) to encourage His army to move forward. He is the One leading us all on!

Genesis 3:15 says, "And I will put enmity between you (satan) and the woman, and between your seed (the tares) and hers (the barley and the wheat); her seed shall crush your head, and you shall bruise His heel."

The Book of Judges Chapter five is the song of Deborah and Barak that they sang together after the great victory over the Canaanites. The song of Deborah and Barak, together… Judges 5.

Let's sing it, or maybe just read it together!

Judges Chapter 5

Then sang Deborah and Barak the son of Abinoam on that

day saying, Praise ye the Lord YHVH for the avenging of Israel, when people willingly offered themselves. Hear, O ye kings; give ear, O ye princes; I, even I, will sing unto YHVH; I will sing praise to the Lord God of Israel. (And we will sing too.) Hear, O ye kings; give ear, O ye princes; I, even I, will sing unto YHVH; I will sing praise to the Lord God of Israel. YHVH, when You went out of Seir, when You marched out of the field of Edom, the earth trembled, and the heavens dropped, the clouds also dropped water. The mountains melted from before YHVH, even that Sinai from before YHVH God of Israel. In the days of Shamgar the son of Anath, in the days of Jael, the highways were unoccupied, and the travelers walked through byways. The inhabitants of the villages ceased, they ceased in Israel, until that I Deborah arose, that I arose a mother in Israel. They chose new gods; then was war in the gates. Was there a shield or spear seen among forty thousand in Israel? My heart is with the governors of Israel, that offered themselves willingly among the people. Bless ye YHVH. Speak, you that ride on white donkeys, you that sit in judgment, and walk by the way. They that are delivered from the noise of archers in the places of drawing water, there shall they recount the righteous acts of YHVH, even the righteous acts toward the inhabitants of His villages in Israel; then shall the people of YHVH go down to the gates. Awake, awake, Deborah; Awake, awake, utter a song; Arise Barak, and lead your captivity captive, thou son of Abinoam. Then He made him that remains to have dominion over the nobles among the people. YHVH made me have dominion over the mighty. Out of Ephraim, there was a root of them against Amalek. After you, Benjamin, among your people; out of MacHir came down rulers, and out of Zebulun they that handle the pen of a writer. *And the princes of IssacHar were with Deborah; even IssacHar, and also Barak.* He was sent on foot into the valley. For the divisions of Reuben there were great thoughts of heart. Why do you abide among the sheepfolds, to hear the bleating of the flocks? For the divisions of Reuben there were great searchings of heart. Gilead abode beyond Jordan: and why did Dan remain in ships? Asher continued on the seashore, and abode in his breaches. Zebulun and Naphtali were a people that jeopardized their lives unto the death in the high places of the field. The kings came and fought, then fought the kings of Canaan in Ta'anacH by the waters of Megiddo; they took no gain of money. They fought from heaven; the stars in their courses fought against Sisera. The River of Kishon swept them away, that ancient river, the River Kishon. O my soul, You have trodden down strength. Then were the horse hooves broken by the means of the prancings, the prancings of the mighty ones. Curse you Meroz, said the angel of YHVH, curse you bitterly the inhabitants thereof; because they came not to the help of YHVH, to the help of YHVH against the mighty. Blessed above women shall Jael, the wife of Heber the Kenite be, blessed shall she be above all woman in the tent. He asked for water, and she gave him milk; she brought forth butter in a lordly dish. She put her hand to the nail, and her right hand to the workman's hammer; and with the hammer she smote Sisera, she smote off his head, when she had pierced and stricken through his temples. At her feet he bowed, he fell, he lay down; at her feet he bowed, he fell; where he bowed, there he fell down dead. Three times this scripture says he bowed at her feet. Three is the number of completion as well. In the Hebrew, it signifies, It is finished, it is sealed. The mother of Sisera looked out at a window, and cried through the lattice, Why is his chariot so long in coming? Why tarry the wheels of his chariots? Her wise ladies answered her, yea, she returned answer to herself. Have they not found? Have they not divided the prey, to ev-

> ery man a damsel or two; to Sisera a prey of divers colors, a prey of divers colors of needlework, of divers colors of needlework on both sides, meet for the necks of them that take the spoil? So, let all Your enemies perish, O YHVH; but let them that LOVE HIM be as the sun when He goes forth in His Might. And the land had REST forty years.

The words to this song are prophetic for the days to come. They are what happened in the TanakH, or Old Testament, a specific event that points to an event that will surely come to pass again on a much greater scale. It speaks of the War at Megiddo (Judges 5:19). This is the coming Armageddon where Yeshua will come and fight for His people. There will be great sadness in that day for those who do not know Him, but yet great Victory for those who do! A Final Victory for a thousand years…

Deborah, a prophetess with a name that comes from the Hebrew root dibber, "She speaks, dibrah," with a spirit lit on fire like torches (Holy Spirit fire); she spoke truth no matter what the cost. She judged Israel for forty years.

And then (after the war) the land has rest forty years…We enter into the millennial age, the Sabbath Rest, where under Yeshua, the land will have rest for a thousand years, and then forevermore.

> "Amen. Even so, Come, Lord Yeshua," Come! (Revelation 22:20).

Bo, Yeshua, Bo! Yesh bi Ahava ve'hi titorer ve'tiga. Yesha bi Ahava ve'hi tenatzeacH. Yesh bi Ahava! A beautiful song in the Hebrew language about LOVE, YHVH God's Love that wins the VICTORY.[24] You can find the Yesh Bi Ahava Song on youtube.

Shoshana of David, the Lily of David, the Bride of Messiah,

SoD (means mystery or secret in Hebrew), סוד A Mystery being revealed in our day!

As the lily (Shoshana) among thorns, so is my love among the daughters. Song of Songs 2:2

"Your neck is like the tower of David built for an armory, whereon hang a thousand shields, all the quivers of warriors" (Song of Solomon 4:4).

"Return, return O Shulamite; return, return, that we may look upon thee. What will we see in the Shulamite? As it were the company of two armies" (Song of Songs 6:13).

The Bride, beautiful, fierce in battle, the Tabernacle of David, the army of God, returning to Him in the beautiful dance of the MacHanaim מחנים (the dance of the two armies), Jewish and Gentile together, men and women filled with the Holy Spirit, heaven and earth together again in the city of Jerusalem.

> Sing and rejoice O daughter of Zion; for lo, I come, and I will dwell in the midst of you, says YHVH. And many nations shall be joined to YHVH in that day and shall be My people; and I will dwell in the midst of thee, and you shall know that the Lord of hosts has sent me unto you. And the Lord shall inherit Judah, His portion in the holy land, and shall choose Jerusalem again. Be silent, O all flesh, before YHVH, for He is raised up out of His holy Habitation.
>
> Zechariah 2:10-13

"I will rejoice in YHVH, I will joy in the God of my Salvation. The Lord YHVH is my strength, and He will make my feet like deer's feet, and He will make me to walk upon mine high places" (Habakkuk 3:18-19).

Grace and the Law together
Jewish and Gentile believers in Yeshua together
Holy Spirit filled man and woman together
Prophesy!

Recommended Reading

Bernis, Jonathan, A Rabbi Looks at the Last Days, Surprising Insights on Israel, the End Times, and Popular Misconceptions, Bloomington, MN, Chosen Books, 2013.

Bible Things in Bible Ways, Was The New Testament Written in Greek or Hebrew?, biblethingsinbibleways.wordpress.com/2013/11/14/was-the-new-testament-written-in-greek-or-in-hebrew/

Edwards, Gene, The Christian Woman Set Free, Women Freed from Second-Class Citizenship in the Kingdom of God, Jacksonville, FL, SeedSowers Publishing, 2005.

Finto, Don, Your People Shall Be My People, Updated and Expanded, Bloomington, MN, Chosen Books, 2001, 2016.

Finto, Don, The Handbook for the End Times, Hope, Help and Encouragement for Living in the Last Days, Bloomington, MN, Chosen Books, 2018.

Hagee, John, In Defense of Israel, The Bible's Mandate for Supporting the Jewish State, Lake Mary, Florida, Frontline Charisma House Book Group, 2007.

Hagee, John, Why Israel?, The Jewish State's Biblical Roots, Miraculous Rebirth and Modern Trials, (Booklet), San Antonio, TX, CUFI, 2019.

Pressfield, Steven, The Lion's Gate, On the Front Lines of the Six Day War, New York, New York, Penguin Group, 2015.

Rosenberg, Joel C., The People, The Land, and the Future of Israel, Israel and the Jewish People in the Plan of God, Grand Rapids, MI, Kregel Publications, 2014.

Roth, Sid, They Thought for Themselves, Ten Amazing Jews, U.S.A., Sid Roth, 2009.

Stern, David H. PH.D., Restoring the Jewishness of the Gospel, A Message for Christians, Clarksville, MD, Lederer Books, 2009.

Wolff, Robert F., Awakening the One New Man, Shippensburg, PA, Destiny Image Publishers, Inc., 2011.

Bible Resources

Hebrew-English New Covenant, Prophecy Edition, Powder Springs, GA, presented to the Jewish Nation by Hope of Israel Publications, hopeofisrael.net, 2009.

The Israel Bible, תנ"ך, edited by Rabbi Tuly Weisz, New Milford, CT, and Jerusalem, Israel, Menorah Books, 2018.

The Holy Bible, Old and New Testaments, Authorized King James Version, Thomas Nelson, Inc., 2003.

Messianic and Israel Ministries

One for Israel

Fellowship of Israel Related Ministries (FIRM)

Jews for Jesus

God TV–specifically, Shelanu.tv

Israel Media Ministries

MaOz Israel

Chosen People

International Christian Embassy Jerusalem (ICEJ)

Jewish Voice

Lev Ha'Olam (works against BDS Movement)

Magen Adom David (non-profit emergency rescue in Israel)

Sid Roth's One New Man Ministry

Friends of Zion (CUFI)

CBN Israel and TBN Israel

And Many Others

Now YHVH had said unto Abram, Get thee out of your country, and from your kindred, and from your father's house,

> unto a land that I will show you. And I will make of you a great nation, and I will bless you, and make your name great; and you shall be a blessing; and I will bless them that bless you and curse him that curses you. And in you shall all the families of the earth be blessed.
>
> Genesis 12:1-3

It is a promise from our heavenly Father. He will bless those of the nations who bless Israel and her people. We are grafted into the family of God when we understand where we came from and how we have been immensely blessed by the Jewish people.

Endnotes

1 Spurgeon, The Church of Christ NPSP 1:213-214 archive.spurgeon.org/misc/eschat2.php#55

2Why Israel? The Jewish State's Biblical Roots, Miraculous Rebirth, and Modern Trials, CUFI, 2019.

3 Yonatan Adler, Watertight and Rock Solid, Stepped Pools and Chalk Vessels as Expressions of Jewish Ritual Purity, Biblical Archaeology Review, Spring 2021.

4 Palestine: The History of the Word Will Surprise and Liberate You, Jewish Journal, Jennifer Karlan, April 28, 2020.

5 https://www.jpost.com/tags/temple-mount

6 https://www.jewishvoice.org/read/article/update-building-third-temple Jewish Voice, Update on the Building of the Third Temple

7 The Jerusalem Post, July 11, 2018, When a Major Earthquake rippled through Jerusalem, by Sarah Levi.

8 https://www.facinghistory.org/weimar-republic-fragility-democracy/politics/casualties-world-war-i-country-politics-world-war-i Casualties of World War I: Facing History and Ourselves

9 https://courses.lumenlearning.com/boundless-worldhistory/chapter/impact-of-war-world-ii/ Impact of World War II

10 mediadefense.gov, Sept. 1, 2020, 2020 China Military Plan Report–Department of Defense; EndTimesTruth.com>tag>200millionmanarmy, and more.

11 Baxter, Irvin, "One of the 5 Greatest Prophetic Fulfillments in 2000 years! posted January 28, 2010, End Time Magazine, https://www.endtime.com/articles-endtime-magazine/november-3-2009/

12 Noah's flood approximately 2348 BC; Exodus of Moses 1491 BC (answersingenesis.com).

13 Ham, Ken, https://www.answersingenesis.org/age-of-the-earth

14 Constantine and the Foundations of Anti-Semitism, article, https://free.messianicbible.com/feature/constantine-foundations-of-anti-semitism/.

15 Anyone but Him, Christian Antisemitism and Faith in Messiah, by Sam Nadler. https://www.messianicassociation.org/ezine04-him.

16 Maltz, Steve, *How the Church Lost the Way*, Saffron Planet, 2009.

17 The Reformation at 500: Grappling with Martin Luther's Anti-Semitic Legacy, Michael Coren, October 25, 2017.

18 The Israel Bible, edited by Rabbi Tuly Weisz, and Hebrew-English New Covenant, Prophecy Edition.

19 www.ektinteractive.com

20 ektinteractive.com

21 Reuters, Update 2 – "Israel starts exporting natural gas to Egypt under Landmark Deal by Aidan Lewis and Ari Rabinovitch, January 15, 2020; https://www.reuters.com/article/israel-egypt-natgas/update-2-israel-starts-exporting-natural-gas-to-egypt-under-landmark-deal-idUSL8N29K1R8

22 https://www.reuters.com/article/us-iran-china/iran-and-chi-

na-sign-25-year-cooperation-agreement-idUSKBN2BJ0AD

23 Sorko-Ram, Shira, Father of Modern Hebrew Language, Part 3, MaOZ Israel Magazine, November 2018

24 www.youtube.com/watch?v=J98XBmoZAi4 Yesh Bi Ahava, Hebrew song (I have in me Love), September 3, 2019.

CPSIA information can be obtained
at www.ICGtesting.com
Printed in the USA
BVHW061205211121
622063BV00004B/71